COLOMBIA BEFORE COLUMBUS

The People, Culture, and Ceramic Art of Prehispanic Colombia

by Armand J. Labbé

Foreword by William B. Lee, Ph.D.

AN AMERICAS FOUNDATION BOOK
IN ASSOCIATION WITH THE BOWERS MUSEUM,
SANTA ANA, CALIFORNIA

RIZZOLI
NEW YORK

Project Director: Stephen Kramer
Assistant to the Director: Elizabeth B. Krauss
Editor: Eugene H. Davis
Photography: Studio Sergei, Hadley, Massachusetts
Armand J. Labbé (#4, 7, 9, 47, 116, 153, 167)
Illustrations: Paul Apodaca
Maps: Paul Johnson and Michael Mitchell

Designer: Arnold Skolnick
Art Associates: Nancy Crompton and Kathleen Unruh
Typography: Larry Lorber, Ultracomp, Inc., New York
Production Services: Martin Cook Associates, Inc., New York
Printed and Bound by: Bookbuilders, Ltd., Hong Kong
Layout, Design and Production: Chameleon Books, Inc., New York

First published in the United States of America in 1986 by
RIZZOLI INTERNATIONAL PUBLICATIONS, Inc.
597 Fifth Avenue, New York, NY 10017

Library of Congress Cataloging-in-Publication Data

Labbé, Armand J.
Colombia Before Columbus.

"An Americas Foundation Book."
"In association with the Bowers Museum, Santa Ana, California."
Published to celebrate the exhibition at the Bowers Museum, 1986, sponsored by The Americas Foundation, Greenfield, Massachusetts.
Bibliography: p. 200
Includes index.
1. Indians of South America — Columbia — Antiquities. 2. Colombia — Antiquities. I. Americas Foundation. II. Bowers Museum. III. Title.
F2269.L33 1986 986.1'01 86-20289
ISBN 0-8478-0770-3 (pbk.)

Front Cover: Chimila-style burial urn
Back Cover: Sinú moon deity

This book is dedicated to the people of Colombia, past and present.

ACKNOWLEDGMENTS

The present volume is the result of three years of research involving the examination of thousands of prehispanic Colombian artifacts in public and private collections in North and South America. The project reflects the contributions of many individuals without whose assistance it could not have been undertaken.

For their support and encouragement, I would like to thank: William B. Lee Ph.D., Director of the Bowers Museum; The Americas Foundation for providing research and financial support and for organizing the exhibition and for producing this book; and its president, Stephen Kramer; and Mr. Hector Godinez and Mrs. Ruth Seigle of the Bowers Museum Blue Ribbon Committee.

Special thanks are due Mr. Kenneth Klassen for the extended loan of his personal library and for his financial contribution. Grateful acknowledgement is extended to those who made their collections available for study and for exhibition: the Bowers Museum, the Denver Art Museum, Harvey and Clavia Aronson, Isnardo Bautista, Dr. and Mrs. Edward Blair, Dr. and Mrs. Paul Blair, Dr. Stephen Blair, Mr. and Mrs. James Byrnes, Jose Castellanos, Guy and Donna Devito, Agusto and Luz Miriam Granados, Saulo and Constanza Granados, Mr. and Mrs. Greg Grinnell, Stephen and Claudia Kramer, Mrs. Susie Lieberman, Mr. Ernest Mailloux, Francisco and Cristina Olano, Mr. and Mrs. Eduardo Rivas, Gerardo and Nora Roca, Dr. and Mrs. Lawrence Sporty, Luz Miriam Toro, and Mr. and Mrs. Emerson Woelfer.

Many individuals contributed their time and efforts by offering their advice and assistance. I would like to thank: the staff of the Bowers Museum and, particularly, Paul Apodaca, Curator of Folk Art, Paul Johnson, Exhibits Specialist, Michael Mitchell, Graphics Illustrator, Margaret Key, Registrar, Margaret Willard, Assistant Registrar, Tracy Ledin, Public Relations Coordinator, Pat Rice, Gini Nishigaya, Nancy Fister, and Elizabeth B. Krauss.

I would like to personally thank Mrs. Gloria Bogdan, who selflessly contributed her secretarial, clerical and considerable research skills to help make this project a success; and Kathleen Gallagher for her tireless typing of the manuscript.

Special thanks are also due: Robert Stroessner, Curator, Denver Art Museum, Mr. Alex Bright, formerly with The Gold Museum, Bogotá, Colombia, Marlene Dobkin de Rios Ph.D., California State University, Fullerton, and Tom Hoskinson, Research Associate, Bowers Museum.

Armand J. Labbé

While working in Bogotá in the 1970s, my travels took me through much of Colombia. The varied topography, the raw beauty of the landscape, and the opportunities to exchange ideas made a lasting impression on me. I was fascinated with the diversity and quality of indigenous handicrafts, some of the finest in South America, which local artisans exhibited with pride. Naturally this interest in folk art led me back to Bogotá's noted museums—El Museo de Oro, El Museo Nacional, and El Museo Archaeológico del Banco Popular. Viewing the splendid gold and ceramic artifacts, evocative still of great extinct cultures, I was impressed with how clearly some of the works of contemporary artisans pointed to the mysterious veiled iconography of the past. It became evident that there was more to discover about the lifeways, religion, rituals, and arcane ceremonies of Colombia's ancient cultures.

As an amateur ceramist, I was particularly drawn to these venerable objects of clay. Often from mere shards, archaeologists attempt to reconstruct detailed images of life lived centuries ago. The fashioning of ceramics heralded a significant step in man's development; it demonstrated his early understanding of the laws of nature and of rudimentary science. Now, with fire, he could model and preserve articles of utility, improving the quality of life through convenience and storage. Inevitably, primitive technology fostered ritual: to hunt and farm is to petition the elemental forces for beneficence and mercy. Shamans, the masters of ritual, directed planting, harvesting, and sacrifice. Thus, a cosmology of man's relationship to his universe evolved. Funerary artifacts offer a rich account of the indigene's expanding comprehension and his accruing mastery of the environment.

Upon returning to North America in 1980, I searched further for texts on Colombia's ceramic past, only to discover that most books were regionally envisioned and often fragmented as site reports. After discussions with anthropologists and archaeologists in North and South America, I became convinced of the need for an updated reference work to synthesize and correlate the existing information, as well as discuss extant and emerging theories. Thus, I was encouraged to pursue the idea of such a volume, and perhaps, an exhibit of the ceramics as well.

Late in 1982, I was introduced to Armand Labbé, Curator of Anthropology at the Bowers Museum in Santa Ana, California. With the support of the Bowers Museum, the possibility of producing a text written by Mr. Labbé and a comprehensive exhibition began to crystalize. The Americas Foundation is a non-profit organization that promotes cultural and educational exchanges among peoples of the Americas. Its participation made possible in North America, for the first time in this century, an exhibition devoted entirely to the ceramics of prehispanic Colombia. The book was to be an independent contribution to the body of research and scholarship on Colombian culture as well as a reference guide to the exhibition.

It is our hope that *Colombia Before Columbus* will generate a renascence of interest in Colombia among scholars, as well as among those curious about these remarkable clay records of the past, which not only shed light on early and current inhabitants, but also bespeak the shared, universal heritage of all peoples.

The creation of this text and the exhibition has been possible through the combined efforts of many individuals. The work of author, anthropologist, and Americanist, Armand Labbé, will mark the beginning of an era of understanding and recognition of Colombia's ancient ceramic history. Dr. William B. Lee and his staff at the Bowers Museum have provided assistance and encouragement since the inception of this project.

Special thanks to: Kenneth Klassen for his expertise and contributions; my assistant Elizabeth Krauss; Stephen Calcagnino; Eugene H. Davis, my friend of 25 years; Frederick U. Fierst; Sergei Starosielski and Steve Hoffenberg.

Conservation of the objects was done by Alfonso Ramirez, Judith Levinson, John Dennis and Cliff Craine. Additional mounts were made by Daniel Krauss of Authentic Designs, Kevin Butler, William Skibel, and David Tassianari, and Hal Flyn Sr.

A special thanks to my wife, Claudia, and to Sra. Nelly Muñoz. Finally, I wish to acknowledge my gratitude to the late Jorge Guillermo Muñoz, who helped make this vision a reality.

Stephen Kramer, President
THE AMERICAS FOUNDATION

CONTENTS

FOREWORD

Colombia occupies such an unusual position in the geography and history of the Americas that it is puzzling why more research has not been forthcoming on this fascinating region.

As a crossroads between North and South America, Colombia reflects most of the influences which have moved between continents. The region is also the source of many cultural influences and is now recognized as having the earliest ceramic art produced in the Americas. (G. Reichel-Dolmatoff, 1985)

This book is intended as a significant contribution to the body of literature describing the cultural history of Colombia before the arrival of Europeans.

Colombia Before Columbus assembles the most recent archaeological data from Colombia and compares it with previous reports, historical chronicles, and ethnographies. Older hypotheses are critically examined, and new hypotheses on the cultural development of the region are formulated.

This work serves not only as a history of prehispanic Colombia, but also as a resource text for Colombian ceramic art. The Bowers Museum in Southern California has been privileged to sponsor author Armand Labbé in his development of both the text and a major exhibit. With the considerable support of the Americas Foundation, this joint effort has resulted in an outstanding new contribution to anthropological understanding and appreciation of the wonderful legacy of the prehispanic Colombian artistic tradition. For too long the focus on Colombia has been exclusively on the products of the goldworking traditions. At last a study of the Colombian ceramic art has emerged on a level that commands worldwide recognition.

William B. Lee, Ph.D.

AUTHOR'S PREFACE

Almost five hundred years have passed since Columbus set sail from Spain on August 3, 1492. What Columbus discovered was far more than new lands. He also discovered new peoples with ideas about the world radically different from those shared by his fellow Europeans.

Although the 15th-century European embarked upon a new era of discovery and exploration, he was ill prepared psychologically to accept the diversity of cultures, religions, and moral values to be found in the Americas. His own immediate experience was the Judaeo-Christian-Islamic world of Europe, North Africa, and the Middle East.

From the earliest centuries of the Christian era, differences of opinion within Christianity had divided and polarized the Christian world. Various heresies continued to emerge well after the Council of Nicaea in 325 A.D. had been convened to suppress the Arian heresy and establish, once and for all, a central unalterable body of dogma for the Christian world. Subsequent heresies were mercilessly suppressed by the prevailing orthodoxy. The numerous crusades launched against the Muslims from the 11th to the 13th centuries served to temporarily galvanize and bolster the authority of the Church. This created even greater intolerance of the "heretic" and "infidel."

Although Charles Martel had defeated the Saracens at Tours in 732 A.D., Moorish power in Spain was not broken until the 15th century. In 1453, Byzantium fell to the Ottoman Turks, thereby closing the eastern Mediterranean to Christian commerce. This also effectively blocked Europe's access to trade with India and the East. This state of affairs stimulated serious efforts to find alternate routes to these important markets.

European exploration from the outset, therefore, was motivated by trade and commercial gain. The merits of newfound lands were argued before the courts of Europe on the basis of their financial value to the Crown and to other underwriters of expeditions.

From the perspective of commercial gain, the newly discovered lands in the Americas were at first rather disappointing. In place of the rich markets of silk, spice, and precious stones the Europeans were seeking in India, they discovered small rural farming communities typical of the islands of the Indies. Columbus had not discovered a new route to India, but had chanced upon lands unknown to 16th-century Europeans. These lands had already been discovered tens of thousands of years before by men from Asia.

The Indians, as they were mistakenly called, did wear a few small ornaments of gold and tumbaga, an alloy of gold and copper. Since gold was universally accepted throughout Europe as the medium of exchange, the promise of finding more in the New World excited the European imagination and became a persuasive argument for continued exploration of the newfound lands.

By 1520, Cortez had conquered Mexico, and significant quantities of gold and silver were acquired as gifts, trade, or booty obtained in conquest. Gold, fiefdoms in the form of land grants to successful conquistadors, and other visionary promises of instant wealth gave rise to feverish and obsessive pursuits of fortune.

The barbarous slaughter of the native inhabitants and the unbridled madness that ensued was conveniently rationalized as patriotic nationalism and religious fervor. The newly discovered lands, it was argued, belonged by God-given right to the Crown, and the newfound "souls" belonged to the Church. The wanton looting and destruction of the native peoples and their cultures was undertaken for love of God and country.

The conquest of Mexico was followed by that of Peru and shortly thereafter by the conquest of the lands of "El Dorado," which became New Granada, now known as the Republic of Colombia.

Colombia, the legendary land of "El Dorado," has long captured the popular imagination. The fabulous cities of gold are now known to have been the exaggeration of rapacious conquistadors. The Indian of Colombia did work gold into beautiful ornaments, figurines, and other forms, but the true wealth of prehispanic Colombia far exceeded the merits of its renowned goldwork. The real treasure lay in her people, their rich culture and traditions.

Colombia Before Columbus investigates the realities of Colombian Indian culture as they have been pieced together by the collective efforts of modern scholars, such as archaeologists, ethnologists, linguists, historians, ethnobotanists, mythologists, art historians, and other specialists. *Colombia Before Columbus* is a voyage into the fascinating world of the prehispanic Colombian Indian. It is an exploration of religion, magic, myth, and culture.

INTRODUCTION

The present volume fills an important gap in the available literature on prehispanic civilization in the Americas. Although many books have been written concerning the civilizations of pre-Columbian Mexico and Peru, there is little material available to the interested nonspecialist on the important cultures of prehispanic Colombia. For over twenty years, the only available text in English serving as a scholarly introduction and overview of pre-European-influenced Colombia has been *Colombia: Ancient Peoples and Places*, published in 1965 and authored by the eminent Colombianist G. Reichel-Dolmatoff. Important discoveries in Colombian archaeology and ethnography brought to light since 1965 have forced scholars to rethink old hypotheses with respect to Colombian prehistory.

This book documents many of these new discoveries and integrates this data with supporting information gleaned from a number of interrelated disciplines. The book is organized into nine chapters. Each chapter introduces the reader to a major prehispanic Colombian culture area: Tumaco-La Tolita, Calima, Middle Cauca, Sinú, Magdalena River, San Agustín-Tierradentro, Highland Nariño, Muisca, and Tairona.

The chapters are organized in such a manner that each area covered in the text geographically borders and logically precedes the region covered next.

Each chapter can be read as an independent unit introducing the reader to a particular culture area. However, those readers interested in a more in-depth understanding of the book's major hypotheses and theses are better served by carefully reading the material in the order presented.

There is a basic format followed throughout the book. The reader is first briefly oriented to the basic geography and essential topographical features of the area under investigation. This information falls into three categories: archaeology, ethnohistory, and the ceramic record. Ethnographic information on existing Colombian and other South American Indians is used to support interpretations of findings in archaeology, to expand our understanding of customs only cursorily referenced in the ethnohistorical accounts, and also to assist in the interpretation of iconography used on ceramics. The maps, graphics, and particularly the photographs of ceramic art supplement and illustrate topics and concepts presented in the text.

Our purpose is to try and understand the realities of prehispanic Colombia. The reconstruction of culture history is never an easy task. One cannot overemphasize the fact that our knowledge to date of the prehistory of Colombia is at best fragmentary. The boundaries of archaeological cultures may change markedly through time. By nature, archaeological evidence is incomplete and prone to bias. For example, changes reflected in burial practices may or may not be related to changes in subsistence patterns, cultural philosophy, or movements of people. Habitation sites, in close proximity to burial sites, may or may not indicate cultural correlation. As you get closer to the present, such affinities increase in direct proportion to contemporaneity. Archaeological explanation is characteristically hypothetical and incomplete, and it is therefore subject to change and adjustment. This is reflected in the professional literature, where the same investigators devise and redevise typologies, chronologies, and other classificatory schemes as additional data comes to light. It is incumbent upon researchers that they provide cogent premises for inferences about archaeological data, so that these inferences reflect the prehistoric realities as accurately as possible given the limitation of archaeological and anthropological methodology.

The usual problems encountered in archaeology elsewhere are compounded in large areas of Colombia, where environmental conditions, such as extreme moisture and acidity of soil, in addition to cataclysmic events, such as volcanic mudslides, floods, and earthquakes, either obliterate or alter the archaeological record. Add to this the fact that systematic, scientific archaeology in Colombia is of very recent heritage, and one begins to appreciate the obstacles posed to any valid reconstruction of culture history. The situation is further complicated by the equally fragmentary nature of the ethnographic literature. It is an unfortunate fact of history that the native American cultures which were flourishing at the time of European contact were, in the main, either rapidly reduced by conquest and disease or hybridized and assimilated by their European antagonists. Here and there, however, pockets of native culture survived and continue to persist, ever so tenaciously, into the present. These surviving cultures, albeit somewhat modified, offer us a glimpse into the lost worlds of their pre-Columbian forebears. They form the basis for the corpus of ethnographic data available to modern research.

Another important source of information is the eyewitness accounts of the Europeans who encountered these cultures firsthand, as conqueror, proselytizer, or explorer. This source of information, however, must be used very cautiously, as what these informants tended to see was not the indigenous American cultures as they actually were, so much as the projected fantasies of the observers themselves, who looked with the peculiar values, aesthetics, and perspectives dictated by their own cultural conditioning.

How could the European understand that among some people human sacrifice, eating the flesh of sacrificed victims, or drinking the ashes of cremated relatives were all activities imbued with deep religious meaning and sentiment? How could the native, on his part, comprehend that a yellow metal the Europeans called gold was more valued by them than life itself, inasmuch as so many of them were willing to endure the cruelest hardships, deprivations, and even the loss of their very lives, in search of it?

To the European, the Indian was idolatrous. He prayed to figures of wood, clay, and stone, did he not? To the Indian, his own rites before idols of wood and stone seemed not so very different in kind from the Spaniard's prayers, masses, and other rituals, performed before foreign idols of similar materials. Both the European and the Indian suffered culture shock, each from the other. Both felt that their respective customs, laws, and mores derived from a higher authority. Each, however, had a strikingly different perception and understanding of what the nature of that higher authority might be. Although they did not realize it at the time, both were being confronted with the fact of cultural relativism. Not only were they experiencing a separate reality, but they each stressed a different mode of expressing and communicating their respective realities. The European had his written word, his bible, his various books of written law and canon. The Indian had his art, his symbols, and his iconography.

Another problem lies in how one perceives and interprets prehispanic art. The ceramic art documented in this volume is employed as a partial record of the prehistoric past. Every culture contains within itself its own peculiar statement concerning man, cosmos, life, and the human condition. Particularly in those cultures that lacked a written language, such statements are encoded and enshrined in their art. We tend to forget that the transition from preliterate metaphoric thought patterns is effected at the expense of limiting the vivid imagery and creative latitudes afforded by nonliterary poetic modes of expression. Metaphoric symbolism as used in preliterate societies and found in prehispanic Colombia, is apt to evoke streams of culturally related images and ideas. Art is more often used to communicate culturally shared perceptions about the nature of man, the natural world or cosmos. It functions in part as an integrative force, relating the individual to the culture as a whole. Even when it is used in the acquisition and manifestation of personal power, as in magic or sorcery, culturally recognized imagery is always employed. In such societies, the artist is often either a practitioner of the sacred, like a shaman or priest, or an agent of such. This is not to say that these societies are devoid of secular artistic expression, only that such expressions are of secondary importance vis-a-vis art as communicated culture. Here, the artist's freedom lies not so much in creating new artistic canons and metaphors as it does in expressing and manipulating culturally recognized and sanctioned canons and imagery. An understanding of prehistoric, preliterate art depends, in large measure, on uncovering and reconstructing the underlying canons and iconography employed. This cannot be accomplished without recourse to ethnography, which can assist us in determining which metaphors are used and which aspect of culture, myth, or cosmology is being communicated.

It becomes apparent, therefore, that prehispanic Colombian art is an expression of prehistoric thought patterns. If skillfully employed, it gives us insights into and understanding of the pre-Columbian mind.

Pre-Columbian art history examined without the benefit of anthropology and related disciplines can never uncover the psycho-cultural perspective of the prehispanic Indian artist. Art history should never be separated from culture history. Conversely, anthropologists and archaeologists must not limit themselves by viewing prehistoric art objects as simple artifacts and interesting curios whose main value lies in the comparative and relative dating of sites. Nor should they restrict themselves to developing typologies used in correlating material found at one site with that found at others. The perspective taken in this volume is holistic. All data should be skillfully employed to maximize its ability to yield information. An important aspect of cultural art lies in its potential capacity to open doors of perception which enable us to see the inner working of minds that conceived and experienced realities separate from our own.

It should be clear from what has been said that the task of the prehistorian is beset from the onset with formidable problems. The resulting story that emerges is fragmentary and incomplete. It cannot be read as one would read a novel in which all the characters, the plot, the drama, and the denouement are controlled by the author.

The prehistory of Colombia is not one history, but numerous individual histories. Some of these are interrelated, while others are quite distinct. One cannot relate the story in a simple linear, chronological format. The realities of Colombian prehistory do not lend themselves to such a facile ordering.

The earliest evidence of man in Colombia is that of the Paleo-Indian big-game hunters. The sparse proof of their existence consists of a few crude, undated tools fashioned of stone. These tools, mainly projectile points and scrapers, are forms associated with big-game hunters elsewhere in the Americas.

Around 7000 B.C., a gradual shift from the Paleo-Indian subsistence pattern took place. The new economy depended less on hunting large game and relied more on exploiting other available food resources, such as fish, shellfish, plants, and smaller game.

This subsistence pattern is characterized by seasonal campsites. Along the northern coast of Colombia, these sites often contain huge deposits of discarded seashells. The trend in the north was a gradual transition to more sedentary lifeways, which eventually included the manufacture of fired clay vessels.

The oldest dated ceramics discovered anywhere in the Americas were unearthed by G. Reicher-Dolmatoff (1985) at Monsu, North Colombia, a site less than four miles from Puerto Hormiga, which formerly vied with Valdivia in Ecuador for that distinction. The Monsu pottery sherds were uncovered in a stratigraphic-layer radiocarbon dated to 3350 B.C. According to the excavator, the dated material overlays a deposit of undated sherds over a meter deep.

Five distinct cultural periods are represented at Monsu: Turbana, Monsu, Pangola, Macavi, and Barlovento. The oldest of these is the Turbana period. The earliest dated ceramics were obtained from the upper levels of the Monsu Period (3350 B.C.). [The lower levels of the succeeding period, the Pangola, have been dated to 2250 B.C.]

The evidence from the earliest levels of the Monsu site suggests that the local economy was based on fishing, hunting, and foraging. Certainly by the Barlovento Period, ca. 1200 B.C., comestibles such as root crops were systematically grown. Reichel-Dolmatoff feels that root crops may have been grown even earlier in the sequence at Monsu.

Systematic horticulture based on root-crop growing gave rise to new patterns of culture, in the north as well as in other parts of Colombia. These changes began sometime before 1000 B.C. Although some of the shell-mound dwellers and related riverine people adopted some of the new horticultural culture patterns, there are indications that these patterns developed elsewhere and were either exported to or imported into the region, possibly from Ecuador or perhaps more directly from the tropical forest regions of Amazonia. A case in point is the Malambo site, which is located on a lagoon of the lower Magdalena River. Malambo represents one of the early root-crop-growing communities of Colombia (early 1st millenium B.C.). Noteworthy is the fact that Malambo ceramics, although somewhat reminiscent of the pottery of the shell-mound dwellers, are technologically and aesthetically more sophisticated and contain forms and decorative techniques not found in the preceding cultures. More significantly, however, molluscs were not part of the Malambo diet, although they were ecologically available. The fact that molluscs were not eaten would suggest that they were not part of the subsistence pattern of the early Colombian horticulturalists. Of particular interest, in this respect, is the fact that recent excavations undertaken by the French in the south coastal region of Colombia revealed that although molluscs were abundant there, they do not appear to have played a part in the diets of the prehistoric coastal mangrove dwellers, whose economy also seems to have been based on fishing and horticulture.

Although we do not know exactly when corn growing was introduced into Colombia, we know that it was fairly early on, perhaps ca. 500 B.C. The available evidence suggests that this new economic pattern diffused into Colombia from Ecuador.

One of the central issues in Colombian archaeology has consisted in determining the origins of settled village life, corn agriculture, and other attributes of civilization in Colombia.

In 1965, when *Colombia: Ancient People and Places* was written, the prevailing opinion leaned heavily in favor of attributing significant Mesoamerican influences to the formation and development of civilization in Colombia. The book strongly supported the Mesoamerican hypothesis. Over the years, other researchers as well as popular writers on Colombian prehistory continued to uncritically repeat the arguments supporting this hypothesis.

In 1975, the Mesoamerican hypothesis was challenged by new data presented by Donald Lathrap in the book *Ancient Ecuador*. Lathrop persuasively argued that Ecuador, rather than Mesoamerica, was the source of many culture traits formerly attributed to the latter. He further postulated that the complex of traits found in Ecuador could ultimately be traced to influences originating in the tropical-forest cultures of Amazonia. Reichel-Dolmatoff himself is now in full agreement with the main tenets of Lathrop's argument (see Monsu, 1985). Because this argument is central to understanding developments in Colombia, and because many writers continue to promote the older hypothesis, it is necessary to review in detail the evidence originally used to support the older hypothesis and the more recent discoveries which now make it untenable. This is addressed in Chapter One of this volume, which explores the cultures that flourished within the Tumaco-La Tolita archaeological zone, an area along the Pacific Coast of southern Colombia and northern Ecuador. It was here that early influences from Mesoamerica were thought to have entered Colombia.

In Chapter One, additional new evidence is presented which supports and gives added weight to Lathrap's position. Major cultural developments along the Pacific Coast of South America are placed within a wider regional developmental context. The ceramic art uncovered in the region is examined in the light of ethnographic data which indicates that many of these artistic forms and figural representations are linked to the manioc-root crop-growing traditions of tropical Amazonia.

In Chapter Two, the reader journeys across the mountains of Colombia's Western Cordillera eastward and northward to the Calima region of the Department of Valle Del Cauca. Some of the earliest known shaft graves found in Colombia have been discovered in this region. Ethnographic data obtained on tribes living in the northwest Amazon area of Colombia shed new light on the iconographic significance of such graves. A major focus of the chapter consists in examining the importance which the concept of duality played in the culture and art of the region, as well as elsewhere in Colombia during prehispanic times.

Chapter Three continues the voyage of exploration into the Middle Cauca Valley region, which is found to the north of the Calima archaeological zone. An important question addressed in this section centers on determining the ethnic composition of the peoples who inhabited this part of the Cauca Valley. Other important issues raised are such customs as cannibalism, corporeal trophy taking, and human sacrifice. These customs are examined in the light of current ethnographic information, which relates these practices to belief systems rooted in tropical-forest Indian mythology and religion.

North of the valley lies the Atlantic watershed region of northern Colombia. This area had its own unique cultural development in antiquity. Its archaeology and ethnohistory are covered in Chapter Four. The introduction of manioc-based horticulture and the later addition of corn-growing to the subsistence base gave rise to new cultural patterns which radically altered the surface characteristics of the natural environment. Enormous engineering projects, consisting of mound building and the construction of entire networks of irrigation and flood-control canals, were undertaken by the Indians of this region. By the 16th century, large areas within the region were under the political control of Indians the Spanish collectively referred to as the Sinú.

East of the Sinú lay the great Magdalena River, which formed the major artery connecting northern Colombia with areas to the south. About 1000 A.D., groups of fierce, cannibalistic peoples known as Caribs, originally from Brazil, began entering and invading Colombia. The Magdalena River was used in their southward advance into the interior of the country. By the 16th century, Carib culture and influence dominated the Magdalena River Valley.

Chapter Five examines the custom of secondary urn burial as it was practiced by peoples living along the Magdalena River and surrounding areas. Many of these peoples are now believed to have been either Caribs or Carib-influenced groups. Evidence of this is found in iconographic elements portrayed on the secondary burial urns. The significance of secondary burial practices is examined. The custom consisted of first defleshing the cadaver, which was effected in a number of different ways. The defleshed bones were then placed in ceramic urns, which were usually buried in shaft-and-chamber tombs. Of particular relevance in understanding this practice are the widespread South American Indian beliefs concerning the physical and spiritual nature of man and the special esoteric significance of bones.

Following the Magdalena River southward to its source, one enters the fascinating regions of San Agustín and Tierradentro, long known for their extensive necropolises. Because their elaborate tombs are the most impressive surviving relics, it is easy to overlook the fact that they were also centers of important cultural development. Their artists produced powerful expressions of their belief systems in stone. The sculptures are evidence of the influence of powerful shamanic traditions in the lives of these people—traditions firmly rooted in the tropical-forest cultures of South America.

The jaguar imagery and alter-ego representations found in the art of this region are examined and are compared with similar imagery used by tropical-forest Indians. The cultural development of the region is outlined and is placed in archaeological perspective.

The section of this chapter devoted to Tierradentro, which lies slightly to the north of San Agustín, re-examines the problem of shaft graves and secondary burials in the light of recent archaeological discoveries in the region.

The highland cultures of Andean Nariño, found to the south of San Agustín, are the subject of Chapter Seven. Many of them were identical to those found in adjacent parts of Ecuador. In protohistoric times, these cultures were the first in Colombia to come in contact with the advancing Inca empire.

Previous hypotheses explaining cultural developments in the southern highlands are critically evaluated. Special attention is given to the ritual significance of certain ceramic forms uncovered in the region. Emphasis is also placed on deciphering some of the iconography used to decorate the ceramics of various highland Indian cultures.

Chapter Eight begins our exploration of the important cultures which flourished in the eastern mountains of Colombia, known as the Cordillera Oriental. Especially noteworthy were the Muisca Indians, who inhabited the high plateau of the modern departments of Cundinamarca and Boyaca. The Muiscas were territorily the most extensive of all Colombian cultures, with their wealth and power based on trade. Within their territories lay huge deposits of salt and copper, as well as significant quantities of emerald-bearing ores.

Muisca beliefs and philosophy were reflected in their myths and ceremonies. A simple Muisca ceremony gave rise to the legend of El Dorado, which in the 16th century lured three European armies of conquest to the region, now dominated by Bogotá, the capital of the Republic of Colombia. The conquest of the Muisca by the European forces ushered in a new epoch—the historical era.

Our exploration ends far to the north in the Sierra Nevada de Santa Marta, an immense solitary mountain formation bordering the Caribbean Sea. In Chapter Nine we encounter the Tairona culture, perhaps the most highly advanced of all prehispanic Colombian societies. Famed for their goldwork, ceramic art, and civil-engineering projects, the Tairona, like the Muisca, were in the process of forming large federations of culturally related villages. As with the Muisca, the impetus for federation was most likely a defense against hostile groups of different cultures living in the surrounding areas, as well as the control of trade routes. The Tairona territory, however, was small compared to that of the Muisca.

The chapter emphasizes the interpretation of Tairona ceramic art in the light of contemporary Kogi myth and ethnography. The Kogi of the Sierra Nevada de Santa Marta are the descendents of this once-powerful and fascinating people.

In the pages that follow, we will explore in greater detail the main themes outlined in this introduction. The various threads of evidence recovered from archaeology, ethnohistory, ethnography, and iconography will be employed as warps and wefts used in the restoration of a prehistoric tapestry, the state of which remains unfinished. It is hoped that the results of this endeavor will offer a graphic, textured image of the completed work.

CHRONOLOGICAL TABLE OF CULTURE REGIONS

I PACIFIC COASTAL REGION

TUMACO-LA TOLITA CULTURE		300 B.C.	– 200 A.D.

II CAUCA VALLEY

A. CALIMA REGION

LLAMA PHASE		1500 B.C. (?)	– 100 B.C.
YOTOCO PHASE		100 B.C. (?)	–1300 A.D.
SONSO PHASE		1200 A.D.	–1600 A.D.

B. MIDDLE CAUCA REGION

MIDDLE CAUCA COMPLEX		1000 A.D.	–1500 A.D.
CALDAS COMPLEX		1000 A.D.	–1400 A.D.

III ATLANTIC COASTAL REGION

MONSU: TURBANA PHASE		?	–?
MONSU PHASE		?	–3000 B.C.
PANGOLA PHASE		3000 B.C.	–?
MACAVI PHASE		?	–1200 B.C.
BARLOVENTO PHASE	ca.	1200 B.C.	–?
PUERTO HORMIGA	ca.	3200 B.C.	–2000 B.C.
CANAPOTE	ca.	2000 B.C.	–1200 B.C.
BARLOVENTO	ca.	1200 B.C.	–?
MALAMBO	ca.	900 B.C.	– 700 B.C.
MOMIL I	ca.	700 B.C.	– 100 B.C.
MOMIL II	ca.	100 B.C.	– 600 A.D.
ZAMBRANO	ca.	600 A.D.	–1200 A.D.
CRESPO	ca.	1200 A.D.	–?

IV SINÚ REGION

GROUP I (LOWER RIO SAN JORGE)	ca.	400 A.D.	–1000 A.D.
GROUP I (GREATER SINÚ REGION)	ca.	100 A.D.	–1600 A.D.
GROUP II (LOWER RIO SAN JORGE)		1400 A.D.	–1600 A.D.

V MAGDELENA VALLEY

LOWER MAGDELENA (TAMALAMEQUE STYLE)	ca.	1200 A.D.	–1500 A.D.
MIDDLE MAGDELENA (RIO DE LA MIEL)	ca.	1100 A.D.	–?

VI SAN AGUSTÍN

HORQUETA PERIOD	ca.	600 B.C.	– 1 A.D.
PRIMAVERA PERIOD	ca.	1 A.D.	– 100 A.D.
ISNOS PERIOD	ca.	100 A.D.	–1000 A.D.(?)
SOMBRERILLOS PERIOD	ca.	1000 A.D.(?)	–1600 A.D.

VII HIGHLAND NARIÑO REGION

PIARTAL COMPLEX	ca.	750 A.D.	–1250 A.D.
CAPULI COMPLEX	ca.	850 A.D.	–1500 A.D.
TUZA COMPLEX (may have been considerably earlier)	ca.	1250 A.D.	–1500 A.D.

VIII EASTERN CORDILLERA

MUISCA (majority of dated material is 1000 A.D.–1500 A.D.)	ca.	300 A.D.	–1540 A.D.

IX SIERRA NEVADA

TAIRONA (may be older but majority of ceramics date from 1000 A.D.)	ca.	1000 A.D.	–1600 A.D.

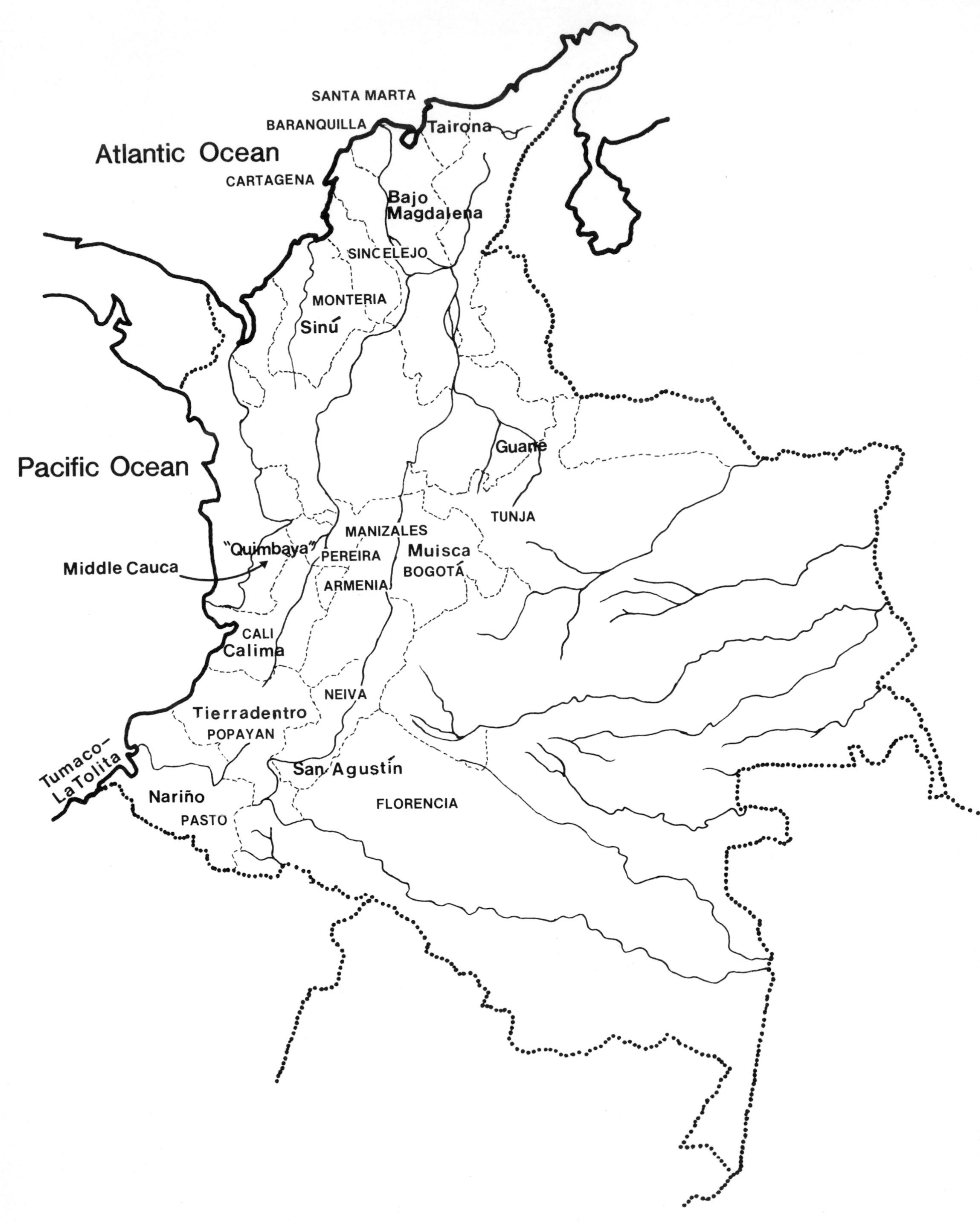
SANTA MARTA
BARANQUILLA
Tairona
Atlantic Ocean
CARTAGENA
Bajo
Magdalena
SINCELEJO
MONTERIA
Sinú
Guané
Pacific Ocean
TUNJA
MANIZALES
"Quimbaya"
PEREIRA
Muisca
BOGOTÁ
Middle Cauca
ARMENIA
CALI
Calima
NEIVA
Tierradentro
POPAYAN
San Agustín
Tumaco-
La Tolita
Nariño
FLORENCIA
PASTO

CHAPTER I

TUMACO-LA TOLITA

Images of Shaman, Jaguar, and Myth in the Coastal Wetlands

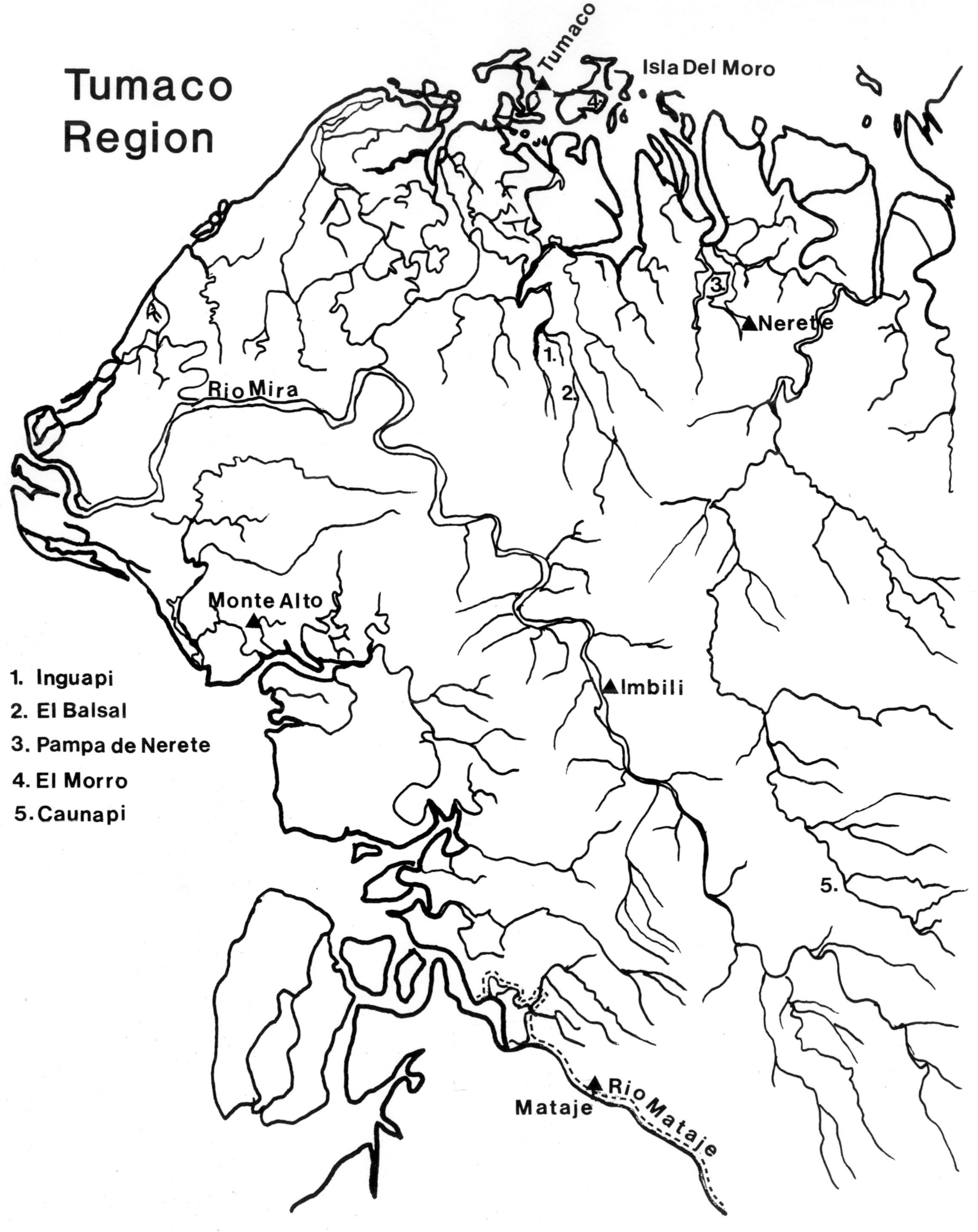
Tumaco Region
Tumaco
Isla Del Moro
4.
3.
Nerete
1.
2.
Rio Mira
Monte Alto
Imbili
5.
Rio Mataje
Mataje
1. Inguapi
2. El Balsal
3. Pampa de Nerete
4. El Morro
5. Caunapi

GEOGRAPHY

The Tumaco-La Tolita culture area extends from the southern Pacific coast of Colombia down through the northern coast of Ecuador to the province of Esmeraldas. While the Colombian side of the zone is generally referred to as the Tumaco Zone, Ecuadorian researchers refer to the Ecuadorian side as the La Tolita Zone. The archaeological evidence, however, indicates that both zones formed one culture province, although there were apparent changes of culture and peoples through time.

The coastal plain of the Tumaco-La Tolita archaeological zone is generally quite flat, with minor topographical variations as one moves from the foot of the Western Cordillera to the coast. Rain falling along this range gives rise to numerous streams and waterways which interconnect with great rivers, such as the Mira, Mataje, Patia, Santiago, and Satinga. Annual precipitation is extremely high along the Pacific coast of Colombia north of Buenaventura (26 ft. / 7.9 cm per yr.). Just south of Buenaventura lie immense mangrove swamps, which seem to have deterred any extensive habitation of this area in antiquity. For these reasons, the Tumaco-La Tolita archaeological zone was a preferred zone of habitation along much of the Colombian and Ecuadorian Pacific coasts.

ETHNOHISTORY

The area was first observed by Europeans when a group of Pizarro's ships explored the coast in 1526–27. They found the coastal area densely populated and villages highly fortified. Individual houses were built over trees or rested on tall wooden piles. Access to these dwellings was restricted by retractable ladders or steps. Francisco Lopez de Gomara (1552 A.D.), commenting on the natives of Esmeraldas in Ecuador, stated that their hair was cut front to back at the center but was allowed to grow along the sides. Ears and nostrils were pierced and adorned with small objects fashioned of gold and emeralds and other precious stones. De Gomara noted that the inhabitants wore short shirts which extended to, but did not cover their privates. [Garments fitting this description are represented on ceramic figures from Nayarit, Mexico. These figures belong to a cultural complex known as the Shaft Tomb Cultures, which flourished in the West Mexican states of Colima, Jalisco, and Nayarit between 200 B.C. and 500 A.D.]

Certain cultural traits, such as the wearing of nose plugs and the piercing of the body for the placement of ornaments, were common to both the prehistoric and historic peoples. We cannot assume, however, that the peoples who inhabited this region at the time of the Spanish contact were in the fact the direct descendants of the people responsible for the various archaeological phases uncovered in the region.

ARCHAEOLOGY

Prior to the 1970s, little scientific archaeology had been undertaken in the region. The first scientific excavations on the Colombian side of the zone were conducted at Monte Alto by Cubillos (Cubillos, 1955). This relatively minor site is said to have attracted as many as 400 treasure seekers, who sifted the sands in search of gold jewelry and other relics. No radiocarbon dates were obtained during Cubillos' excavations at Monte Alto.

Much of the material found in the Tumaco-La Tolita Zone is believed to have been made during a period of habitation popularly called Classic Tumaco, in Colombia, and Classic La Tolita, in Ecuador. Based on current but admittedly scarce data, Classic Tumaco-La Tolita flourished sometime between 300 B.C. and 200 A.D., within more restricted areas of the zone.

Based on his work at this site and previous observations made at Isla Del Morro, Cubillos suggested that Tumaco culture (i.e., Classic Tumaco-La Tolita) may have originated outside of Colombia, perhaps resulting from successive periods of contact with Mesoamerica.

Later excavations were conducted by G. Reichel-Dolmatoff (1965) at a site called Mataje, along the Mataje River, near the Ecuadorian border. On the basis of a series of radiocarbon dates, Reichel-Dolmatoff divided Mataje into three major chronological periods: Mataje I (?–400 B.C.); Mataje II, which began around 300 B.C. and continued to about 10 A.D.; and Mataje III, which followed Mataje II but lacks a firm C-14 date to establish a terminal period. Double-spouted vessels with bridge handles, tall tripods, and bowls with bulbous supports were among the oldest pottery forms found. Reichel-Dolmatoff relates the cultural material of the Period II at Mataje with material found at the Cantaguero site (250 B.C.) on the lower Calma River.

On the basis of his excavations and surveys in this area, Reichel-Dolmatoff hypothesized that Mesoamerican influences entered Colombia along the Pacific coast. According to his reasoning, there were two major periods of Mesoamerican influence. The first, beginning as early as 1200 B.C., brought in such elements as the jaguar cult, maize cultivation, burial mounds, monolithic sarcophagi, and obsidian mirrors. The second, beginning about 500 B.C., ushered in such elements as deep-level shaft graves with lateral chambers, elaborate figurines, occipito-frontal head deformation, pottery with multiple supports, flat and cylindrical stamps, elaborate spindle whorls, biomorphic whistles, and perhaps double-spouted vessels. He further believed that both these periods of significant Mesoamerican influence gave rise to a new culture pattern characterized by an economy based on seed agriculture and sedentary village life, with subsequent increases in population, social stratification, craft specialization, and trade.

Other investigators, such as Betty Meggers (1966), have also argued in favor of Mesoamerican influences on Tumaco-La Tolita culture. In contrast, Lathrap (1975) has argued for the existence of efficient agricultural systems based on maize, manioc, sweet potatoes, arrowroot, and peanuts in Ecuador by 3000 B.C. He further suggests that Mesoamerica received important cultural and artistic influences from Ecuador, rather than vice versa. An important corollary of Lathrop's argument is his belief that many of the cultural elements found in the Formative levels of culture in Ecuador have their roots in the tropical lowland cultures of South America.

Let us examine more closely some of the arguments proffered in support of the hypothesis which holds that Mesoamerican influences entered Colombia via the Pacific coast and moved inland.

It has been suggested that elements such as the jaguar cult, maize cultivation, burial mounds, and monolithic sarcophagi were introduced into Colombia ca. 1200 B.C. by sporadic settlers, who penetrated from the Pacific coast toward the east. Granted, the fanged-feline motif, indicating a jaguar cult, is present in the Olmec and Olmec-influenced cultures of Mesoamerica at this time. However, the form of feline representations found in Colombia seems unrelated to the Olmec, or Olmecoid forms.

It is possible that the Olmec, San Agustín, and Chavín (Peru) cultures may all have their roots in the tropical forest region of northern South America. Cultural elements that are common to two or more of the three — fanged jaguar personages, the depiction of the alter-ego motif, stone sarcophagi — are perhaps the result of a common origin and heritage, rather than the direct influence of one on the other. Even today, the jaguar figures prominently in the cultures of the Vaupes region of Colombia and other parts of Amazonia. Although jaguars ranged as far north as New Mexico in prehispanic times, their most significant area of concentration appears to have been, and remains today, the tropical forest regions of South America.

While stone sarcophagi, notably the La Venta sarcophagus, are found in Olmec culture, they certainly were not common there, but appear to have been an elite and exceptional form of burial. Stone sarcophagi are more common at San Agustin.

The second period of major Mesoamerican influence presumably brought in its wake such cultural elements as deep-level shaft graves with lateral chambers, elaborate figurines, occipito-frontal head deformation, pottery with multiple supports, flat and cylindrical stamps, and biomorphic whistles. However, most if not all of these traits have prototypes in earlier Ecuadorian cultures. Moreover, the shaft-tomb-complex ceramic figures of West Mexico, which date to between 200 B.C.–500 A.D., show no notable stylistic affinities with the ceramics associated with the shaft tombs of Colombia. Some ceramic figures, notably a few from Colima, West Mexico, indicate stylistic similarities with the elaborate ceramic hollow-spouted figures of the Chorrera culture of Ecuador. Chorrera, however, antedates the Mexican complex. Additionally, both roller and flat stamps were already present in Chorrera prior to the purported importation of these forms from Mesoamerica after 500 B.C.

Finally, tripods and vessels with multiple supports are present in Ecuador as early as the Valdivia culture, well before 1800 B.C. On the basis of the available data, the evidence does indeed support contact between Pacific coastal South America and Mesoamerica. The main direction of influence appears to have been from the south to the north during Formative periods.

The 1970s was a period of increased archaeology and surveys in the Tumaco-La Tolita Zone, among which should be mentioned: *La Mision Española en Esmeraldas*, undertaken between 1970–76, with preliminary findings published by Alcina Franch from 1971–73; a French expedition, *El Proyecto Tumaco*; and ongoing investigations undertaken by El Museo de Banco Central de Ecuador. Outlines and site reports of the French work have been reported by Jean-François Bouchard (1982–85). An outline of the research strategy of the Museo de Banco Central was delivered to the 45th Congress of Americanists, Bogotá, Colombia in 1985 by Francisco Valdez.

Recent archaeology conducted in the region during the 1970s and 1980s indicates that cultural development along the Pacific coast of southern Colombia and northern Ecuador was far more complicated than previously realized. We now know that cultures different from but contemporaneous with Classic Tumaco-La Tolita coexisted within the region.

Evidence in the form of radiocarbon dates and stratigraphic and cross-site comparison of pottery types suggests that Classic Tumaco-La Tolita flourished between 300 B.C. and 200 A.D. Dates obtained for the Colombian manifestation of this culture fall between 300 B.C. and 100 A.D. Surprisingly, those obtained for the La Tolita site in Ecuador cluster between 100–300 A.D. As only three dates have been secured for this site, it is difficult to determine whether they reflect its real chronological depth. Bouchard (1983) feels that additional archaeology at the site will yield earlier dates. Unfortunately, La Tolita, one of the most important centers of the Classic Tumaco-La Tolita culture, has been seriously and irrevocably altered by unsupervised diggings over the years.

French excavations of site T1 at Inguapi uncovered cultural material clearly related to Classic Tumaco-La Tolita. The site is divided into three distinct periods: Inguapi I, II, and III. Classic Tumaco-La Tolita is represented by Inguapi I and II. The ceramics of Period I include tripods, ceramic graters, and figurines. The graters are indicative of root-crop horticulture. Numerous fishnet weights associated with Period I were uncovered at Inguapi. This suggests that fishing formed an important part of the economy.

Inguapi II is also represented by fishnet weights, but graters are not reported for this period. This does not necessarily mean that root crops were no longer being grown. Graters may have been made, but perhaps of more perishable material than those of Period I, which were fashioned of clay. Moreover, the clay graters are possibly ceremonial replicas of more utilitarian forms fashioned of wood and inset with sharp, pointed stone chips. The ceramics of Period II differ little from those of Period I. In fact, Bouchard believes that they essentially belong to the same complex.

There is one notable difference, however, between Periods I and II. For some as yet unknown reason, during Period II, people began building houses over artificial mounds which raised the level of the house site well above that of the natural topography. This may have become necessary because of changes in climate and environment. Another possibility is that the mounds served as the foundation for buildings different from and possibly larger than those built during Period I. There is simply too little data to draw a conclusion with respect to why these mounds were built.

During Period III, Inguapi appears to have been occupied by people culturally unrelated to those of Periods I and II. New types of pottery were made, with decoration consisting of incised and hachured triangles, rectangles, and other geometrics. Population density also appears to have declined markedly during this period as compared with previous ones. Excavations at Inguapi therefore uncovered two distinct cultures: Classic Tumaco-La Tolita, represented by Periods I and II, and another unrelated culture, represented by Period III.

Classic Tumaco-La Tolita cultural material has been found at additional sites in the region, but none of these has been systematically excavated. The information obtained by research at Inguapi gives us an overview of local developmental sequences. Cultures such as Classic Tumaco-La Tolita, however, must also be placed in wider regional perspective. Observed from this broader viewpoint, it becomes clear that Classic Tumaco-La Tolita ceramics, such as those of Period I at Inguapi, derive from forms associated with coastal cultures heavily influenced by the Terminal Formative Chorrera culture in Ecuador, which ended about 300 B.C.

The next regionwide developmental sequence is called the Period of Regional Development by Ecuadorean researchers. This sequence is divided into three stages. Classic Tumaco-La Tolita flourished during the first stage, and there is some chronological overlapping between this stage and the next. Stage II begins about 50 A.D. and is represented by the Balsal complex at El Balsal and by the Nerete complex at Pampa de Nerete. Bouchard (1982–1985) feels that this stage marks a change from Classic Tumaco-La Tolita, although its significance is unclear. The evidence derives mainly from observable changes in the ceramics. Notably, the conical tripod supports of the preceding stage are replaced by bulbous mammiform supports.

The last stage of the Regional Development, however, does represent a cultural strata different from that of the previous two periods. This stage is represented by the upper levels of the El Morro site. Its people, like their predecessors, enjoyed an economy based on farming and fishing. However, there appears to be little relationship between their ceramics and those of the previous stages.

The research conducted to date leaves many questions unanswered. A satisfactory chronology for this coastal region of Colombia and Ecuador cannot be established without additional in-depth archaeology.

THE CERAMIC RECORD

Most of the ceramic forms represented in this chapter belong to the Classic Tumaco-La Tolita culture. The Tumaco-La Tolita people have left a rich legacy of ceramic art in the form of vessels, figures, figurines, molds, rollers, graters, and other artifacts. Many of these objects have been heavily eroded by time and environmental factors. However, they still offer a vivid account of various attributes of their ceremonial and mythical life, including items of dress and adornment, house and temple models, depictions of fantastic mythical figures, characteristic physical attributes, disease patterns, certain aspects of sexuality, and other vestiges of culture.

It is probably safe to assume that the ceremonial pottery, and perhaps most if not all of the ceramic figures and figurines, were fashioned by a relatively small group of specialists. This would conform with the patterns of production determined for many other areas of prehispanic America.

Much of the surviving prehispanic art of Colombia, as well as of Ecuador, was manufactured as funerary art. Many of the ceramics have been uncovered by treasure seekers from the numerous artificial mounds which are found within the zone. The inclusion of Classic Tumaco-La Tolita ceramic fragments within the mounds may be due to their original deposition in soils used in the construction of the mounds. Only thoughtful, meticulous archaeology can assist us in determining how we should interpret the context in which an object is found. Mere stratigraphic and contextual provenance at the time of discovery is no clear indication of its original deposition.

In general, it can be stated that the ceramic vessels were fashioned using a coiling technique. No prehispanic vessels fashioned by means of a potter's wheel have been documented for the Americas. Fine to medium sand was a common tempering material. Figurines were either modeled by hand or cast from molds. Added decoration included paint and incising. Red, probably obtained from achiote (the seed of the annato tree), and white were the preferred colors; but green, blue-green, brown tones, and yellow were also used. More often than not, it is extremely difficult to determine which colors were used, as they have washed away through erosion and water action. Slip baths, fine solutions of clay applied over the object prior to firing, were also employed.

The most common firing technique was reduction firing. As a result, the surface colors of the vessels are usually various shades of gray, although pinkish grays and light browns are also known. As is true for much of the Americas, the Tumaco-La Tolita Zone has considerable stylistic variation within its ceramic inventory. This consequently leads to divisions and subdivisions generating complex typologies which are best left to specialists to sort and classify.

Articles in popular publications about the Tumaco-La Tolita culture frequently proclaim that its ceramic art offers a dramatic documentation of the everyday life of the people. A careful examination of this art, however, suggests that a literal reading may be misleading: the imagery represents mythical rather than mundane aspects of life. A case in point is the innumerable figurine heads documented in public and private collections. These are commonly discovered in situ, devoid of a body, or purposely broken off from the figurine body. We may include within this category the numerous disembodied feet, arms, and phalli, many of which were obviously cast as such (#18). The numerous bodiless heads remind us of the same phenomenon evident in Mesoamerica, particularly at Teotihuacan and Gulf Coast, Veracruz.

The key to a proper interpretation of these disembodied parts is to be found in the mythological structure of horticultural societies. A common mythic structure among peoples, whether in Southeast Asia, Melanesia, Polynesia, or tropical America, is the belief that plants originate from the burial of a body part of a mythical or legendary personage. For example, in the Tuamotuan version of a popular Polynesian plant-origin myth, the protagonist, Maui (Wonder-worker), engaged and defeated Te Tuna (Monster Eel, The Phallus) in a struggle of wits, endurance, and prowess, which in every aspect assumed the trappings of a bizarre and exotic male dominance ritual, culminating with Maui disappearing into Te Tuna's body and tearing him apart, from the inside out. Maui cut off Te Tuna's head. Maui's mother, Hua-hega, instructed him to take the head and bury it. From this buried head arose the first coconut, whose flesh became a meat for all, and whose shell was fashioned into cups.

Among the Desana Indians of the Vaupes region of Colombia, the following origin myths have been recorded by G. Reichel-Dolmatoff:

A man had two sons, one married, one a bachelor. The unmarried son had intercourse with his sister-in-law. Learning of this, his brother lay in wait and ambushed him, cutting the penis off the wounded man. He threw the penis into the river and from it, the unyu fish was born.

In another myth, we are informed that the first Desana had a son, who, because he was an adulterer, was given a second head by the Sun. Appalled, the boy's father petitioned for help. The Daughter of the Sun intervened, tearing off the extra head and positioning it in a tree, replacing a termite's nest. Some of the termites remained and established themselves in the head, which then transformed into a beehive, while the termites turned into bees. Thus, we are told, were bees and honey born from the head.

An origin myth from the Tariana Indians of the Vaupes region, recorded by the 19th-century French traveler Henri Coudreau, relates how Yurupary, born of a virgin after she had drunk Kashiri (manioc beer), killed and devoured a number of boys who had broken his dietary laws. Some men of the village then tricked him into intoxication and threw him into a fire. From the ashes of Yurupary emerge the paxuiba palms, which are said to be his bones. From these palms, the men fashioned the sacred trumpets believed to represent his voice.

Of significance in these myths is the common belief that various plants and other comestibles originated from the buried or discarded body parts of mythical or legendary figures. The fact that at Teotihuacan the small ceramic heads appear to have been intentionally tossed into the agricultural fields reinforces the interpretation that these heads were used in vegetation fertility rites.

We may conclude from this that the ceramic heads and other clay body parts found in Classic Tumaco-La Tolita culture are linked to similar plant-origin myths.

Another group of artifacts which appear to be rooted in the horticultural traditions of the tropical forests are ceramic graters in the form of a fish (Plate II) or anthropomorphic fish (#13). Usually interpreted as having been used to grate manioc (yucca), it is unlikely that these objects were actually used for such purposes. More probably they were ceremonial or ritual objects linked to manioc-growing traditions. This is suggested by the relatively few specimens that have been uncovered, as well as by the iconography. Utilitarian forms, on the other hand, would likely have been made of wood and inlaid with sharp flakes of stone.

Among the Trumai Indians of the upper Xingu, Brazil, there is an important ceremonial ritual known as the Ole, or manioc ceremony. During this ritual, offerings of fish, placed on manioc cakes, are made each day before posts which have been erected in the center of the village for this purpose (Zerries, 1969). Little else is known concerning this Trumai ritual. The picture is somewhat clarified, however, in the Kwarup ceremony of the Camayura, a neighboring group. The Kwarup ceremony appears to be the Camayura version of the Trumai Ole ceremony. The purpose of the Kwarup ritual is to promote the fertility and growth of plants. The posts which they erect represent the *mama'e* (the "mothers"), the spirit masters of various vegetable and animal species. It is said that manioc and the instruments used to cultivate it were given to the Cayamura by fish-like *mama'e*.

Among both the Trumai and the Camayura, therefore, an association is made between fish and manioc. It is common knowledge that graters are used to process manioc. Is it not possible that the Tumaco-La Tolita ceramic graters, in the form of a fish, are linked to traditions similar to those found among the Camayura and Trumai? The argument is given added weight when we consider that some of the fish-form graters are anthropomorphized, perhaps to represent the fish-like *mama'e*.

Another art motif common in Tumaco-La Tolita sculpture is the anthropomorphic fanged feline, often depicted with an erect phallus (#12). Such a being is not analagous to any ordinary living animal and therefore falls within the category of the fantastic.

Descriptions of fantastic beings are common among the mind-altering, drug-using cultures of the tropical forests of South America. The Tukanoans of the northwest Amazon, for example, believe in a forest spirit known as the *boraro*. The *boraro* is imagined as "a monstrous man-like being, covered with shaggy black hair, with huge pointed fangs protruding from his mouth. He has big pointed ears and a large penis." (G. Reichel-Dolmatoff, 1975). The *boraro* is essentially a phallic being, which, according to Reichel-Dolmatoff, represents an image of unbridled male sexual power, particularly dangerous because it is not subject to traditional cultural norms.

It is uncertain whether some of the Tumaco-La Tolita fanged felines are representations of a fantastic being, or class of beings, analogous to the *boraro*. But given the other cultural homologues with tropical-forest culture patterns, it would seem advisable not to dismiss such analogies out of hand. Certainly we should not consider realistic depictions of fanged felines (#6) as falling within the category of *boraro*-like representations. Anthropomorphized, fanged jaguars with huge, erect phalli, however, are common in Tumaco-La Tolita art. It is this latter genre that appears to fit the ethnographic descriptions of the *boraro*.

Relatively common are graphically depicted sexual themes which lacked any pornographic intent on the part of the artist. Anal coitus, auto- and mutual masturbation, and other forms of sexual fondling are common. Conspicuously absent are depictions of frontal coitus. This thematic approach to sex is also typical for north coastal Peru, where frontal coitus is also noticeably absent from the art. It is also significant that homosexuality is not portrayed in Tumáco-La Tolita art. As previously speculated (Labbé, 1980) with regard to Moche art of north coastal Peru, the absence of portrayals of frontal coitus, in combination with an artistic emphasis on alternative modes of sexual expression, may indicate an artistically communicated emphasis on birth control.

Other stock themes portray couples in intimate embrace; women depicted holding one or both breasts, alluding to their role as nurturers; and mothers holding infants (#5), a related theme. Women holding one or both breasts is also a common theme in West Mexican shaft-tomb art, but it appears there somewhat later than in Tumaco-La Tolita.

Figures in ritual garb (#2) are fairly common and indicate a rich and varied ceremonial life. Bird forms are often an important aspect of ritual headdresses, and feathers are often depicted on costumes. Both men and women are shown with alter-ego figures surmounting the back and peering overhead (#2). In Tumaco-La Tolita art, the alter ego is more often than not anthropomorphized, rather than zoomorphized, a clear deviation from the alter-ego motif found on the stone sculpture of San Agustin. [A common form of this motif at San Agustin is the lizard. We may observe in this respect that the Waica of the upper Orinoco River hold the belief that each child possesses an alter ego in the form of a brown lizard (Zerries, 1969). The alter-ego concept is firmly rooted in shamanic ideas. Archaeological examples of this motif, in the form of stone figures with zoomorphs surmounting their back, have been found in the Amazonian lowlands. Unfortunately, these figures cannot be dated.]

Among animals depicted, the most common are birds (#3), felines, armadillos, serpents, and opossums. Both felines and caymans are often rendered in anthropomorphized form. A most remarkable rendition is that of a quadrupedal, winged, fanged creature (#7), which undoubtedly belongs to the class of fantastic beings. Considering the importance of the use of mind-altering plants among Colombian Indians, it is tempting to view the many depictions of fantastic beings as a result of visions experienced under the influence of psychomimetic plant substances. Similar visions are widely reported in Colombian ethnographies. "From the Carribean coast to the highlands of the interior, from the Pacific to the Orinoco, the Indians told of strange beings, who appeared to them in the shapes of monsters armed with pointed fangs, terrifying beings, with glowing eyes and roaring voices..." (G. Reichel-Dolmatoff, 1975).

Representations of dwellings, most probably temple models, are fairly common (#9). These structures are characterized by a square or rectangular floor plan. The roofs are generally relatively high-pitched, often with pronounced gables. Steps at the front of the edifice are sometimes indicated, and entrances lack doors of any kind. Some of these models, particularly those with pronounced gables and frontally sloping roofs, are remarkably similar to house types found in parts of Oceania and island Southeast Asia, most notably the Batak house types of Indonesia.

We have little information on the contextual use of musical instruments. Clay whistles and ocarinas are well represented in public and private collections. Whistles come in a variety of polymorphic forms, usually anthropomorphic, zoomorphic, or combinations of both. Ocarinas are commonly fashioned in the form of half-man, half-alligator. Other instruments may have been made of perishable material, such as wood. Double pan-pipes, graduated from the outer toward the center pipes, are depicted on figurines (#23).

Double-spouted bridge-handle vessels are a prevalent form (#15, 17) also found in the Calima Zone, the Middle Cauca region, Tierradentro, and San Agustín. The early Calima types are commonly anthropomorphic or zoomorphic jars, a tradition which continued there in modified form during the

Yotoco Phase, as well as in contemporary Middle Cauca ceramics. Vessels from Tierradentro, San Agustin, and the coast are usually devoid of zoomorphic or anthropomorphic elaboration, although these forms are occasionally encountered.

Except for a few such jars from the Tumaco-La Tolita region, it is doubtful that these vessels were used to contain liquids. Their only opening is at the end of the spouts, which are extremely narrow in diameter, making them difficult to fill. It is more likely that the form of this vessel held symbolic significance, as suggested by vessels (#16) in which one spout is phalliform and the other is wide-mouthed. Such sexual dimorphic symbolism is well documented for Colombian Indians, particularly by groups such as the Kogi of the Sierra Nevada de Santa Marta and the Desana of the Vaupes region of southeastern Colombia. The use of form as symbolism has unfortunately been ignored by most investigators.

As a final note, other observations which reveal aspects of Tumaco-La Tolita culture inform us that:

- Cranial deformation was practiced by at least some of the population (#4).
- As observed by Gomara in the 16th century, the custom of piercing the ears and nose septum for the placement of ornaments was also practiced by the prehistoric populations (#22, 24).
- Women generally seem to have worn a wraparound skirt to cover their privates, but otherwise went around bare-breasted (#1).
- Headgear appears to have been quite common, typically covering the head, but not the ears (#21).
- A number of figurines portray diseased individuals suffering from acromegaly, syphilis, elephantiasis, facial paralysis, and a variety of tumors.
- Old age is clearly represented.
- The use of molds for the mass production of art objects tends to indicate a dense population along the coast (#31–34), requiring large quantities of ritual art.
- Trophy heads are occasionally portrayed, usually held by a primary figure, perhaps signifying that head-hunting was practiced or that severed heads were used in certain rituals (#36).

1
Standing female figure
Grayish-white, decorated with modeled and incised detail
h: 13½ in. (34.3 cm) × w: 4¾ in. (12.1 cm)
Tumaco-La Tolita culture (ca. 300 B.C.–300 A.D.)
Southwest coastal Colombia–northwest coastal Ecuador

The figure is wearing a short wraparound skirt. A necklace with a circular pendant is indicated by deeply incised lines and relief.

2
Standing figure in ritual garb
Gray, with added red paint
h: 8⅝ in. (22 cm) × w: 4¾ in. (12.1 cm)
Tumaco-La Tolita culture (ca. 300 B.C.–300 A.D.)
Southwest coastal Colombia–northwest coastal Ecuador

The figure probably represents a shaman or priest. An alter-ego figure can be seen peering from above the head. The figure is wearing a feathered headdress, ear spools, a nose ring, a labret (lip plug), and arm bands. A shell ocarina hangs from the neck. Great emphasis was placed on the details of the face and costume and little on the hands and feet.

3
Bird
Grayish-white, decorated with relief and incised details
h: 5½ in. (14 cm) × l: 8 in. (20.3 cm)
Tumaco-La Tolita culture (ca. 300 B.C.–300 A.D.)
Southwest coastal Colombia–northwest coastal Ecuador

This is a stylized depiction of a parrot.

4
Female figure
Gray
h: 7¾ in. (19.8 cm) × w: 6 in. (15.2 cm)
Tumaco-La Tolita culture (ca. 300 B.C.–300 A.D.)
Southwest coastal Colombia–northwest coastal Ecuador

This is a modeled figure of serene demeanor wearing ear ornaments, an elegant necklace, and a nose ring. The figure's head is swept back, probably indicating artificial skull deformation. Skull deformation, a modification of the cranium, may be intentionally produced (by tying boards in the front and back of the head); or it may be the accidental result of such customs as binding a child to a cradle board. Skull deformation is known from as early as 1500 B.C. in Ecuador and about 1200–1000 B.C. in Mexico.

5
Seated female figure with child
Grayish-white
h: 6⅞ in. (15.9 cm) × w: 3¼ in. (8.3 cm)
Tumaco-La Tolita culture (ca. 300 B.C.–300 A.D.)
Southwest coastal Colombia–northwest coastal Ecuador

This genre emphasizes the nurturing role of the mother.

6
Fanged feline
Grayish-white
h: 4¼ in. (10.8 cm) × l: 5¼ in. (13.3 cm)
Tumaco-La Tolita culture
(ca. 300 B.C.–300 A.D.)
Southwest coastal Colombia–northwest coastal Ecuador

This is a stylized depiction of a jaguar.

7
Lid from an *incensario*, with fanged feline
Grayish-white
h: 6⅜ in. (16.2 cm) × d: 7 in. (17.8 cm)
Tumaco-La Tolita culture
(ca. 300 B.C.–300 A.D.)
Southwest coastal Colombia–northwest coastal Ecuador

8
Stylized shark
Grayish-white, decorated with modeled and incised details
l: 10½ in. (26.6 cm) × w: 6½ in. (16.5 cm)
Tumaco-La Tolita culture (ca. 300 B.C.–300 A.D.)
Southwest coastal Colombia — northwest coastal Ecuador

9
Temple model
Grayish-white
h: 4⅞ in. (11.8 cm) × w: 4¼ in. (10.8 cm)
Tumaco-La Tolita culture (ca. 300 B.C.–300 A.D.)
Southwest coastal Colombia–northwest coastal Ecuador

10
Mythic fish, with the front of the head modeled in the form of a temple
Grayish-white
h: 4 in. (10.2 cm) × l: 9¾ in. (24.8 cm)
Tumaco-La Tolita culture (ca. 300 B.C.–300 A.D.)
Southwest coastal Colombia–northwest coastal Ecuador

The manner in which the teeth are formed suggests that the artist was using them iconographically. Triangles placed point to point are symbols of interacting male and female dyads, connoting fertility. (See Labbé 1982 for the significance of temples in pre-Columbian civilizations.)

11
Anthropomorphized-jaguar head
Grayish-white
h: 4¾ in. (12.1 cm) × w: 5½ in. (14 cm)
Tumaco-La Tolita culture (ca. 300 B.C.–300 A.D.)
Southwest coastal Colombia–northwest coastal Ecuador

12
Anthropomorphized jaguar
Grayish-white
h: 6½ in. (16.5 cm) × w: 3 in. (7.6 cm)
Tumaco-La Tolita culture (ca. 300 B.C.–300 A.D.)
Southwest coastal Colombia–northwest coastal Ecuador

13
Fish-form grater with human head
Grayish-white, with traces of red paint
l: 9 in. (22.9 cm) × w: 3⅜ in. (8.6 cm)
Tumaco-La Tolita culture (ca. 300 B.C.–300 A.D.)
Southwest coastal Colombia–northwest coastal Ecuador
This is a ceremonial grater that probably represents the spirit progenitor of the manioc plant.

12

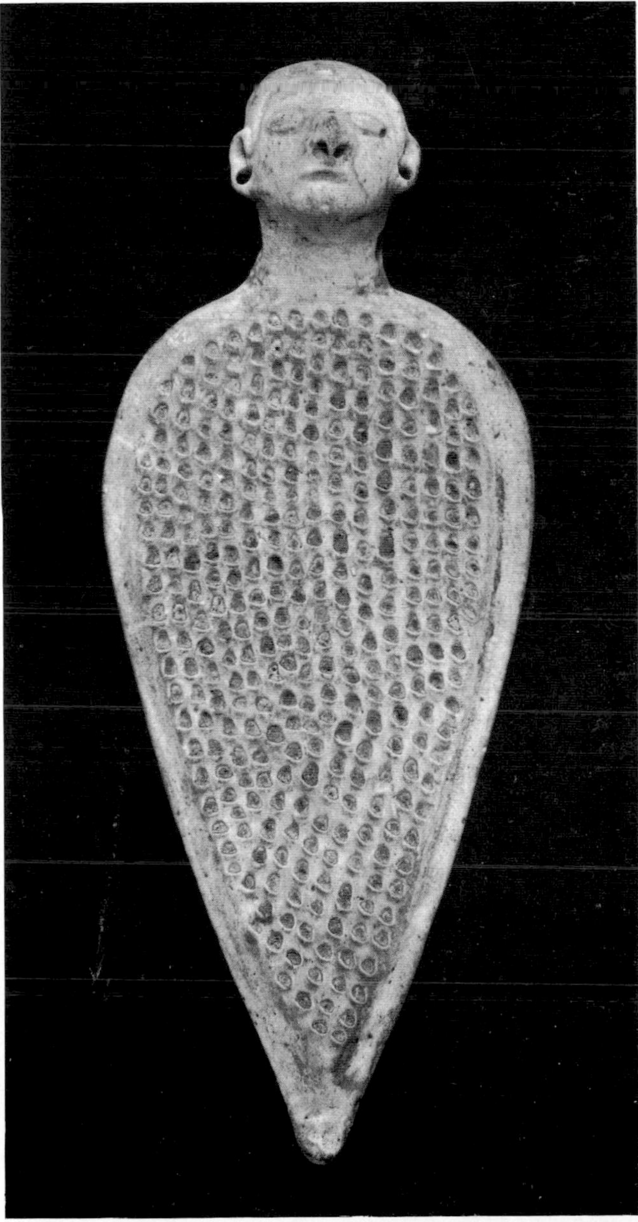

14
Poporo
Grayish-white, decorated with black painted stripes
h: 5¾ in. (14.6 cm) × d: 5½ in. (14 cm)
Specific culture undetermined.
Southwest coastal Colombia–northwest coastal Ecuador

These containers were used to store lime, which is mixed with the coca leaves before it is chewed. Among some Colombian Indians, such as the Kogi of the Sierra Nevada de Santa Marta, the *poporo* is regarded as female, and the stick that is dipped in it to extract the lime is regarded as male; the process of extracting the lime is symbolic, therefore, of sexual intercourse.

15
Anthropomorphic-zoomorphic pedestal *alcarrazas*
left: Light gray, with traces of black paint
h: 5⅝ in. (14.4 cm) × circum: 14¾ in. (36.9 cm)
right: Dark gray
h: 5¾ in. (14.6 cm) × circum: 14 in. (35.6 cm)
Tumaco-La Tolita culture (ca. 300 B.C.–300 A.D.)
Southwest coastal Colombia–northwest coastal Ecuador

The anthropomorphic head on the left is depicted with a quid of coca leaf in the cheek. The head on the right is that of a fanged feline.

16
Double-spouted *alcarrazas*
left: Gray, with traces of white paint
h: 8¼ in. (21 cm) × d: 6 in. (15.2 cm)
right: Gray
h: 6¾ in. (17.2 cm) × d: 7¼ in. (18.4 cm)
Tumaco-La Tolita culture (ca. 300 B.C.–300 A.D.)
Southwest coastal Colombia–northwest coastal Ecuador

These vessels are distinguished by dimorphic spouts. In the context of prehispanic Colombian and Ecuadorian Indian symbolism, the wide-mouthed spout represents the female form while the phalliform spout represents the male form.

17
Double-spouted *alcarraza*
Grayish-white
h: 6½ in. (16.5 cm) × w: 5½ in. (14 cm)
Tumaco-La Tolita culture (ca. 300 B.C.–300 A.D.) (?)
Southwest coastal Colombia–northwest coastal Ecuador

The body of the vessel is modeled in the form of an ithyphallic human male.

18
Phalli fragments
Grayish-white
left: l: 5½ in. (14 cm)
right: l: 4 in. (10.2 cm)
Tumaco-La Tolita culture (ca. 300 B.C.–300 A.D.)
Southwest coastal Colombia–northwest coastal Ecuador

These phallic fragments represent uncircumsized specimens.

19
Phalliform vessel
Grayish-white, with traces of red paint
l: 4½ in. (11.4 cm) × w: 2¼ in. (5.7 cm)
Tumaco-La Tolita culture (ca. 300 B.C.–300 A.D.)
Southwest coastal Colombia–northwest coastal Ecuador

This possibly was a ceremonial mortar used to grind plants or soft mineral substances. The edge of the shallow receptacle is notched along the sides. The prominent, exposed glans may indicate that circumcision was performed in the Tumaco-La Tolita culture, although other phallic specimens clearly indicate intact foreskins.

20
Phalliform winged insect
Gray, decorated with incised details
l: 4½ in. (11.4 cm) × h: 1⅝ in. (4.1 cm)
Tumaco-La Tolita culture (ca. 300 B.C.–300 A.D.)
Southwest coastal Colombia–northwest coastal Ecuador

The transposition of wings on this grub-like, phalliform body would indicate a composite symbolic imagery that connotes fertility and transformation. The shape and incising of the wings suggests the female sexual organ with labia.

21
Head with headdress
Dark gray, decorated with incised details
h: 5½ in. (14 cm) × w: 4¼ in. (10.8 cm)
Tumaco-La Tolita culture
(ca. 300 B.C.–300 A.D.) (?)
Southwest coastal Colombia–northwest coastal Ecuador

22
Ceramic heads
Grayish-white
Avg. h: 2¼ in. (5.7 cm) × Avg. w: 2½ in. (6.4 cm)
Tumaco-La Tolita culture (ca. 300 B.C.–300 A.D.)
Southwest coastal Colombia–northwest coastal Ecuador

23
Fragment of a figure playing pan pipes
Gray
h: 3¾ in. (9.5 cm) × w: 2⅞ in. (7.3 cm)
Tumaco-La Tolita culture (ca. 300 B.C.–300 A.D.)
Southwest coastal Colombia–northwest coastal Ecuador

24
Human heads
Grayish-white
left: h: 5¼ in. (13.3 cm) × w: 3½ in. (8.9 cm)
right: h: 3⅞ in. (9.8 cm) × w: 1⅞ in. (4.8 cm)
Tumaco-La Tolita culture (ca. 300 B.C.–300 A.D.)
Southwest coastal Colombia–northwest coastal Ecuador

25
Human head fragment
Grayish-white
h: 4 in. (10.2 cm) × w: 2¾ in. (7 cm)
Tumaco-La Tolita culture (ca. 300 B.C.–300 A.D.)
Southwest coastal Colombia–northwest coastal Ecuador

26
Head with neck collar
Grayish-white
h: 4½ in. (11.4 cm) × w: 3¾ in. (9.5 cm)
Tumaco-La Tolita culture (ca. 300 B.C.–300 A.D.)
Southwest coastal Colombia–northwest coastal Ecuador

26

27
Head fragment
Grayish-white
h: 3 in. (7.6 cm) × w: 2¾ in. (7 cm)
Tumaco-La Tolita culture (ca. 300 B.C.–300 A.D.)
Southwest coastal Colombia–northwest coastal Ecuador

28
Seated anthropomorphic figure
Grayish-white
h: 5¼ in. (13.3 cm) × w: 4½ in. (11.4 cm)
Tumaco-La Tolita culture (ca. 300 B.C.–300 A.D.)
Southwest coastal Colombia–northwest coastal Ecuador

29
Figure seated on a bench
Grayish-white
h: 6¾ in. (17.1 cm) × w: 3 in. (7.6 cm)
Tumaco-La Tolita culture (ca. 300 B.C.–300 A.D.)
Southwest coastal Colombia–northwest coastal Ecuador

30
Figural jar
Dark gray
h: 5¾ in. (14.6 cm) × w: 4½ in. (11.4 cm)
Tumaco-La Tolita culture (ca. 300 B.C.–300 A.D.)
Southwest coastal Colombia–northwest coastal Ecuador
This is a Tumaco-La Tolita version of the Calima-style *canastero*.

31
Mold for mask
Grayish-white
h: 7⅜ in. (18.7 cm) × w: 8 in. (20.3 cm)
Tumaco-La Tolita culture (ca. 300 B.C.–300 A.D.)
Southwest coastal Colombia–northwest coastal Ecuador

32
Molds for casting standing figures in ritual attire
Gray
left: h: 5½ in. (14 cm) × w: 3 in. (7.6 cm)
right: h: 7 in. (17.8 cm) × w: 5 in. (12.7 cm)
Tumaco-La Tolita culture (ca. 300 B.C.–300 A.D.)
Southwest coastal Colombia–northwest coastal Ecuador

28

29

30

31

32

33
left: Roller stamp
Grayish-white
h: 3⅝ in. (9.3 cm) × w: 1½ in. (3.8 cm)
right: Flat stamp
Grayish-white
h: 4 in. (10.2 cm) × w: 3 in. (7.6 cm)
Tumaco-La Tolita culture
(ca. 300 B.C.–300 A.D.)
Southwest coastal Colombia–northwest coastal Ecuador

34
left: Mold for casting fanged felines
Grayish-white
h: 3⅜ in. (8.6 cm) × w: 3 in. (7.6 cm)
right: Mold-cast fanged feline
Grayish-white
h: 3¾ in. (9.5 cm) × w: 3½ in. (8.9 cm)
Tumaco-La Tolita culture
(ca. 300 B.C.–300 A.D.)
Southwest coastal Colombia–northwest coastal Ecuador

35
Mold-cast mythic monster maskette
Gray
h: 4¾ in. (12.1 cm) × w: 5½ in. (14 cm)
Tumaco-La Tolita culture
(ca. 300 B.C.–300 A.D.)
Southwest coastal Colombia–northwest coastal Ecuador

36
Mold-cast figure of a priest or shaman holding a trophy head
Grayish-white
h: 4⅛ in. (10.5 cm) × w: 3⅜ in. (8.6 cm)
Tumaco-La Tolita culture
(ca. 300 B.C.–300 A.D.)
Southwest coastal Colombia–northwest coastal Ecuador

37
Death mask and mold-cast fanged-feline mask
Grayish-white
left: h: 3¼ in. (8.3 cm) × w: 4⅜ in. (11.1 cm)
right: h: 4 in. (10.1 cm) × w: 5 in. (12.7 cm)
Tumaco-La Tolita culture
(ca. 300 B.C.–300 A.D.)
Southwest coastal Colombia–northwest coastal Ecuador

33

34

35

36

37

38

Mold-cast figures
Grayish-white
left: h: 3¼ in. (8.3 cm) × w: 2⅛ in. (5.4 cm)
right: h: 4¼ in. (10.8 cm) × w: 2¾ in. (7 cm)
Tumaco-La Tolita culture (ca. 300 B.C.–300 A.D.)
Southwest coastal Colombia–northwest coastal Ecuador

CHAPTER II

THE CALIMA REGION

Cycles of Life and Death in the Valle del Cauca

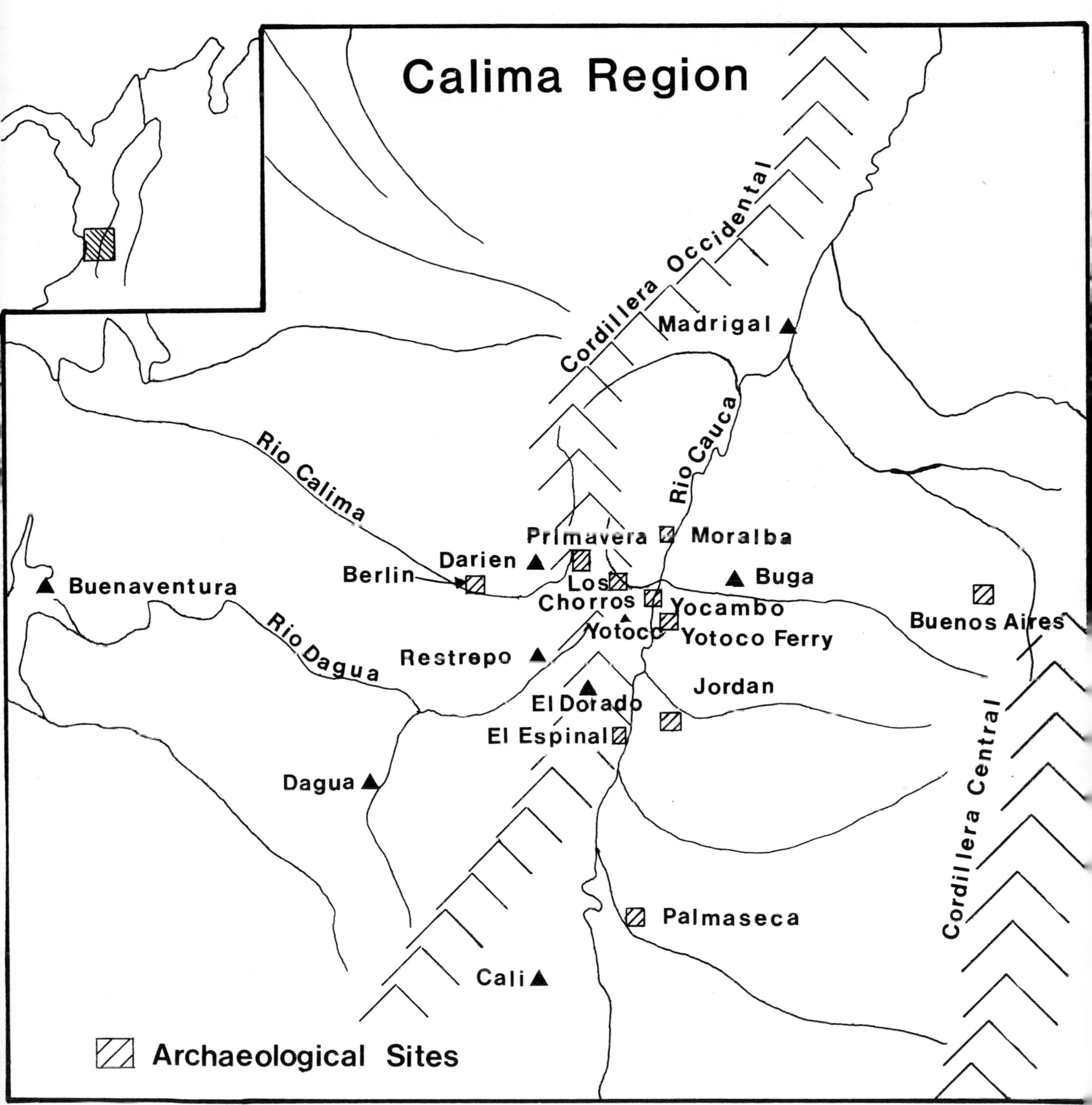
Calima Region
Cordillera Occidental
Madrigal
Rio Cauca
Rio Calima
Primavera
Moralba
Darien
Berlin
Buenaventura
Los
Chorros
Buga
Yocambo
Yotoco
Yotoco Ferry
Buenos Aires
Rio Dagua
Restrepo
Jordan
El Dorado
El Espinal
Dagua
Cordillera Central
Palmaseca
Cali
Archaeological Sites

The term "Calima" has been used in Colombia to refer to certain styles of ceramic ware and goldwork found in restricted areas of the Department of Valle Del Cauca, without regard to specific internal stylistic variation or chronology. In more limited popular usage, Calima has been used to designate the earliest ceramic ware found in the region, a brown-slipped and incised ware now classified as belonging to the Llama cultural phase. Calima is also employed to describe an archaeological zone within the Department of Valle Del Cauca. The full extent of the zone, however, has not been determined.

GEOGRAPHY

The Calima region lies within the Department of Valle del Cauca and embraces the upper Calima Valley and surrounding areas of the Western Cordillera (Cordillera Occidental), as well as adjacent lands along both sides of the Cauca River. This region is naturally rich and fertile, with a mean annual rainfall of about 96.5 cm (38 in.). The western part of the area is crossed by the Calima and Dagua rivers, while the Cauca flows through the eastern reaches, between the Western and Central Cordilleras.

THE LLAMA PHASE

In recent years, a sequence of distinct and important cultural phases has been designated for this region: the Llama, the Yotoco, and the Sonso. Additional cultural complexes, such as the Moralba phase, which stratigraphically overlays the Sonso, are poorly represented archaeologically and appear to have had very limited duration or regional significance. The Llama phase, formerly Early Calima, is a recent designation for a cultural manifestation within the Calima Zone.

Recent archaeological surveys and excavations in the area have located over sixteen cemeteries, each consisting of from six to twenty tombs (Schrimpff, Herrera, Bray, 1982). The cemeteries are commonly located on the sides of hills. Burial offerings sometimes consist of only one or two ceramic vessels. More commonly, a number of vessels, including ornaments of stone and gold, are found (ibid). Occasionally a tomb is discovered empty. Skeletal remains, which would permit a study of the physical characteristics and pathological patterns of Llama-phase people, have not been unearthed. This may be due to high acid soil conditions, which are not conducive to the preservation of bone and other organic materials (ibid), or it may be due to other as yet undetermined cultural factors.

A problem encountered by archaeologists lay in locating Llama-phase habitation sites. The vicinity of the Llama-phase cemeteries yielded ample evidence of the presence and activities of peoples from the later Yotoco and Sonso phases, but no clear evidence of the existence of Llama-phase people. It has been suggested that peoples of the succeeding phases destroyed the evidence in the process of constructing dwellings and terracing the hillsides for agriculture. However, the El Topacio site within the municipality of Darien did yield Llama-phase cultural remains, overlain by Yotoco and Sonso remains, respectively.

Llama-phase ceramics are recovered from tombs of the shaft grave variety (Perez de Barradas, 1954; Dussan de Reichel, 1965; in Bray, 1978).

Ceramic sculptures include anthropomorphic, zoomorphic, and phytomorphic double-spouted jars (*alcarrazas*) (#39, 42); anthropomorphic and zoomorphic jars with a receptacle at the back (*canasteros*) (#45); and other polymorphic jars, open-mouthed at the top (#46, 47). Llama-phase ceramics are commonly surfaced with a brown to reddish-brown slip. Less common forms in the Llama-phase style are masks (#49, 50) and pipes.

Decoration is usually effected by means of modeling, incising, or excising. The most common renditions are modeled human or animal forms. According to a study undertaken by Ann Legast (1982), both the frequency and variety of animal depictions are greater for Llama-phase ceramics than they are for the succeeding Yotoco phase. Among the fauna represented are birds, armadillos (#42), felines, monkeys, bats, kinkajous, turtles, iguanas, and amphibians. The serpent, not depicted per se, is used in the formation and elaboration of other animal and human forms (Plate V). On the more highly incised specimens, human faces are typically well-defined, with prominently delineated cheeks, noses, and lips. Eyes are executed in a variety of styles: incised with hollow elongated centers; hollow, puffed, and incised; or simple incisions.

As is general for prehispanic Colombia, great emphasis is placed on the head. There is a distinct lack of emphasis on genitalia, making it often difficult to determine which sex is indicated. Arms and legs are given secondary importance, often only slightly distinguished from the trunk of the body. Figures with receptacles on their backs (Plate VII) have more distinctive limbs than figural jars open at the top (#43). On figures with receptacles, hands are usually placed on the knees, while on figural jars open at the top, they are generally held inward and placed on the abdomen. The predominant posture is crouching or sitting, rarely standing (#48). Although it might be presumed that figures in a sitting posture with hands on knees are seated on a bench, the bench itself is not indicated. After 500 A.D., the bench is a commonly rendered art motif in the ceramic art from the Caribbean coast through the Magdalena River valley and the Sinu, Middle Cauca, Popoyan, and highland Nariño regions. It is notably rare or absent in the ceramic art of cultures from areas such as the southern Pacific lowlands, San Agustin, Tierradentro, and the Calima region.

Body tattooing is indicated by means of incised geometrics on the chest and abdomen of many figures, particularly those of the *canastero* genre (Plate VII). Common tattoo motifs are concentric rectangles and concentric ovoids. The human figures are generally naked. Figures are commonly shown wearing a necklace. On some, a seashell is shown suspended from the neck (#48). The shell is incised, and it suggests both in appearance and decoration the decorated ceramic shell ocarinas found in highland Nariño shaft graves of the Piartal and Tuza phases (750 – 1500 A.D.).

It is often difficult to determine on some figures whether hairstyle or headgear is indicated. A common style is the lobed variety, usually in three rows, but also quite often in two. A cross-hatched band may signify a headband, or it may form the base of the headgear. Clearly in one figure (#45), a hairstyle is indicated. As opposed to the *canastero* genre, where the lobes are three-dimensional and rise above the head, the hair of human figures of the *alcarraza* genre (#41) is generally unobtrusive and is indicated merely by incised detail. Hair or headgear is not portrayed on the flat-topped figural jars (#48), but it is partially rendered on flat-topped jars which flare outward at the rim (#43). Each genre artistically conforms to distinct and recognized canons specific to itself.

A common decorative element is the incised circle (Plate VIII) widely used over much of prehispanic Colombia. It has been found at Monsu and in the Tairona, Muisca, Tierradentro, and other regions. In Llama-phase Calima art, the circle is commonly employed to indicate breasts, the navel, and occasionally the eyes. It is probable that there is added but as yet undetermined symbolism involved.

Llama-phase ceramic masks are extremely rare. The two specimens documented in this chapter are in a style clearly related to that of a ceramic mask ascribed by Alcina Franch to the Tumaco-La Tolita culture (300 B.C.–300 A.D.) and reproduced in *Pre-Columbian Art* (José Alcina Franch, 1983, plate 166, p. 340). In all three specimens, old age is indicated by deep curving furrows. The Calima specimens differ from the Tumaco-La Tolita mask in that the furrows are divided by the nose and nose bridge, while in the latter, the brow furrows extend uninterrupted across the top of the mask, although the lower furrows are indeed divided by the nose. The mouth on the Tumaco-La Tolita specimen is a solid concavity, while that on the Calima masks is open front to back.

In the Mesoamerican context, old age was often characteristic of certain deity representations. Huehueteotl (the Old, Old, Sacred One, i.e., the Lord of Fire) was so depicted, as was Kinich Ahau, an aspect of the sun, among the Maya (Labbé, 1982). Some depictions of old personages found in Tumaco-La Tolita culture are almost identical with Mesoamerican depictions of Huehueteotl, while others look remarkably like Kinich Ahau.

THE YOTOCO PHASE

In 1964, surveys and excavations in the Cauca River valley uncovered a distinct cultural complex called the Yotoco phase (W. Bray and M. E. Moseley, 1976). Yotoco-phase culture was centered in the Cauca River valley, extending in the north to the southern region of the Department of Quindio and in the south to just north of the city of Cali. Yotoco-phase material has been uncovered to the east and west of the Cauca River, and is widely found in areas once occupied by Llama-phase people.

In addition to their fine ceramics, Yotoco-phase people worked stone into celts and grinding implements and fashioned a variety of ritual and ornamental objects out of gold.

The Yotoco-phase economy appears to have been based on corn agriculture and the cultivation of other plant comestibles, supplemented by fishing and some hunting. Faunal and floral remains are notably rare or absent from the archaeological record because of highly acidic soil conditions, which do not favor preservation. Corn agriculture, however, seems to be indicated by the grinding stones.

During this phase, cultural activity in the region, such as agricultural terracing of the countryside, house building, and other modifications of the local environment, increased markedly. From surveys conducted thus far, the population density, at least toward the end of the Yotoco phase (around 1200 A.D.), seems to have been quite high.

It should be understood that some of the radiocarbon dates obtained for this phase are highly suspect (radiocarbon dates for Yotoco range from 900 B.C.–1770 A.D.) Considering the fairly consistent dates for the succeeding Sonso phase (ca. 1200 A.D. to the Spanish conquest) obtained thus far, and in view of the fact that Sonso-phase material is commonly found stratigraphically deposited over Yotoco material, a terminal date somewhere between 1200–1300 A.D. seems reasonable.

Determining a commencement date for this phase is somewhat more difficult. The preceding Llama phase appears to have ended sometime between the first century B.C. and the first century A.D. A comparison of one Llama-phase anthropomorphic *alcarraza* (#39) with a second (#53) demonstrates a stylistic continuity between the two vessels. The latter vessel, however, is decorated by means of the resist technique. It is possible that this vessel and other similar examples represent a transitional period between Llama and Yotoco. If this proves to be true, early Yotoco would date to the first centuries A.D.

YOTOCO PHASE CERAMICS

The post-firing technique of resist, or negative painting, is typical for Yotoco-phase ceramics (#53, 57). First the vessel is covered with slip, a fine solution of clay, which is polished or burnished prior to firing. After firing, it is painted with a plant resin. Areas of the vessel intended to remain the color of the slip are covered with additional slip, and the entire vessel is then held over a flame. The plant resin is converted by the refiring to a shiny black. After the vessel has cooled somewhat, the added slip, which has served to protect the underlying one, is brushed away, revealing the polished slip beneath. The entire process, which has been described by Bruhns for Middle Cauca resist wares, results in a black-on-red design (Bruhns, 1976).

The classic Yotoco resist designs are similar to related designs found to the north in the Middle Cauca region. The Middle Cauca ceramics date to between 1100–1400 A.D., which is contemporary with the latter part of the Yotoco phase.

The oldest dated resist ware discovered in Colombia was unearthed during archaeological investigations in the San Agustin area in 1960. Luis Duque Gómez reported finding sherds and fragments decorated in the resist technique at the base of the Northwest Mound of the Mesita B complex of the Archaeological Park. These sherds and fragments, which were decorated in resist black-on-red as well as resist red-on-red, were in a strata composed of refuse dated to the second century A.D.

The resist technique probably originated in Ecuador, where it is found in Early Cerro Narrio deposits, in highland Ecuador. According to Lathrap (1975), the Cerro Narrio material predates the Chorrera resist-painted pottery by many centuries. This suggests that the resist-painting technique in Ecuador originated early in the second millenium B.C.

There is a marked difference in the clay paste used to fashion Yotoco-phase funerary pottery and that used for Llama-phase pottery. Yotoco ceramic pastes are usually finely textured and durable, whereas the Llama-phase paste is typically coarse.

The surface of Yotoco-phase vessels was decorated by means of slips effecting white, red, and orange-tan. These color schemes were often mixed, although the most common combination was red and white, arranged in bands or selectively applied to certain areas of the sculpture. The choice of color may have had symbolic significance.

THE SONSO PHASE

The next major cultural phase, the Sonso, began sometime around 1200 A.D. and continued to the Spanish conquest. Much of what we know about the Sonso people, some of whom were encountered by the Spanish in the 16th century, was recorded by chroniclers such as Pedro Cieza de Léon. Cieza observed the living cultures of a number of different tribes occupying the Cauca Valley. It is not known, however, how these groups were organized politically. It is evident that population densities were quite high and that the various groups shared many cultural traits.

The Gorrones in the northwestern part of the Calima Zone lived in large round houses with straw roofs. Villages were composed of groups of fifteen or so dwellings and were dispersed along the slopes of hills and valleys. Their economy was based on corn, beans, squash, and root crops, supplemented by fishing. The diet was also augmented by a large variety of fruits, including pineapples, *aguacate*, and *guayabas*. The Gorrones were said to have been named after a fish they caught and commonly sold at market.

The Gorrones may have practiced headhunting and other forms of trophy taking. According to Cieza, heads and other human body parts were hung inside some Gorrone huts. The eating of human flesh, particularly that of captive enemies, seems to have been widely practiced. Trophy heads, in some instances, were kept as assurance of power over one's enemy. The hanging of hands and feet may actually have been a reverential act, from the perspective of the indigene. We should recall the importance that severed body parts played in the mythology of the root-crop growng societies. In other cases, as is recorded for the fierce Pijao Indians of the upper Magdalena valley, there appears to have been a distinct and deliberate cult of dominance exercised over the bodies of slain enemies.

Gorrone society was somewhat stratified. The deceased elite had their bodies wrapped in fine cloth of considerable length and width. Gold jewelry and other small funerary offerings were placed between the layers of cloth. The enclothed body was then tightly bound with a long cordage. The disposition of the body afterwards is not known. Cieza states that others were buried in deep graves. Undoubtedly, these are the shaft graves uncovered archaeologically.

There appears to have been a marked decline in the quality of metalworking when compared with the Yotoco phase. We can infer that wood was worked into sculpture, but most perishable materials have long since disappeared from the archaeological record.

Other groups of people were also living in the region. The Liles were a relatively small group, distinct from the Gorrones but perhaps somewhat under their authority. They inhabited lands just to the south. The Bugas occupied lands to the east of the Cauca River, while the Aguales were settled in the Cauca Valley.

From the available information, we can surmise that there was no central authority for the area as a whole. The highest level of organization was perhaps a small group of loosely federated townships, under the authority of a chieftain. Most townships appear to have enjoyed relative autonomy and were governed by their own chieftain or headman, who had some authority in the settlement of disputes. However, personal wrongs were usually avenged by friends and relatives of the injured party. Aberrant behavior was controlled by community disapproval rather than by dint of vested legal authority.

Some groups apparently practiced polygamy, but we do not know if this was a general custom or restricted to the elite. According to Cieza, where polygamy was practiced, one wife was the principal, while others held inferior status. Still others had even lower status, being little more than servants. According to Juan de Castellanos, another chronicler, women enjoyed relative parity with men and played an important role in community affairs—even in warfare, taunting the enemy with insults and rantings.

War between rival groups was rather common. Defeated enemy warriors, according to Cieza, were sometimes taken into the conqueror's hut. There the body was flayed and the flesh removed for later consumption. The skin was stuffed with ash and presumably sewn up tight. The defleshed skull was modeled with wax, so that it took on the appearance of the slain warrior. This zombie-like effigy was then placed on a special table and positioned in such a manner that it appeared to be alive. This custom has also been reported for the Pijao Indians, who lived in the upper Magdalena Valley. According to a popular tale, a Pijao killed an enemy Paez, flayed the body and ate the flesh. He then restored the bones to the skin, stuffing the body with *iutse* plants. [*Iutse* is thought to be the hallucinogenic plant, *echyutse chime*, which is chewed by shamans during curing rituals.] According to the tale, the slain man was thereby temporarily restored to life, zombie-like, and sent back to his people (G. Reichel-Dolmatoff, 1975).

Little is known about the religion of these people, other than that they had established feast days of a solemn nature. The dead were honored at some of these festivals. Slaves, generally obtained as prisoners of war, were used as labor and were occasionally ritually sacrificed, presumably as part of a religious rite or ritual.

SONSO PHASE CERAMICS

Sonso-phase ceramics are markedly different from those of the preceding Yotoco phase. They are commonly thicker-walled and coarser. The ceramic forms, as well as the decorative techniques employed in their embellishment, bear little resemblance to those of the previous phase. Extremely rare are the double-spouted bridge-handle vessels. Also rare is the use of the negative painting technique. The most common decorative techniques include appliqué, impressing, incising, and modeling.

Fairly common are stylized anthropomorphic jars; the faces are often framed with impressed fillets of appliquéd clay (#61, 62). Similar fillets of clay are used to indicate necklaces. The zoomorphic jars are globular, some terminating at the top in the form of a wide-mouthed, flaring spout. Gourd-shaped vessels, with a small opening along the upper stem, are also known, as are double-effigy anthropomorphic vessels. Also common are globular jars, with two lugs above on one side of the vessel and one lug, positioned toward the bottom, on the other.

Sonso-phase ceramics are poorly documented in the literature, and notably few specimens are known in either public or private collections outside Colombia. The evidence at hand would suggest that Sonso represents the intrusion of new people or ideas into the region. These people would appear to have displaced or culturally absorbed those responsible for the Yotoco phase.

Negative painted sherds have not been found associated with Sonso habitation sites in the sedimentary deposits of the Cauca River. Few examples of this technique have been found associated with Sonso-phase funerary offerings from the Cauca River Valley. Thus, it is unlikely that negative painting is a true Sonso-phase characteristic. It has been reported that the technique is better represented in Sonso-phase tombs of the Calima River Valley and other parts of the Western Cordillera. The *alcarraza* form reportedly associated with Sonso tombs is also largely restricted to parts of the Western Cordillera and probably represents a surviving vestige of Yotoco-phase culture and ideology.

FUNDAMENTALS OF CALIMA ICONOGRAPHY

The use of the serpent in the formation of body parts of anthropomorphic-zoomorphic beings is of significance (#46). It is evident that the artist is conveying the impression that the entire body of these beings is composed of serpent forms. As previously hypothesized (Labbé, 1982), in Mesoamerican art, as well as in the art of Chavin in Peru, the serpent is iconographically employed as a symbol denoting the life force. The concept of lifeforce is well developed among the Tukano and other tropical-forest Indians of Colombia.

Such ideas are clearly elaborated in Mexican thought in concepts of *teotl* (lifeforce) and in ideas concerning the Cosmic Duality, Ometeotl (Ometecuhtli-Omecihuatl, the Lord and Lady of Duality). Quetzalcoatl, the Feathered Serpent in his aspect as Ehecatl, Lord of the Wind, represents the Breath of Ometeotl. If we focus on the esoteric and sacred nature of the concept, we will perceive that the term *Quetzalcoatl* actually signifies the lifeforce, which is said to be composed of both male and female forms of energy. Quetzalcoatl can mean "Quetzal-feathered serpent," in a literal sense, or "precious twin," in a figurative and metaphoric sense. That which was precious was the dual, dimorphic energy of the Lord and Lady of Duality, who poured forth their essence, Quetzalcoatl, into the universe.

Ometeotl is also called the Lord of Fire and of Time. Fire represents undifferentiated energy, or lifeforce, hidden in all things.

As one Nahuatl poet sang:

> Mother of the gods, father of the gods, the old god,
> spread out on the navel of the earth,
> within the circle of Turquoise,
> He who dwells in the waters, the color of the bluebird,
> He who dwells in the clouds.
> The old god, He who inhabits the shadows
> of the land of the dead,
> the Lord of fire and of time.
> (Florentine Codex, Book VI, fol. 71, V)

The great duality of male-female, positive-negative forces permeates the universe, from the highest heaven to the lowest underworld. As essence, Ometeotl is symbolized by fire; as essence taking living form, the great duality is symbolized by the serpent. It was from this perspective that the life-giving rays of the sun were called *xiuhcoatl* (fire-serpent). The sun, according to prehispanic Mexican cosmology, was sacrificing its lifeforce, so that life on earth could exist. This energy was dispensed in the form of sun rays, the *xiuhcoatl* that impregnate and nourish the earth-mother, thereby giving birth to the biosphere. One should understand that the physical sun was but an effect of a more esoteric and hidden principle. This concept is not so different from a Colombian Desana Indian concept, recorded by G. Reichel-Dolmatoff (1971):

> The Sun Creator, nevertheless, was not the same sun that now illuminates our earth, but a creative principle that, although continuing in existence, is now invisible and can be known only by the beneficial influence that emanates from it. After the act of creation and of the establishment of the moral norms, the Sun returned to Ahpikondia, the region of Paradise, not to remain there as a deus otiosus, but continuing to participate in his Creation. He sent on his eternal representative, this sun, that we see today in the sky, and it is through it that the Creator Sun exercises his power, giving his Creation light, heat, procreation, and above all, fertility."

The dimorphic, binary dualism of the Mexican is also mirrored in the cosmology of the Colombian Desana. As Leon-Portilla (1975) has said of the Mexican system:

> There was always the need for an active masculine aspect and a passive or conceiving feminine counterpart.... Generation and conception were moments inseparably unified in the dual divinity (Ometeotl).

This bears close resemblance to a homologous concept among the Desana:

> So the energy of procreation-creation is a masculine power that fertilizes a feminine element that is the world. Of course the biosphere has both masculine and feminine aspects, but seen in its totality, as a field of creation, it has primarily a feminine character over which the Sun exercises its power. (G. Reichel-Dolmatoff, 1971, pp. 42–43)

From the foregoing, it would seem justifiable to interpret the serpent forms of Calima as symbols of the lifeforce as well. In the aforementioned Calima figures, the artists intentionally use the serpents to delineate different parts of the body, intimating that underlying the form perceived as a whole is a sustaining and unifying essence, as symbolized by the serpent.

Fangs are often closely associated in prehispanic art with symbols of life, such as the serpent, and with concepts of fertility and procreation. Fanged felines are closely associated with concepts of sexuality, impregnation, and fertilization. For example:

> ...among the Paez Indians...the jaguar-spirit, or jaguar monster, has shamanistic qualities and is the shaman's guide and helper. Moreover, he is associated with thunder, rain, and lakes. Many of his attributes are related to sexual aggression. (G. Reichel-Dolmatoff, 1975, p. 54)

Associations between fanged personages and sexuality are widespread for indigenous groups within Colombia who draw a clear relationship between eating–devouring and sex–procreation (G. Reichel-Dolmatoff, 1975). Such associations are also evident in prehispanic Mexican art. This is graphically portrayed by the sculpture of Tlaltecuhtli-Coatlicue in the National Museum of Anthropology in Mexico City, which depicts a fanged personification of the great Earth-Duality, whose body is composed of serpents and whose mouth is fanged. A huge serpentiform phallus hangs between the legs, while sacrificial hearts and hands adorn the chest, presumably nourishing the flaccid breasts. The associations are clear. Life is derived from death. Life and death form an inseparable cycle. Life devours and feeds on life, in order to sustain itself. Death is a transformation, the conversion of the energies of one form into yet another form of life. The same concepts are implied in the serpentiform fanged "monsters" of Calima.

Similarly, we should not imagine that depictions of armadillos, bats, monkeys, or felines are intended solely or primarily to represent the species involved. Each animal more probably was intended to represent a particular aspect or attribute of the mythic and cultural world of the people. The armadillo (#42), for example, may be used by the Desana Indians of the northwest Amazon as a character in a creation myth, or as a symbol having uterine connotations. As G. Reichel-Dolmatoff has pointed out:

> There is a difference between the symbol as replica and the symbol as model. On the other hand, a symbol can be conceived and interpreted on different levels of abstraction. An armadillo can be a uterine symbol and, as a consequence, can be compared with a drum, the uterus of the sib, and from there, with the structure of the Universe. (1971)

Our approach to the indigenous art of prehispanic Colombia must not lose sight of the cultural context in which the art is found and the native perspectives which are still evident among living ethnographic groups. However problematic the symbolism, the fact remains that it is an integral and inseparable aspect of the traditional art of the native peoples of Colombia. Furthermore, as is true for the Kogi of the Sierra Nevada de Santa Marta, the Desana of the northwest Amazon, and many other groups, form is as much a part of the symbolic repertoire as is graphic iconography. We shall address ourselves more directly to form as symbolism later.

Certainly, archaeology divorced from other methodologies is incapable of reconstructing such integrated aspects of the prehistoric ethnographies. Nonetheless, consistent cultural patterns, such as the use of form as symbolism or the use of animal forms in an ideologic, iconographic manner, when persistent cross-culturally over wide geographic areas have a greater degree of reliability when used as models of ethnographic analogy than any form of random speculation.

Each culture attempts to devise schemes by which it may viably classify experienced phenomena. Such schemes become a means of storing knowledge in a way orderly and meaningful to the culture which created it. Cross-cultural studies have demonstrated that one culture's classificatory scheme may seem totally irrelevant and inapropos when applied to the sociocultural needs of another culture.

Many Indian societies in northern South America employ in varying degrees a classificatory system based on sexual dimorphism, a system wherein structure and function are both identified as consequences of the interaction of male and female forces. In such systems, geometric forms are themselves perceived to be essentially "male" or "female." Concavities, for example, are receptive and therefore essentially female, while convexities or protruding forms, which "expand," are essentially male. The use of a sexually dimorphic scheme is also true for Mesoamerican civilization, with its strong emphasis on the Ometeotl (Divine Duality) concept, and among the Desana Indians of the northwest Amazon in Colombia.

There are essentially two worldwide perspectives on dimorphic dualism. The more recent of the two is the western model, which appears to have been formulated in Iran sometime between the 13th and the 8th century B.C. This perspective states that all pairs of dualities are essentially oppositional and absolute in and of themselves. Zoroaster's concept of the Lord of Light, Ahura Mazda, in combat with the Lord of Darkness, Ahriman, is the epitome of this perspective. In the 6th century B.C. in Greece, this perspective was debated and reinforced by the teachings of the Eleatic school, which ultimately spawned the atomist theories of Democritus and influenced the dissecting, analytical methodologies of Aristotle. One cannot overly stress the influence and consequences this view has had on Western civilization. In addition to dichotomizing the individual human being into an opposing higher and lower nature, it created the concepts of perfection and free will, which were then used to persuade the individual to align himself with the equally opposed forces of good and evil. In the realm of science, man was pitted against nature. According to the Eleatic perspective, nature could be taken apart, studied, exploited, and remade to conform to man's needs. This sounded the death knell for the archaic animism and nature religions of the West.

The Western concept of dualities of absolute opposition was essentially formulated at a time when the Bronze Age was coming to a close and the age of ironworking was taking precedence. Old theocracies were on the decline, and new warrior-based secular authority was coming into power.

The Eastern perspective has clung to an older view of interacting, functionally relative dualities of complementarity. This view is essentially cyclical and reciprocal. The complementary dualities are not perceived as absolutes, but rather as varying combinations and degrees of both positive and negative principles. The tendency toward absolutism is perceived as creating imbalance and is thereby inherently destructive to dynamic harmony. Sickness and misfortune result. The Eastern point of view is iconographically represented by the symbols of Yin-Yang.

The indigenous Colombian Indian perspective (Desana et al.) differs from the Eastern viewpoint in the particulars, but not with respect to the general: the same two forces are perceived to govern the world, which the Indian calls the male and female principle. Harmony and balance between the two conduce to health and prosperity; disharmony and imbalance lead to sickness and misfortune. Each Indian culture prescribes its own laws and customs, which must be followed if harmony and balance is to be maintained.

Understanding the base from which the Indian classifies his world gives us a perspective with which to view and interpret his art. By itself this may not give us the specific meaning of the artwork, but it does increase the likelihood of validity on the general interpretive level.

The underlying concept behind the sexual dimorphic classification scheme is the perception that the interaction of male and female principles governs the dynamism and order of the world. Male forms of energy are seen to invest, i.e., impregnate, extend, and move outward. Female energies receive and convert male energies into new forms, thereby conceiving.

> So the energy of procreation-creation is a masculine power that fertilizes a feminine element that is the world... In the first place, the creative principle is masculine (Sun, yellow) and acts upon the biosphere (red) that, although composed of a masculine element and a feminine one, is imagined essentially as a feminine element. (G. Reichel-Dolmatoff, *Amazonian Cosmos*, 1971, pp. 46–47)

Accordingly, the Desana classify the color yellow as containing within itself the fertilizing energy of the sun and therefore elements of the male principle. Yellow-colored honey, semen and semen-colored saliva, yellowish or milky-white semen-colored quartz crystals, yellow squirrels, the macaw, manioc starch (white), cotton (white), and other elements of like color are similarly classified. Color symbolism then becomes a means of identifying whether an element partakes of either the male of the female principle. It should be noted that the seminal symbolism of the quartz crystal exists among other groups within Colombia, for example, the Kogi Indians of northern Colombia (G. Reichel-Dolmatoff, 1951). Far to the north in Mesoamerica, the association of semen and saliva is graphically rendered in a Quiche Maya story, recorded in the Popul Vuh, where in a talking skull impregnates a young girl by spitting into her hand and informing her that therein lies the heritage of the race.

In general, bones and skeleton result from the action of the male principle, blood and flesh from that of the female principle. We should recall that in one of the mythic legends of Mesoamerica, the hero Quetzalcoatl descends to the underworld of Mictlan in order to retrieve the bones of mankind, which he reanimates by bleeding his virile member over the dessicated bones. The action of the red blood (female principle) transforms the dead bones to life.

Lightning is perceived to be an action of the male principle, metaphorically described as an ejaculation of the sun (G. Reichel-Dolmatoff, 1971), which can fertilize the land. The idea that lightning has the ability to fertilize the land is common to the corn-growing cultures of the American Southwest and Mesoamerica, as well as over wide areas of Colombia.

Among the Desana Indians, the interaction of the male and female principles takes place within a circuit of energy called the *boga*. The energy which flows within the *boga* is not only composed of male and female principles, but also of benevolent and malevolent aspects. That which promotes health, harmony, life, and well-being is benevolent; that which promotes sickness, disease, disharmony, and death is malevolent. In general, the principle of malevolence decreases the total energy of the energy circuit.

With regard to the believe that female energy is transformative, one may consider that the uterus is described in Desana metaphor as the place where one cooks, or transforms energy. The *boga* in this respect is seen as a vehicle of transformation and creation that is essentially a female principle (i.e., it contains and transforms), but the *boga* itself results from the action of a complementary male principle called *tulari*. *Tulari* causes boga; it makes *boga* function. "Thus, Tulari is masculine energy, and boga is feminine energy. The two together — tulari boga and uhuri boga — are fertilization and fecundity; they are the great current that circulates." (G. Reichel-Dolmatoff, *Amazonian Cosmos,* 1971, pp. 54–55). And though we are speaking of people far removed in time and space from the formulations of the Nahuatl philosophers of Ometeotl in ancient Mexico, there is an unmistakable correspondence between the two in the perception of how the forces of the world interact and effect creation. We must emphasize once again that the kinds of correspondence we are observing and noting are not on the level of mythic structure, but rather on that of basal mythic perspective: the way one sees the world, rather than the way one describes what one sees of the world. The concept of complementary duality is an important common perspective shared by Indians over large areas of the Americas; yet the way this concept is elaborated, or described artistically, varies markedly from one group to another.

Mention was made in the foregoing that form itself can have symbolic significance. Vertical elements in general, but especially tubular vertical elements, are often perceived as male or phallic. Inverted U-shaped forms are generally female or uterine, connoting protection and sometimes transformation. Turtle shells, armadillo shells, and house roofs are often employed as uterine symbols. Cavities or open receptacles and containers depict a female capacity. Among the Desana, we are told that:

> As the *recipient* of masculine semen, the female finds diverse symbolic expression. Her *receptivity* is compared with the gesture of soliciting or joining her hands before her breasts in the form of a *concave receptacle*. (ibid p. 61; emphasis added)

In general, concavity has female significance and connotations. Caves, mouths, and similar concavities are felt to be female forms. Relevant to the above description of Desana symbolism is the use of words like *recipient*, *receptivity*, and *concavity* on the part of the ethnographer to translate the Desana symbolic intent into a European language. And again, we are told:

> Symbolically the hearth represents the uterus... the vessels and the plate represent the Creation. The hearth is thus an instrument of cosmic transformation, a crucible. The pot-stands... symbolize sexual organs, be it the penis (cylindrical and 'canal'-shaped form) or the vagina (tubular and funnel-shaped form). (ibid, p. 109)

Sexual dimorphic symbolism is used to portray the dynamic interaction of cosmic and terrestrial forces. In the prehispanic Indian view, the universe and all of creation constantly and cyclically manifest the interaction of the two primal forces, symbolized as male and female. Centrifugal force, an outward movement, is an expression of the male principle. Centripetal force, a drawing inward (gravity), is an expression of the female principle.

The female principle, however, does more than just receive; it also transforms what is received. The Sun Father may impregnate the Earth Mother with his sunlight rays, his fire-serpents, his semen, but it is the Earth Mother that receives and absorbs this energy and converts it into the biosphere. The seed gestates within the earth, but the earth converts it into a sprout (minor male force), which grows into the strong corn stalk (major male force), which then throws out leaves (uterine, protective female form) from which the corn emerges and grows (male action). The corn is then eaten (mouth, cavity, female form) and transformed (female action) into blood (female principle of nourishment — male action of moving out). The blood is consumed by the cells as a nourishment (primary female action) and converted into flesh (transformational female action). We may observe that there are two female and two male cycles involved in this system. The first female action is to receive; the second is to transform. The first male action is to emerge and move outward; the second is to mature and finally decay. The second female process gives birth and rise to the first male process. The woman receives the seed of the male (first female action);

the seed is transformed through fertility and gestation into new life (second female process). The new life reaches critical mass and emerges from the womb, the cavity of darkness, into the world of light (first male process); there, it grows, matures, and dies (second male process). The body is then received by the earth (first female process) and is subsequently transformed through decay (second female process) to emerge once again as part of the biosphere.

In Mesoamerica, these cycles of interaction and transformation were symbolized by the sun's movement along the cardinal directions in its diurnal journey through the sky. The sun rises and is born in the east. It grows to maturity at its zenith in the south, then wanes toward the west, where it is, metaphorically speaking, received by the earth. From the Mesoamerican's point of view, the sun continued its journey through the night, being transformed in the north, only to be reborn once again in the east, at dawn, where it would emerge at the horizon from the bosom of the Earth-Mother. Thus: Emergence–Dawn–East; Descent–Dusk–West; Zenith–Midday–South; Nadir–Midnight–North.

From what has been stated above, it is clear that the very shape of the shaft-and-chamber tombs found within the Calima zone were most probably patterned after the human birth canal and womb. Through burial in the shaft grave, the bones of the deceased were being returned, both literally and figuratively, to the womb of the Earth-Mother, in the hope that they would thereby be transformed and the spirit of the dead might emerge once more as new life. This interpretation is supported by Desana Indian beliefs:

> The association of ideas is clear if we understand that the grave in which the corpse is buried is the uterus to which the corporeal part of man returns, while the spiritual part goes to the uterus of Ahpikondia. (G. Reichel-Dolmatoff, *Amazonian Cosmos*, 1971, p. 75)

If impregnation–fertility, gestation–transformation, birth–growth, nourishment–protection, and life–death are processes of great significance in the thought of the indigene today, should we not suspect that this is perhaps reflected in the art of previous Colombian Indian societies, particularly in those instances where such art has been placed in a womb-like, shaft-and-chamber grave, along with the deceased? We must bear in mind that the Yotoco artist is following his own cultural art canons. He may intentionally give to a form one symbolic significance, on one level of abstraction, and employ the very same form differently, on another level. For example, a small figural jar (#44) appears to depict a frog when observed as a complete composition. Closer examination reveals that the artist also intended to communicate that the frog's head and face is formed by the interfacing of two serpent heads seen in profile. Those readers familiar with Mexica-Aztec art will recall that the head of the colossal stone statue of Coatlicue-Tlaltecuhtli is formed in the very same manner, by means of two interfacing serpents representing the interaction of male and female principles in the formation of the lifeforce (Labbé, 1982). Viewed from this perspective, the small figure in question connotes dimorphic sexual interaction, hence fertility.

The principle of dimorphic interaction is restated in a common Yotoco-phase vessel form, the double-spouted jar known as an *alcarraza*. It is highly unlikely that the primary function of these vessels was to contain liquid. Instead, their use as iconograms seems indicated. Observing these vessels from the perspective of prehispanic geometry and form employed as symbolism, we may hypothesize that the upper part of the vessel, the inverted U-shaped handle, represents a womb, and the spouts on this level of abstraction represent splayed legs. This is not only a posture for intercourse, but also for birth-giving. The lower element, distinguished by the knob and body, signifies the male organ of generation. The overall configuration suggests intercourse, with fertility implied. The fertility connotations of the genre are reinforced in other examples (#54, 55), where breasts are explicitly portrayed and testicles implied. Again, the intent is to connote fertility. A similar interpretation is implied for many other specimens. Does this mean that intercourse and fertility are explicit for each and every *alcarraza*? Certainly not, as is evident from other examples (#56). Such ideas, however, may be implicit, as the artist employs the basic form for additional purpose and effect.

It may be observed that on Llama-phase *alcarrazas*, which are earlier than the Yotoco-phase examples, the sexual dimorphic iconography is not clearly indicated. In general, Llama–phase *alcarrazas* in no way suggest a phallus. It may be that we are witnessing a more refined level of abstraction wherein phalli are suggested by the spouts, but perhaps not. It is also possible that an earlier form (Llama phase), originally devoid of dimorphic sexual symbolism, was later (Yotoco phase) employed as a means of communicating fertility.

39
Double-spouted anthropomorphic *alcarraza*
Reddish-brown slip, decorated with incised details
h: 8⅝ in. (22 cm) × d: 7 in. (17.8 cm)
Llama phase (ca. 800 B.C.–100 B.C.)
Calima zone, Valle Del Cauca

The figure shown is possibly playing a shell-shaped ocarina. Hair, jewelry, and other details are indicated by incising, and the figure wears a necklace with a skull-pendant bead.

40
Globular *alcarraza*
Brown slip, decorated with incised details
h: 6½ in. (16.5 cm) × circum: 18 in. (45.7 cm)
Llama phase (ca. 800 B.C.–100 B.C.)
Calima zone, Valle Del Cauca

The zigzag pattern most probably represents lightning as a symbol of the lifeforce.

41
Anthropomorphic *alcarraza*
Reddish-brown slip, decorated with incised details
h: 8¼ in. (21 cm) × w: 7¾ in. (19.7 cm)
Llama phase (ca. 800 B.C.–100 B.C.)
Calima zone, Valle Del Cauca

The nipples and navel are indicated by means of incised circles. The artist appears to be portraying an almost amorphous male figure in a seated or crouched position. The figure's skeleton appears on the back of the vessel. The intention is to convey the dual nature of existence, encompassing the process of life and death. In prehispanic thought, death is viewed not as a finality, but as a transformation process. The cross-hatching of the skeletal ribs signifies that the potential for new life exists in the bones (see Chapters Five and Six for the meaning of bones in prehispanic thought).

42
Armadillo-effigy *alcarraza*
Reddish-brown slip
h: 8 in. (20.3 cm) × l: 9½ in. (24.1 cm)
Llama phase (ca. 800 B.C.–100 B.C.)
Calima zone, Valle Del Cauca

43

44

43
Human-effigy jar
Reddish-brown slip
h: 11 in. (27.9 cm) × w: 6¼ in. (15.9 cm)
Llama phase (ca. 800 B.C.–100 B.C.)
Calima zone, Valle Del Cauca

44
Frog-effigy jar with serpent-form details
Brown slip, decorated with incised details
h: 3 in (7.6 cm) × l: 4½ in. (11.4 cm)
Llama phase (ca. 800 B.C.–100 B.C.)
Calima zone, Valle Del Cauca

45
Anthropomorphic-effigy *canastero*
Reddish-brown slip, decorated with incised details
h: 7⅞ in. (20 cm) × w: 4⅝ in. (11.8 cm)
Llama phase (ca. 800 B.C.–100 B.C.)
Calima zone, Valle Del Cauca
The figure's hair is elaborately styled, and tattoos may be indicated on the abdomen by the incised lines.

46
Zoomorphic-effigy jar
Brown slip
h: 6¾ in. (17.1 cm) × w: 7 in. (17.8 cm)
Llama phase (ca. 800 B.C.–100 B.C.)
Calima zone, Valle Del Cauca

45

46

47

47
Anthropomorphic-zoomorphic-effigy jar
Reddish-brown slip
h: 6¼ in. (15.9 cm) × l: 5½ in. (14 cm)
Llama phase (ca. 800 B.C.–100 B.C.)
Calima zone, Valle Del Cauca

The limbs and form of the mythic figure and the frog it rides are composed of stylized serpent forms.

48
Human-effigy jars

left: Reddish-brown slip
h: 4¾ in. (12.1 cm) × d: 4¾ in. (12.1 cm)
Llama phase (ca. 800 B.C.–100 A.D.)
Calima zone, Valle Del Cauca

right: Tan slip
h: 5¼ in. (13.3 cm) × d: 4½ in. (11.4 cm)
Llama phase (ca. 300 B.C.–100 B.C.)
Calima zone, Valle Del Cauca

49
Anthropomorphic face mask depicting old age
Reddish-brown slip, decorated with incised details
h: 7 in. (17.8 cm) × w: 7 in. (17.8 cm)
Llama phase (ca. 800 B.C.–100 B.C.)
Calima zone, Valle Del Cauca

50
Anthropomorphic face mask depicting old age
Reddish-brown slip, decorated with incised details
h: 7½ in. (19.1 cm) × w: 5¾ in. (14.6 cm)
Llama phase (ca. 800 B.C.–100 B.C.)
Calima zone, Valle Del Cauca

51
Human-effigy *alcarraza*
Reddish-brown slip
h: 8¾ in. (22.2 cm) × d: 8¾ in. (22.2 cm)
Transitional Llama phase–Yotoco phase (ca. 100 B.C.–400 A.D.)
Calima zone, Valle Del Cauca

52
Drum-shaped *alcarraza*
Black-on-red resist painted, decorated with incised details
h: 8¾ in. (22.2 cm) × circum: 17 in. (43.2 cm)
Yotoco phase (ca. 300 A.D.–1300 A.D.)
Calima zone, Valle Del Cauca

53
Anthropomorphic *alcarraza*
Black-on-red resist painted, decorated with incised details
h: 9⅝ in. (24.4 cm) × w: 5½ in. (14 cm)
Transitional Llama phase–Yotoco phase (ca. 100 B.C.–400 A.D.?)
Calima zone, Valle Del Cauca

This specimen appears to have been produced during the transition from Llama phase to Yotoco phase. The form of the figure and the incised details are typical of the Llama-phase ceramics, while the resist-painted design typifies Yotoco-phase ware.

51

52

53

54
Phalliform-mammiform *alcarraza*
Black-on-red resist painted
h: 8½ in. (21.6 cm) × w: 7 in. (17.8 cm)
Yotoco phase (ca. 300 A.D.–1300 A.D.)
Calima zone, Valle Del Cauca

55
Phytomorphic *alcarraza*
Red slip
h: 7¾ in. (19.7 cm) × w: 5½ in. (14 cm)
Yotoco phase (ca. 300 A.D.–1300 A.D.)
Calima zone, Valle Del Cauca

The artist appears to have combined phalliform, mammiform, and phytomorphic elements to create a composite symbolism connoting fertility.

56
Alcarrazas
Reddish-brown slip
left: h: 7 in. (17.8 cm) × circum: 18 in. (45.7 cm)
right: h: 7 in. (17.8 cm) × w: 5 in. (12.7 cm)
Yotoco phase (ca. 300 A.D.–1300 A.D.)
Calima zone, Valle Del Cauca

57
Zoomorphic-quadruped *alcarraza*
Black-on-red resist painted
h: 7¼ in. (18.4 cm) × circum: 18½ in. (47 cm)
Yotoco phase (ca. 300 A.D.–1300 A.D.)
Calima zone, Valle Del Cauca

This *alcarraza* is probably a Yotoco-phase example of a Llama-phase effigy form.

58
Toad-effigy *alcarrazas*
Red and white slips
left: h: 5¼ in. (13.3 cm) × w: 5½ in. (14 cm)
right: h: 6 in. (15.2 cm) × w: 4¾ in. (12.1 cm)
Yotoco phase (ca. 300 A.D.–1300 A.D.)
Calima zone, Valle Del Cauca

57

58

59
Anthropomorphic *alcarraza*
Reddish-brown slip
h: 6¾ in. (17.1 cm) × w: 6⅜ in. (16.2 cm)
Yotoco phase (ca. 300 A.D.–1300 A.D.)
Calima zone, Valle Del Cauca

60
Globular vessel with three lugs
Black-on-red resist painted
h: 12¼ in. (31.1 cm) × circum: 36 in. (91.4 cm)
Cultural complex undetermined (ca. 1200 A.D.–1400 A.D.)
Calima zone, Valle Del Cauca

61
Anthropomorphic-effigy jar
Reddish-brown slip
h: 14 in. (35.6 cm) × w: 8 in. (20.3 cm)
Sonso phase (ca. 1200 A.D.–1600 A.D.)
Calima zone, Valle Del Cauca

62
Anthropomorphic-effigy jar
Reddish-brown slip
h: 11⅛ in. (28.3 cm) × d: 9⅛ in. (23.2 cm)
Sonso phase (ca. 1200 A.D.–1600 A.D.)
Calima zone, Valle Del Cauca
(PHOTO COURTESY OF THE BOWERS MUSEUM)

63
Phalliform secondary-burial urns
Buff terracotta
left: h: 27½ in. (70 cm) × circum: 46¾ in. (118.8 cm)
right: h: 40½ in. (102.9 cm) × d: 15¾ in. (40 cm)
Cultural complex undetermined
Calima zone, Valle Del Cauca

64
Tubular receptacles
left: Red slip
l: 5⅛ in. (13 cm) × d: 2½ in. (6.4 cm)
Yotoco phase (ca. 300 A.D.–1300 A.D.)
right: Brown slip
l: 3¾ in. (9.5 cm) × d: 1¾ in. (4.5 cm)
Llama phase (ca. 800 B.C.–100 B.C.)
Calima zone, Valle Del Cauca
These artifacts may have been snuffing apparati.

63

64

VARIATION IN *ALCARAZZA* FORM AND STYLE BY REGION AND PERIOD

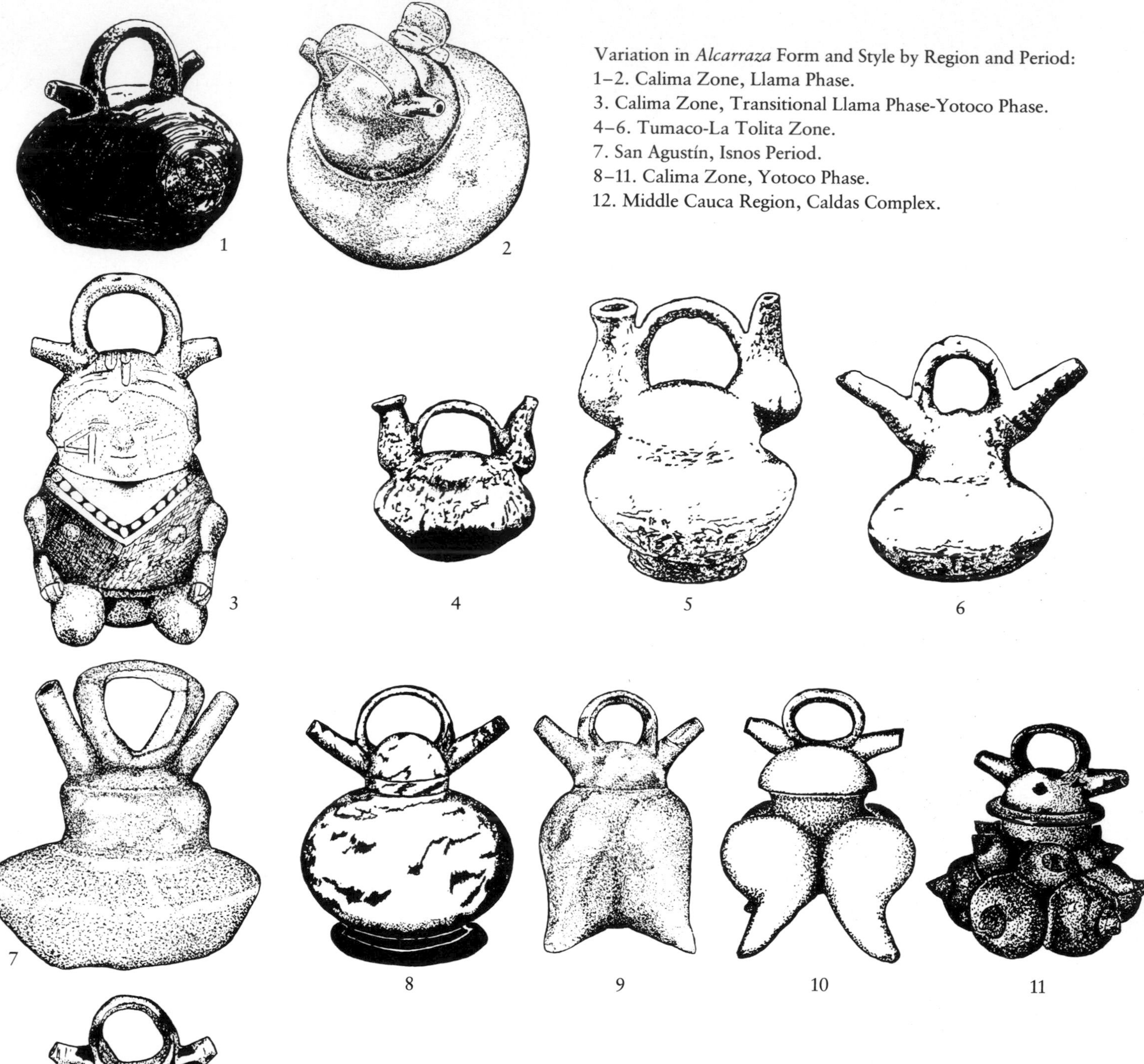

Variation in *Alcarraza* Form and Style by Region and Period:
1–2. Calima Zone, Llama Phase.
3. Calima Zone, Transitional Llama Phase-Yotoco Phase.
4–6. Tumaco-La Tolita Zone.
7. San Agustín, Isnos Period.
8–11. Calima Zone, Yotoco Phase.
12. Middle Cauca Region, Caldas Complex.

(Opposite)

Plate I
Standing figure
Grayish-white
h: 13¼ in. (33.7 cm) × w: 5½ in. (14 cm)
Tumaco-La Tolita culture (ca. 300 B.C.–300 A.D.)
Southwest coastal Colombia–northwest coastal Ecuador

The figure is wearing ear spools and other ear ornaments, a nose ring, and a wrap-around garment. The nipples are prominently depicted, and the navel is indicated by a hole. Bands may be indicated at the knees by incised lines. An unidentified object hangs from the neck.

II

III

IV

V

VI

Plate II
Fish-form graters
Grayish-white, decorated with red paint
left: l: 11 in. (27.9 cm) × w: 3¼ in. (8.3 cm)
right: l: 11 in. (27.9 cm) × w: 3⅞ in. (9.8 cm)
Tumaco-La Tolita culture (ca. 300 B.C.– 300 A.D.)
Southwest coastal Colombia–northwest coastal Ecuador

These are probably ceremonial graters used during manioc rituals. The face and border of fish are painted red.

Plate III
Globular spouted vessel
Grayish-white, decorated with red paint and punctate design
h: 7⅜ in. (19.7 cm) × circum: 20½ in. (52 cm)
Specific culture determined
Southwest coastal Colombia–northwest coastal Ecuador

Plate IV
Sub-globular shouldered jar with median ridge
Gray, decorated with incised geometric designs and red paint
h: 7 in. (17.8 cm) × d: 7¾ in. (19.7 cm)
Specific culture undetermined
Southwest coastal Colombia–northwest coastal Ecuador

Plate V
Zoomorphic *canastero*
Reddish-brown slip, decorated with incised detail
h: 6½ in. (16.5 cm) × w: 4½ in. (11.4 cm)
Llama phase (ca. 800 B.C.–100 B.C.)
Calima zone, Valle Del Cauca

The figure is a mythical fanged creature with serpentiform limbs. The serpent is used by Calima artists to symbolize the lifeforce.

Plate VI
Zoomorphic-effigy *alcarrazas*
Reddish-brown slip, decorated with incised details
left: h: 8½ in. (21.6 cm) × w: 5¼ in. (13.3 cm)
right: h: 7½ in. (19.1 cm) × l: 8 in. (20.3 cm)
Llama phase (ca. 800 B.C.–100 B.C.)
Calima zone, Valle Del Cauca

(Opposite)

Plate VII
Human-effigy *canastero*
Brown slip, decorated with incised details
h: 9¾ in. (24.8 cm) × w: 7 in. (17.8 cm)
Llama phase (ca. 800 B.C.–100 B.C.)
Calima zone, Valle Del Cauca

The naked male figure is profusely incised with decoration representing body tattooing.

Plate VIII
Anthropomorphic-effigy *canastero*
Reddish-brown slip, decorated with modeled and incised details
h: 7¼ in. (18.4 cm) × w: 4½ in. (11.4 cm)
Llama phase (ca. 800 B.C.–100 B.C.)
Calima zone, Valle Del Cauca

Plate IX
Alcarraza
Black-on-red resist painted
h: 8 in. (20.3 cm) × w: 6 in. (15.2 cm)
Yotoco phase (ca. 300 A.D.–1300 A.D.)
Calima zone, Valle Del Cauca

X

XI

XII

XIII

Plate X
Hollow seated anthropomorphic figure with painted face
Buff terracotta, decorated with black-on-white painted details
h: 12¾ in. (32.4 cm) × w: 7 in. (17.8 cm)
Cultural complex unknown
Middle Cauca region

Plate XI
Amphoras
Black-on-red-and-white resist painted
left: h: 6¾ in. (17.2 cm) × d: 6 in. (15.2 cm)
right: h: 7¾ in. (19.7 cm) × d: 6 in. (15.2 cm)
Middle Cauca complex
i(ca. 1000 A.D.–1500 A.D.)
Middle Cauca region

Plate XII
Jar with appliquéd serpents
Black-on-red-and-white resist painted, decorated with appliquéd details
h: 9¾ in. (24.8 cm) × circum: 19¾ in. (50.2 cm)
Middle Cauca complex
(ca. 1000 A.D.–1500 A.D.)
Middle Cauca region

Plate XIII
Anthropomorphic-effigy vessel
Black-on-white-and-red resist painted
h: 10¼ in. (26 cm) × w: 7 in. (17.8 cm)
Middle Cauca complex
(ca. 1000 A.D.–1500 A.D.)
Middle Cauca region

Plate XIV
Phytomorphic vessel
Black-on-red resist painted
h: 7 in. (17.8 cm) × d: 7 in. (17.8 cm)
Middle Cauca complex (ca. 1000 A.D.–1500 A.D.)
Middle Cauca region

Plate XV
Spouted zoomorphic-effigy vessel
Black-on-red-and-white resist painted
h: 7¼ in. (18.4 cm) × l: 9¼ in. (23.5 cm)
Specific complex undetermined (ca. 1000 A.D.–1500 A.D.)
Middle Cauca region

Plate XVI
Double-chambered anthropomorphic vessel
Red-and-white slip
h: 7¼ in. (18.4 cm) × l: 11 in. (27.9 cm)
Middle Cauca complex (ca. 1000 A.D.–1500 A.D.)
Middle Cauca region
(as seen in *Precolumbian Ceramics* by Jesus Arango Cano, 1979, Plate 11)

Plate XVII
Globular vessel with four lugs
Black-on-red resist painted
h: 9¼ in. (23.5 cm) × circum: 26¼ in. (66.7 cm)
Caldas complex (ca. 1000 A.D.–1400 A.D.)
Middle Cauca region

Plate XVIII
Hollow-slab anthropomorphic figure
Light-brown slip, with black resist-painted details
h: 10¼ in. (26 cm) × w: 9¾ in. (24 cm)
Caldas complex (ca. 1200 A.D.–1400 A.D.)
Middle Cauca region

The figure wears a headdress that is sometimes interpreted to represent an eagle with wings spread. The eagle is often associated with the sun in precolumbian iconography.

XIX

XX XXI

Plate XXII
Double-spouted figural vessel
Buff terracotta
h: 9¼ in. (23.5 cm) × d: 8¾ in. (22.2 cm)
Dates undetermined
Sinu region

Plate XXIII
Female figure wearing nose ring
Buff terracotta
h: 8½ in. (21.5 cm) × w: 5 in. (12.7 cm)
Dates undetermined
Sinu region

Plate XIX
Solid-slab anthropomorphic figure with child
Light-brown slip, with traces of resist painting
mother: h: 10¼ in. (26 cm) × w: 7¾ in. (19.7 cm)
child: h: 5 in. (12.7 cm) × w: 2¾ in. (7 cm)
Caldas complex (ca. 1200 A.D.–1400 A.D.)
Middle Cauca region

Plate XX
Hollow-slab anthropomorphic female figure
Black-on-red-and-tan resist painted
h: 9¼ in. (23.5 cm) × w: 7¼ in. (18.4 cm)
Caldas complex (ca. 1200 A.D.–1400 A.D.)
Middle Cauca region

Plate XXI
Hollow-slab anthropomorphic figure
Black-on-red resist painted
h: 14½ in. (36.8 cm) × w: 11½ in. (29.2 cm)
Caldas complex (ca. 1200 A.D.–1400 A.D.)
Middle Cauca region

XXIV

Plate XXIV
Female figure
Buff terracotta
h: 10 in. (24.1 cm) × w: 7 in. (17.2 cm)
Zambrano region (dates undetermined)
Lower Magdalena River region

Multiple perforations along the ears and body characterize figures of this style.

Plate XXV
Globular vessel with lid
Black-on-red slip, decorated with black paint
h: 20½ in. (52.1 cm) × d: 46½ in. (118.1 cm)
Cultural complex undetermined
Sinu region

This is an unusual vessel decorated with black vertical stripes. The lid is a footed cup, which was placed upright into the opening of the vessel (not as photographed).

Plate XXVI
Semiglobular-effigy jar with four figures in relief
Black and red paint, with incised decoration
h: 13½ in. (34.3 cm) × d: 15 in. (38.1 cm)
Cultural complex undetermined
Sinu region

XXV

XXVI

(Preceding pages)

Plate XXVII
Burial urn with lid surmounted by a male figure seated on a bench
Brownish-orange terracotta
h: 29¾ in. (75.6 cm) × circum: 27½ in. (69.9 cm)
Pelaya style (dates undetermined)
Lower Magdalena River region
The urn is decorated with modeled stylized birds. The seated figure is holding a *poporo*.

Plate XXVIII
Burial urn with lid
Buff terracotta, decorated with incised and modeled details
h: 25¾ in. (65.4 cm) × circum: 56 in. (142.2 cm)
Dates undetermined
Middle Magdalena River region
The lid is surmounted by two interfacing birds.

XXIX

XXX

XXXI

CHAPTER III

THE QUIMBAYA REGION

Artists, Graves, and Cannibals of the Middle Cauca

(Opposite)

Plate XXIX
Globular vessel
Burnished dark-brown slip, decorated with punctate design
h: 14 in. (35.6 cm) × circum: 43 in. (109.2 cm)
Horqueta period (ca. 600 B.C.–100 B.C.)
San Agustin cultural tradition
San Agustin archaeological zone
A simple band of punctated lines above and below a middle band of stippled dots comprises the decorative design of the vessel.

Plate XXX
Carinated jar with lid
Burnished dark-brown slip, decorated with punctate design
h: 19¼ in. (48.9 cm) × d: 11½ in. (29.2 cm)
Horqueta period (ca. 600 B.C.–100 B.C.)
San Agustin cultural tradition
San Agustin archaeological zone

Plate XXXI
Double-spouted *alcarraza*
Red slip, with traces of black resist paint
h: 8 in. (20.3 cm) × d: 5½ in. (14 cm)
Isnos period (ca. 100 A.D.–700 A.D.?)
San Agustin cultural tradition
San Agustin archaeological zone

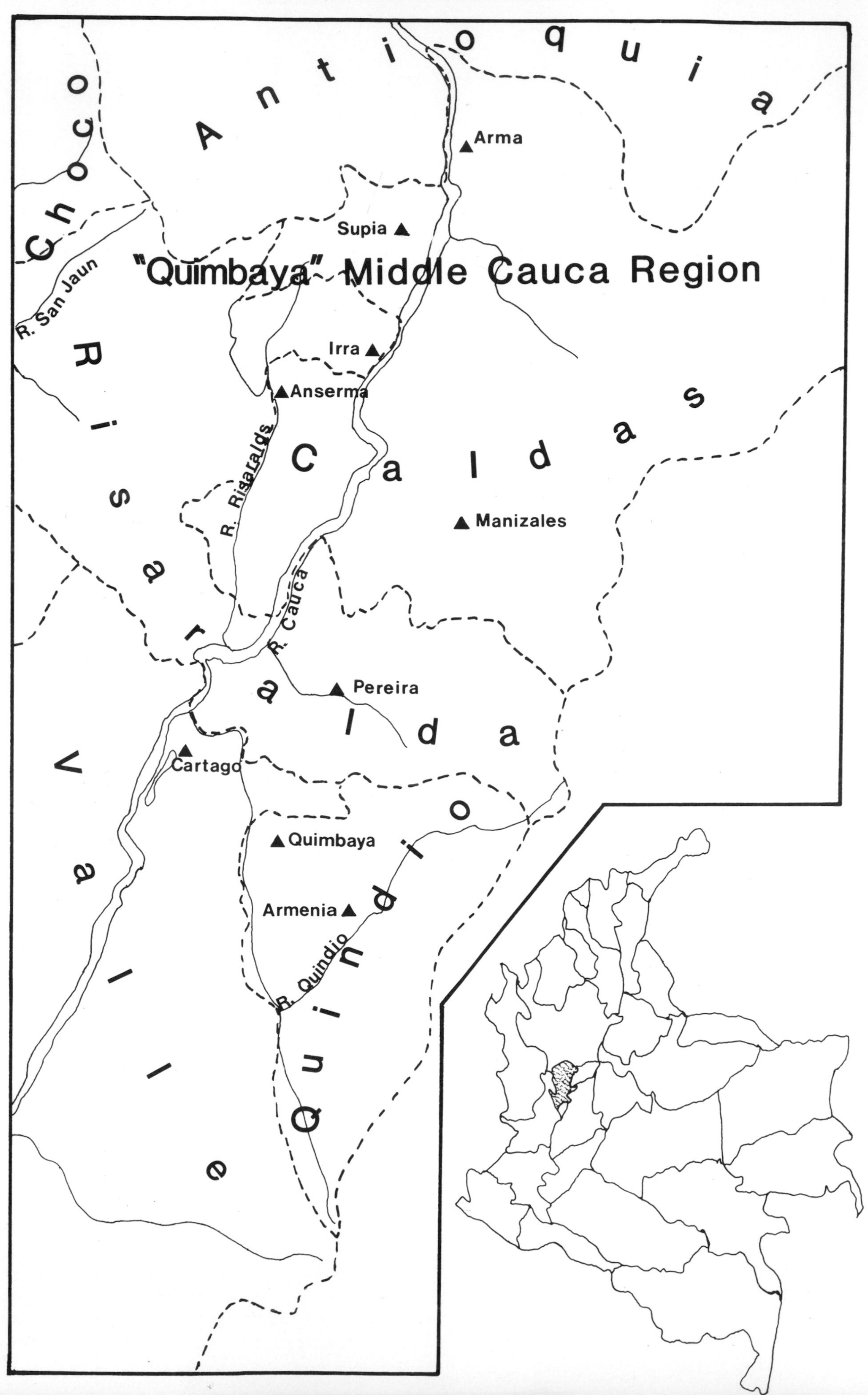
Antioquia
Choco
Arma
Supia
"Quimbaya" Middle Cauca Region
R. San Jaun
Irra
Anserma
Risaralda
R. Risaralds
Caldas
Manizales
R. Cauca
Pereira
Cartago
Valle
Quimbaya
Armenia
R. Quindio
Quindio

GEOGRAPHY

Immediately to the north of the Calima Zone lie the archaeologically and artistically rich provinces of the Middle Cauca River region, which are climatically similar to the Calima Zone.

The term "Quimbaya," as used in the popular literature, refers to the art and artifacts of a number of divergent prehistoric cultures found in the Middle Cauca River Valley and adjacent slopes and mountains of the modern departments of Quindio, Risaralda, Caldas, and southern Antióquia.

ETHNOHISTORY

Who were the tribes that inhabited this region in the 16th century? We know that a small area of the southeast portion of the region was occupied by the Quindos. The Quindio River flowed through their territory. West of the Quindos, the historically noted Quimbayas occupied lands to the Cauca River. Their territory extended from the La Vieja River in the south, to the Manizales in the north. North of the Quimbayas were the Carrapas. West of the Carrapas lived the Irras, who in turn were bordered on the north by the Quinchias. West of the Irras was a larger group known as the Ansermas. The Risaralda and Del Oro rivers ran through their territory. To the west lived the fierce Chancos, described by Cieza de Léon as being the tallest and among the most robust of any of the Indians in the region. They appeared to be small giants among their neighbors. Other groups to the north of the Quinchias and Carrapas included the Zopias, Pozos, Picaras, Paucuras, Cartamus, and Armas.

A problem encountered in reconstructing the prehistory of this region lies in determining the different cultures responsible for the many distinct cultural traits uncovered archaeologically. At the time of the Spanish conquest, the region was inhabited by a number of tribes, speaking different dialects. What is uncertain is which language families were represented by the various dialects. Very few words were ever collected by the chroniclers. The general consensus today is that an older cultural strata consisted of peoples who spoke dialects of the Chibcha language. Chibcha was spoken by groups in the Sierra Nevada de Santa Marta and over wide areas of the Cordillera Oriental, notably in the modern Departments of Cundinamarca and Boyacá—the ancient lands of "El Dorado." It was also spoken in Panama and lands to the south in Colombia, as well as lands south and southwest of the Middle Cauca Valley. Similarities in culture between groups in the Middle Cauca region and known Chibcha-speaking groups, such as the Muisca of the highlands of the Cordillera Oriental, support the hypothesis of a strong Chibcha substratum in the region. In both areas, bodies of the deceased elite were similarly prepared. [The body was slowly heated over a fire, allowing the fat to melt away. According to the chroniclers (Robledo et al.), the dessicated body was then readied and adorned. Decoration was applied using a red paint, obtained from *achiote*. Strings of beads were placed about the wrists and ankles. The body was then wrapped in cloth fashioned from cotton.]

Robledo states that weapons, cups, and bowls of food were placed with the deceased leader in the burial chamber, along with a bench. The grave offerings were intended to be used by the chieftain during the evening hours. Individuals close to the deceased would lie in wait above the grave for many nights, listening to hear him stir and speak from below. Whether this was sincerely believed by the Indians, or whether they were embellishing reality for jocular effect, we do not know. It is known that they took great care to assure that the location of the tomb remain hidden, even camouflaging the site by sowing seeds over the grave. It is possible that the grave was visited at night, as Robledo relates, but this would have increased the probability that the site would become known to others.

The feared Carib-speaking peoples were another important strata influencing the culture of the Middle Cauca region. Carib influence in the region is suggested by such customs as artificial deformation of the cranium, the eating of human flesh, the use of poisoned arrows (the preferred weapon of the Chibcha-speaking people was the *atlatl*, or spear-thrower-propelled javelin), and the binding of the calves and upper arms of the body. The latter custom is graphically documented on certain slab figures attributed to the Caldas ceramic complex. The upper arms and calves were tightly bound, above and below. This caused an artificial depression of the bound part of the limb and a corresponding swelling of adjacent areas. This custom was said to increase the strength of the limbs.

Linguistic studies, albeit based on meager data, also support a Carib presence in the Middle Cauca region. The Carib-speaking peoples appear to have invaded Colombia as part of a massive movement out of their homeland, likely centered in Brazil, between the Tapajos and Xingu Rivers (Duque Gómez, 1970). Moving along the coast like army ants, they conquered and absorbed many of the peoples they encountered along the way. From the coast, some moved into the Caribbean, which in a real sense became their sea. They colonized the islands of the Antilles, conquering and displacing the less aggressive Arawak-speaking Indians. Advancing along the coast of South America and from bases in the Caribbean, they invaded and occupied the coastal areas of Venezuela and parts of Colombia. The Caribs descended into the interior valleys of Colombia along great rivers such as the Magdalena and Cauca. Small pockets of Carib-speaking people established themselves in Central America, in Honduras, Guatemala, and Nicaragua.

The Caribs first entered Colombia perhaps not earlier than 1000 A.D., but possibly much later. We should not imagine that these successive advances and conquests progressed without resistance. However, from the perspective of culture history, the three- to six-hundred-year movement of Carib-speaking peoples into Colombia, and their concurrent occupation and domination of large territories, can only be compared to similar movements of northern Chichimec Indians into the Valley of Mexico.

At the time of the Spanish conquest, Carib-speaking groups were still pushing forth on all fronts, exerting considerable pressure against the older established cultures of the Sinú and the Chibchas of the Cordillera Oriental. Population pressure, frequent warfare, and the abduction of enemy women undoubtedly led to mutual acculturation between Chibcha and Carib-speaking peoples in Colombia.

Among the armaments used by various groups in the region in the 16th century were war clubs, the sling, fire-hardened palmwood spears, the *atlatl*, and the bow. In addition to a number of ingenious snares and traps, the Indians used camouflaged pits containing sharp, poisoned wooden stakes. As in Mesoamerica, human sacrifice was an integral part of the lifeway of many of the tribes who lived in the Middle Cauca region. Children were also sacrificed, as was the practice in other parts of Colombia.

One should bear in mind that the taking of sacrificial life was widespread in antiquity in the Old World as well. Germanic and Celtic tribesmen were observed practicing human sacrifice by Roman historians, such as Tacitus, in the first century A.D. And although the later Romans were appalled by such practices, their own forebears did the same a few centuries earlier, while young Romans of their own day were being sacrificed daily in warfare, in the name of emperor and state. Human sacrifice in Mesopotamia is evident at Sumer and was customary in many early agricultural societies worldwide.

Among horticultural, root-crop-growing peoples, stretching in a broad equatorial belt from island Southeast Asia to the Americas, human sacrifice was often accompanied by ritual cannibalism. In the Americas, the concept of sacrifice seems linked to ideas concerning the maintenance of balance between human, animal, and plant biospheres. In South America this is reflected in concepts surrounding mythic personages, such as the "Master of Animals," who controls the number of animals killed by hunters. Similar personages govern plants and fish.

Among the Tukano, the shaman mediates between the hunters and the "Master of Animals." To compensate for animal energy taken from the biosphere by hunters, a certain number of men and women are figuratively offered to the "Master of Animals." They are believed to be taken by disease or by accident. Among the Desana Indians of the northwest Amazon region of Colombia is the following belief:

> ... to replace the animals that periodically fall prey to the hunters and fishermen, a certain number of souls go to these malocas, considered to be large uterine 'storehouses.' The souls constitute the energy that is converted into new creatures that eventually go forth into the forests and the waters to be caught by men. (G. Reichel-Dolmatoff, *Amazonian Cosmos*, 1971, p. 66)

Implicit in these beliefs is the perception that reality is composed of interrelated, interdependent, and reactive phenomena. The activities of men affect the total balance of the world. There is a mutual dependence between plant, animal, and human biospheres.

In Mesoamerica, the concept of sacrifice was epitomized by the celestial personage of Nanuatzin — in Mexican mythology, a minor deity — who sacrificed himself by leaping into the celestial fire and emerging as the sun, constantly dispensing its essence that life might exist on earth. (See *Florentine Codex*, Book 7, Chapter 1)

Life depended on life. Life was taken in order that it might continue, and death was the means whereby it was sustained. Plants were consumed by animals and converted to animal energy; both plants and animals were consumed by men and converted into human energy.

This fundamental perception of interdependence, reciprocity, and balance, probably formed during hunting and gathering times, may have later led to serious concerns as human populations increased. The inadequacy of the natural ecology to supply a correlative increase in animal protein and the subsequent increase in population may have persuaded these societies to regulate themselves by human sacrifice.

In the Old World, human sacrifice was phased out in areas that combined irrigation farming with animal husbandry. It continued in island Southeast Asia and Oceania, where slash-and-burn agriculture was practiced and where there were few animal domesticates. The frequency of human sacrifice in the Americas was highest in latitudes between Ecuador and central Mexico, an area typified by high population densities and few animal domesticates. Certainly, additional factors were involved in the cultural complex surrounding human sacrifice, but the underlying motivation is linked to concepts of ecological balance. This is exemplified on a more archaic level by the "Master of Animals," and among some of the more complex societies, by sacrifices to the solar entity.

In the Middle Cauca region, Robledo observed that among the Armas Indians, victims were sacrificed on platforms constructed of wood. A stairway led to the top of the platform. Flanking either side of the stairway were two large wood statues, reminiscent of the Mexican sacrificial platforms with median stairway. Atop the great temple pyramid in Tenochtitlan, the capital of the Mexica-Aztecs, were two temples, each with a statue, one representing Huitzilopochtli, a personification of the sun as warrior [i.e., the sun at its zenith in the south (See Labbé, 1982)], and the other of Tlaloc, a personification of the force of nature controlling rain, thunder, lightning, and water. The Colombian idols were said to face the rising sun. In Mexico and in the Middle Cauca region, the heart was extracted and offered up in sacrifice, and the victims' skulls were displayed on racks.

While these rites in part may evince Mesoamerican influence, it is also possible that they have a common origin elsewhere. Human sacrifice in Mesoamerica cannot be definitely confirmed for either the Olmec horizon (Ignacio Bernal, 1969) or for most groups of the Classic Period. Certainly it is not evident prior to the Olmec horizon. Colombian and Mesoamerican sacrificial rites of the 16th century bear close resemblance, but we cannot determine which is earlier. These rites do not appear to have been practiced in Mexico prior to the 10th century A.D. It is more likely that sacrificial rites are ultimately traceable to South American tropical-forest Indian ideology.

The custom of flaying slain enemies and stuffing the skin with ash, as was common among the Gorrones of the Calima zone, was also practiced by the Ansermas, Picaras, Carramantas, Pozos, Paucuras, and Armas of the Middle Cauca region. This custom, along with conserving and displaying corporeal trophies, may be indicative of cults of dominance and acquisition of personal power. Modeling the skull with wax, thereby recreating the features of the enemy, is ideologically linked to Old World concepts of magical power. There was power in art, just as in the spoken word. The ability to name things gave one a certain degree of control. Animals could be persuaded to approach and obey, rather than be frightened away. Words became associated in the mind of both man and beast with particular actions and evoked in each a memory, pleasant and alluring or unpleasant and frightful. Similarly, the image evoked memories. The ability to form an image enabled the image-maker to hold those memories in mind, giving him control and power. It is an unlikely happenstance that the two most important elements of magic are the chant and the image.

[The word *magic* in English is primarily derived from the old Persian word *magu*, referring to the magi priests of ancient Persia, three of whom are mentioned in the Christian New Testament. Magic, in one applied sense, signifying a figure impressed or drawn upon wax, metal, or other material, used as a talisman, an amulet, or for casting spells, is derived from the word *image*. Image, in turn, is rooted in the Latin verb *imitari*, which means to imitate or imagine. At some point in human prehistory, the ability to draw images and configurations came into being, and art was born.]

That power–magic was an underlying aspect of such practices in the Middle Cauca is implied in the descriptions of the chroniclers and has been surmised and suspected by researchers (see Herman Trimborn, 1936).

Similar concepts of magic pervade the ritual consumption of human flesh, also linked to the belief that the soul of the lifeforce of the slain warrior would be absorbed by the conqueror. Ultimately, this act would link the two, giving the consumer a communion with and power over the spirit of the consumed. This interpretation is supported by ethnographic analogy with other groups. Among the Jivaro of Ecuador, the shrunken trophy heads of captured enemies were believed to be imbued with a magic power called *tsarutama*, which accrued to the possessor of the trophy.

A cannibal-myth reenactment festival, the Bai Feast, is held among the Witoto tribes of the Putumayo River, some of whom live in Colombia. According to the myth, Moma, the creative force governing plants and fish, personified as members of Moma's tribe, consumed his own progeny, namely the plants and fish. These consumed personified plants and fish, referred to as the *Bunesai*, were looked upon as conquered enemies, and their "teeth" and "heads" were kept as trophies in Moma's hut (Preuss, 1921; Zerries, 1968). This Witoto myth is directly related to vegetation-renewal rites. The underlying belief is that new life can come only from the death of old life. Thus Moma consumes his own progeny, his own creations, in order to fashion them anew. The Middle Cauca ritual cannibalistic customs and the displaying of corporeal trophies may have been rooted in similar beliefs.

ARCHAEOLOGY

The first archaeological surveys and excavations in the region were undertaken by the Colombian archaeologist Luis Duque Gómez from 1941–43. An attempt was made to classify and categorize the many different types of ceramics found within the region into four major archaeological zones, or provinces: 1. the Northern Zone; 2. the Northwest Zone; 3. the Western Zone; 4. Quindio. Duque Gómez also enumerated and classified the various types of tombs and burials found within the four zones, particularly Quindio. This study, based on his own investigations, also drew upon information recorded by the noted *guaquero* Luis Arango Cano, in his memoirs, *Recuerdos de la Guaqueria en el Quindio* (1924).

Although the typical grave site found in the Middle Cauca region is the shaft-and-chamber tomb, a variety of other types are known. Mention is made of relatively shallow rectangular tombs, in which the body is placed in an extended position, with a single ceramic vessel at the head as a burial offering. No objects of gold have been found with this grave type. A variation of this tomb is the rectangular grave with a small chamber at one end. This type often contains ceramics and a few gold artifacts. Modifications of this basic type include larger chambers and tombs of greater depth.

An elite form of burial is characterized by two rectangular shafts, joined at the base. The chamber is spacious and often lined with slabs of stone. As expected for this grave, offerings tend to include large quantities of gold jewelry.

One interesting burial consists of a deep shaft, at the bottom of which is a rectangular niche containing a body in vertical position. A variant of the shaft-and-chamber tomb consists of a second shaft, which begins at the floor level of the first chamber and leads to a second chamber.

Some tombs are quite elaborate, being comprised of a chamber with two naves supported by distinct columns. Such tombs tend to be rather spacious and are thought to be those of dignitaries or chieftains. Grave offerings generally include large quantities of gold jewelry.

A unique tomb was one with a cruciform floor plan; a skull was placed at the end of each arm of the cross and faced inward toward the center.

The disposition and treatment of the body also varied markedly. Bodies have been found which were first wrapped in cloth, then covered and packed in clay, forming a casing around the corpse. Some graves contain one body, while others have many. Still others hold only heads or disarticulated body parts. [An interesting custom was the placing of copper finger-tip sheaths over the fingers and toes of the deceased.]

Duque Gómez (1970) relates that the famed gold artifacts known as the "Treasure of the Quimbayas" (much of which was uncovered at the site of La Soledad in Filandia, Quindio, in 1891) were found associated with cremation burials. These exquisite gold offerings were later gifted by the Colombian government to the Queen of Spain and are now housed in the Museo de America in Madrid. Cremations and secondary burial of bones were usually placed in ceramic urns, although small rectangular monolithic sarcophagi with lids have been found at Pereira, in Risaralda, and at Manizales, in Caldas.

Little additional archaeology was undertaken in the region until 1970, when Karen Olson Bruhns (UCSF) headed an archaeological survey project. Over sixty sites were located within the departments of Quindio and Valle. A number of tombs were excavated and the first radiocarbon dates obtained. Previously, Bruhns (1966) had attempted a classification of the ceramics found in the Middle Cauca region on the basis of style and technique. The work conducted in 1970 enabled her to refine the classification scheme and date some of the distinct complexes she had discerned.

THE CERAMIC RECORD

As previously mentioned, the ceramic art of the Middle Cauca region is commonly called "Quimbaya" in popular literature. This broad generalization is not useful in understanding culture history. We will employ a version of Bruhns's scheme to distinguish some of the cultural complexes subsumed under the name Quimbaya.

Four major complexes were distinguished by Bruhns. The first is called the Middle Cauca Complex. Radiocarbon dates for this complex would suggest that ceramics were fashioned sometime between 1050 A.D. and 1500 A.D. The sites are situated on level ground, ridge tops, and river terraces. As in the Calima Zone, maize agriculture is inferred from the large number of grinding implements found in association with the sites. The evidence suggests that population density was quite high. Villages were used for relatively short periods and then relocated. Burials are in shaft-and-chamber tombs. Middle Cauca Complex sites are distributed over wide areas of the Middle Cauca Valley and the Cordillera Central.

Vessels were fashioned by means of the coiling technique, tempered with sand and fired in an open pit. True molds were neither employed in forming vessels nor in effecting designs. Vessel surfaces were treated with clay slips, or modified by incising and appliqué. Resist painting was widely used. The finely decorated wares are distinguished by surface treatment and decoration, and fall into three main groups: Three-Color Resist; Punctate-Resist; and Heavy White and Resist-on-Orange.

There are some similarities in form and style of decoration with wares found immediately to the south in the Calima Zone. Others, such as the tricolor resist wares and the shouldered and tiered amphoras (Plate XI), bear little resemblance to Calima Zone types. Genres such as anthropomorphic vessels (#66) have no counterparts in the Calima Zone. Others, such as the stirrup vessels (#65) and wares such as Heavy White and Resist-on-Orange (#69), are unique to the Middle Cauca region. Some vessels share similarities in resist design with the Yotoco style of the Calima region (#73, Plate XV).

The second major complex in Bruhns's scheme is called the Caldas Complex. Caldas sites, found mainly in the Departments of Caldas, Quindio, and Risaralda, are generally smaller and fewer in number than Middle Cauca sites. Among the more common wares is a red-and-black, two-color resist ware, characterized by a highly fired, fine, thin paste. Other wares include rectangular (solid and hollow) slab figures and an appliquéd-and-incised ware found mainly in the northern part of the Middle Cauca in the northern Caldas and southern Antióquia). Radiocarbon dates obtained for the Caldas Complex fall between 1000–1400 A.D.

Although the Caldas resist ware was decorated by means of a two-color resist technique, most of the Caldas forms, with few exceptions, such as the *alcarraza* (#77), are different from those of the Calima Zone. The Caldas amphoras (#79) are closer to Middle Cauca Complex amphoras. Unique to the Caldas Complex are the appliquéd Incised Ware *incensarios* (#80) and the solid-slab (#82) and hollow-slab (Plate XXI) figures.

Considering that the ceremonial bench is depicted in Middle Cauca Complex ceramics and that this genre usually includes female figures seated on the ground without a bench, but executed in the same style as the male figures with benches, it is possible that some Caldas slab figures (#83) may be an abstract version of this genre. If so, then the bench is indicated by the extended slab. (For seated female companion figures, see Plate XX.)

The bench was a symbol of authority in prehispanic societies and is still an important element in native societies of northern South America. In Mexico its use was restricted to the West Mexican Shaft Tomb and the Gulf Coast

Veracruz cultures. Among the Maya, the woven mat held similar significance. Among the Desana of Colombia, the bench is said to be a symbol of wisdom and stability:

> Sitting on a bench is a procreating and protecting posture that, at the same time, forms a yellow-red-blue cosmic axis with the last element, that of communication being expressed by the seated and thinking person. "The flat part of the seat is our earth... above is man with his thought." (G. Reichel-Dolmatoff, *Amazonian Cosmos*, 1971, p. 111)

According to Reichel-Dolmatoff's Desana informant, people who are personally imbalanced and of bad habits should not sit on such benches, as it is said that the "beneficient force of the bench does not find a field to act upon and thus does harm to the person." (op. cit.) The use of the bench should be restricted solely to adult males. Most of the prehistoric societies have held similar beliefs about the bench.

Two other complexes have been defined by Bruhns: Brownware Incised and Tricolor. Neither have been dated. Brownware Incised was described by Bennet in 1944 and detailed by Bruhns in 1973. It is believed to date from before 800 A.D. Aside from Brownware Incised vessels, the known ceramic complexes of the Middle Cauca region all seem to date from after 1000 A.D. Obviously, ceramic-producing cultures must have existed prior in the region. As Bruhns (1976) and others point out, the immense buildup of soil due to volcanic ash, mud slides, and other geological factors may have buried and concealed the earlier sites. Other ceramic forms include roller (#88) and flat stamps (#87) used to impress designs, and the elaborately decorated spindle whorls (#84–86) used to spin thread.

65

66

67

65
Anthropomorphic-effigy vessels
Red and white slips
left: h: 9¾ in. (24.8 cm) × w: 8 in. (20 cm)
right: h: 6¼ in. (15.9 cm) × w: 4¾ in. (12.1 cm)
Middle Cauca complex (ca. 1000 A.D.–1500 A.D.)
Middle Cauca region

66
Hollow seated figures
Black-on-white-and-red resist painted
left: h: 7¾ in. (19.7 cm) × w: 4¼ in. (10.8 cm)
right: h: 6½ in. (16.5 cm) × w: 3¾ in. (9.5 cm)
Middle Cauca complex (ca. 1000 A.D.–1500 A.D.)
Middle Cauca region

67
Amphoras
Black-on-red-and-white resist painted
left: h: 11 in. (27.8 cm) × circum: 20½ in. (52.1 cm)
right: h: 11 in. (27.8 cm) × circum: 21 in. (53.3 cm)
Middle Cauca complex (1000 A.D.–1500 A.D.)
Middle Cauca region

68
Annular-based bowl
Black-on-white-and-red resist painted
h: 4 in. (10.2 cm) × d: 6¼ in. (15.9 cm)
Middle Cauca complex (ca. 1000 A.D.–1500 A.D.)
Middle Cauca region

69
left: Pedestal dish
Heavy white-and-resist on orange
h: 4¾ in. (12.1 cm) × w (diagonal): 8½ in. (21.5 cm)
right: Pot stand
Heavy white-and-resist on orange
h: 5½ in. (14 cm) × w (diagonal): 8¼ in. (13.3 cm)
Middle Cauca complex (ca. 1000 A.D.–1500 A.D.)
Middle Cauca region

70
left: Globular jar
Punctate-and-resist on red
h: 5½ in. (14 cm) × d: 6 in. (15.2 cm)
(as seen in *Precolumbian Ceramics* by Jesus Arango Cano, 1979, Plate 5)
center: Shouldered jar
Punctate-and-resist on red
h: 6¾ in. (17.2 cm) × circum: 17 in. (43.2 cm)
right: Annular-based bowl
Punctate-and-resist on red
h: 3¾ in. (9.5 cm) × d: 5¼ in. (13.3 cm)
Middle Cauca complex (ca. 1000 A.D.–1500 A.D.)
Middle Cauca region

70

71
Alcarraza
Black-on-white-and-red resist painted
h: 9¼ in. (23.5 cm) × d: 7¼ in. (18.4 cm)
Middle Cauca complex (ca. 1000 A.D.–1500 A.D.)
Middle Cauca region

72
Double-chambered anthropomorphic vessel
Red-and-white slip
l: 9 in. (22.9 cm) × w: 4½ in. (11.5 cm)
Middle Cauca complex (ca. 1000 A.D.–1500 A.D.)
Middle Cauca region

73
Anthropomorphic vessel
Black-on-red resist painted
h: 13 in. (33 cm) × w: 9¾ in. (24 cm)
Middle Cauca complex (ca. 1000 A.D.–1500 A.D.)
Middle Cauca region

This vessel is decorated with a design that appears on Yotoco-phase ceramics from the Calima zone.

74
Hollow-slab seated male figure
Black-on-red resist painted
h: 18 in. (45.7 cm) × w: 10¾ in. (27.3 cm)
Caldas complex (ca. 1000 A.D.–1400 A.D.)
Middle Cauca region

75

75
Abstract anthropomorphic figure
Black-on-red resist painted
h: 16¼ in. (41.3 cm) × w: 7 in. (17.8 cm)
Middle Cauca complex (ca. 1000 A.D.–1500 A.D.)
Middle Cauca region

76
Toad- or frog-effigy *alcarraza*
Black-on-red-and-white resist painted
h: 6 in. (15.2 cm) × w: 4¾ in. (12.1 cm)
Middle Cauca complex (ca. 1000 A.D.–1500 A.D.)
Middle Cauca region

77
Tetrapod *alcarraza*
Black-on-red resist painted
h: 8 in. (20.3 cm) × circum: 19 in. (42.3 cm)
Caldas complex (ca. 1000 A.D.–1400 A.D.)
Middle Cauca region

78
Annular-based, shouldered jar
Black-on-red resist painted
h: 6⅞ in. (16.2 cm) × d: 7 in. (17.8 cm)
Caldas complex (ca. 1000 A.D.–1400 A.D.)
Middle Cauca region

79
Amphora
Black-on-red resist painted
h: 16¼ in. (41.3 cm) × circum: 36½ in. (92.7 cm)
Caldas complex (ca. 1000 A.D.–1400 A.D.)
Middle Cauca region

80
Incensarios
Reddish-brown to light-brown slips, decorated with appliquéd and incised details
left: h: 5 in. (12.7 cm) × d: 8 in. (20.3 cm)
center: h: 3¾ in. (9.5 cm) × d: 6 in. (15.2 cm)
right: h: 3¾ in. (9.5 cm) × d: 7½ in. (19.1 cm)
Caldas complex (ca. 1000 A.D.–1400 A.D.)
Middle Cauca region

81
Figure seated on a bench
Buff terracotta
h: 15 in. (38.1 cm) × w: 9 in. (22.9 cm) × d: 12½ in. (31.7 cm)
Popayan (dates undetermined)
Valle Del Cauca

The iconography of this genre (a figure, with diadem and shield, seated on a bench) suggests that the figure represents the sun as First Shaman.

(PHOTO COURTESY OF THE DENVER ART MUSEUM)

82
Solid-slab anthropomorphic figure
Light-brown slip, decorated with black resist painting
h: 13 in. (33 cm) × w: 9¼ in. (23.5 cm)
Caldas complex (ca. 1200 A.D.–1400 A.D.)
Middle Cauca region

83
Solid-slab anthropomorphic figure with child
Light-brown slip, decorated with incised details
h: 14 in. (35.6 cm) × w: 9 in. (22.9 cm)
Caldas complex (ca. 1200 A.D.–1400 A.D.)
Middle Cauca region

The incised decoration indicates the binding of calves, thighs, wrists, and upper arms.

84

85

86

84
Spindle whorls
Black, decorated with white-filled incised details
Avg. h: 1 in. (2.54 cm) × w: 1 in. (2.54 cm)
Cultural complex and dates undetermined
Middle Cauca region

85
Spindle whorls
Brown to reddish-black, decorated with white-filled incised details
Avg. h: 1¼ in. (3.2 cm) × w: 1½ in. (3.8 cm)
Cultural complex and dates undetermined
Middle Cauca region

86
Spindle whorls
Black and brown, decorated with white-filled incised details
Avg. h: 1⅛ in. (2.9 cm) × w: 1½ in.(3.8 cm)
Cultural complex and dates undetermined
Middle Cauca region

87

87
Flat stamp
Buff terracotta
l: 5¼ in. (13.3 cm) × w: 2½ in. (6.4 cm)
Cultural complex and dates undetermined
Middle Cauca region

88
Roller stamp
Grayish-black
l: 5½ in. (14 cm) × circum: 8 in. (20.3 cm)
Cultural complex and dates undetermined
Middle Cauca region

CHAPTER IV

THE SINÚ REGION

Mound Builders of the Atlantic Flood Plain

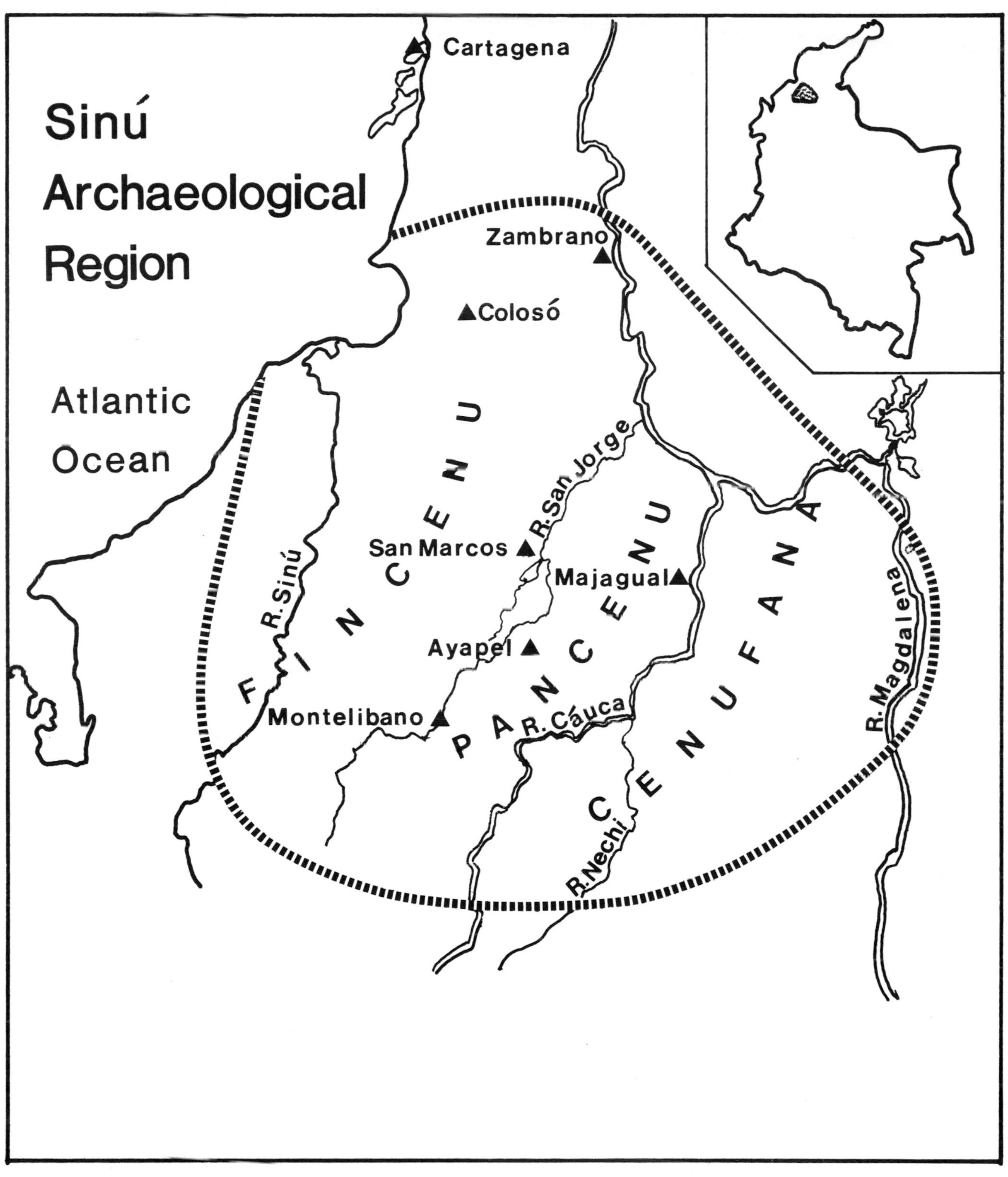
Sinú
Archaeological
Region
Atlantic
Ocean
Cartagena
Zambrano
Colosó
San Marcos
Majagual
Ayapel
Montelibano
R. Sinú
R. San Jorge
R. Cauca
R. Nechi
R. Magdalena
FINCENU
PANCENU
CENUFANA

GEOGRAPHY

Following the Cauca River northward across the Department of Antióquia, one arrives at the northeastern extremity of the Cordillera Occidental known as the Cuchilla Del Mocho and the northwestern extremity of the Cordillera Central. Here, the great valley formed by the Cauca River ends, while the river continues its course through a vast region of grassy lowlands. This region is comprised of a broad flood plain coursed by the meanders of numerous rivers, such as the Rio San Jorge, the Rio Nechi, and the Rio Sinú. The topography is only occasionally broken by an outcrop of highlands. The most prominent of these is the Serrania de San Jacinto in the northern portion of the region, between the Rio Magdalena and the Caribbean coast.

The San Jorge, Sinú, and Nechi Rivers were important centers of culture in antiquity. The San Jorge River has its source in a geological formation know as the Nudo de Paramillo, in the Department of Córdoba, and ultimately joins a tributary of the Magdalena River in the Department of Bolivar. The Sinú has its source in the Department of Antióquia and empties into the Atlantic in the Bay of Cispata. The river bifurcates near Cerete, forming the Aguas Blancas (White Waters) and Aguas Prietas (Dark Waters), which later unite at Lorica, continuing on to the sea. The San Jeronimo range lies between the San Jorge and Sinú rivers.

ARCHAEOLOGY

The term *Sinú*, as used in popular literature, refers to cultural artifacts found in an extensive region situated predominantly in the modern departments of Córdoba and Sucre. In prehistoric times, this was an important area of development for a number of distinct cultures, some of which were still flourishing at the time of the Spanish Conquest. Some of these were relatively new at the time of the conquest, while others had long disappeared, leaving only transient memories in the form of archaelogical vestiges. Little solid evidence exists from which to formulate a detailed prehistory of the region.

Evidence obtained in northern Colombia indicates that manioc growing had become an important regional subsistence pattern by the first millenium B.C. The type site is represented by Momil, situated on a lagoon formed by the lower Sinú River. Momil has been divided into Momil II, which began early in the first millenium B.C., and Momil II, which spanned the first centry B.C. to about 600 A.D. Dates for Momil are estimated based on cross-comparisons with similar artifacts found elsewhere, for which absolute dates have been obtained (G. Reichel-Dolmatoff, 1966).

Momil I represents a stage of development consisting of sedentary villages based on manioc horticulture. Maize agriculture was introduced during Momil II and is indicated by the presence of *manos* and *metate* grinding implements and large ceramic vessels used to contain maize beer. Agriculture was heavily supplemented by hunting and fishing, as shown by the large quantities of turtle-shell fragments and alligator, mammal, and fish bones found in the midden and refuse sites.

The ceramics of Momil I are usually decorated by shallow grooving and incising, although there are some early painted forms. Characteristic shapes include globular and subglobular jars, bowls, and griddles used for making manioc cakes. Momil I figurines are solid, highly abstract forms. Momil I is typified by flat ceramic stamps for impressing designs, presumably on textiles and perhaps on the body. Momil II continues the same vessel forms as Momil I, but adds new forms, such as large globular storage vessels, tripod vessels with tall supports, and clay cylinder stamps.

Formerly, the Sinú region was considerably more forested than it was at the time of European exploration. Human activity was responsible for this change in ecology. Around the first century A.D., a system of artificial canals was developed as a means of controlling the periodic flooding which characterizes much of the region. These canals were later extensively elaborated. Entire systems were built over earlier projects, enlarged, and otherwise modified by successive peoples.

Investigations undertaken by Ana Maria Falchetti de Saenz and Clemencia Plazas de Nieto (1977–78) along the lower San Jorge in the Department of Sucre and along the middle San Jorge in the Department of Córdoba demonstrate the pattern of development.

Two distinct occupations of the region have been identified by investigators. The first group inhabited the region between the 5th and 10th centuries A.D. This culture was centered along the lower course of the San Jorge. A peripheral expression of the culture was located along the middle course of the same river.

High population density necessitated an effective management of land resources. In response, the people constructed an integrated system of canals and artificial mounds, which served as platforms for habitation sites above the flood and water marks. Additional mounds were constructed for burial purposes. Often, a number of burial mounds were grouped together to form cemeteries. Small mounds are usually indicative of a single burial, while larger mounds were used for multiple burials.

Certain cemeteries are characterized by mounds of uniform size, while others have mounds of varying dimensions. The site of El Japon, on the lower San Jorge, and that of Yucatan, in Montelibano, are especially noted for the size of their mounds. Funerary offerings consisted of carved shells, ceramics, textiles, and objects of gold. Sinú-style goldwork is of very high quality and purity. Especially well-executed are the false filagree pendants, cast with great delicacy by the lost-wax process.

Fishing, hunting, and manioc growing played an important role in the local economy. Agricultural ridges were raised for planting.

There are basically two distinct kinds of manioc: bitter and sweet. Archaeologically, the bitter variety is associated with ceramic griddles. West of the Eastern Cordillera, it is found only at an early time horizon. It must be processed and detoxified before ingesting. Later, as processed flour, it is cooked as flat cakes, spread on a griddle, and placed over an open fire. The cakes may be stored and conserved for later use. In areas where bitter manioc is used, it generally forms the basis of the diet, even today.

Sweet manioc was cultivated by the people of the San Jorge, according to Falchetti de Saenz and Plazas de Nieto. It is generally used to supplement the diet of hunting and fishing peoples and doesn't require detoxification.

As population density increased, the San Jorge people spread out along the banks of the river. At Montelibano, a local variant of this culture developed around the 11th century A.D. Along the lower San Jorge, however, the original centers of culture were gradually abandoned late in the 10th century A.D.

The second occupation of the San Jorge began about the 15th century. This group moved along the lower San Jorge River, already vacated by the first group. It is unclear why the old centers were abandoned. The first group had a widespread dispersal pattern within settlements, with distinct agricultural habitation areas and burial sites; the second tended to concentrate on less land, and settlements were more widespread. The latter depended extensively on hunting turtles, fish, birds, reptiles, and mammals. Although the practice of burial-mound interment continued, individuals were also buried within habitation mounds.

Who were the newcomers? They may have been related to a tribe known historically as the Malibu (Falchetti de Saenz and Plazas de Nieto, 1977–78). The Malibu were first encountered by the Spanish, along the lower Magdalena. Described as a communal tribe of gatherers, they practiced a primitive form of agriculture, growing some maize, manioc, cotton, and other plant domesticates. They were co-governed by secular chieftains and a powerful "caste" of priest-shamans, who acted as intermediaries between the unseen forces of nature and their local community. Additionally, they served as healers.

The archaeological discovery of two distinct groups along the San Jorge suggests that the peoples of the Greater Sinú region at the time of the conquest were neither of one ethnicity nor on the same level of sociocultural development.

ETHNOHISTORY

The chronicles shed some light on the sociopolitical realities of the region during the 16th century. Accordingly, Ayapel was an important urban center exercising political and economic control over a large group of satellite villages. These villages were agrarian communities of fishing and hunting folk, with extensive trade relations and a strong dependence on manioc growing. Pedro de Aguado states that the principal towns were composed of well-built houses with elaborate temples constructed of wood. In one temple alone, there were twenty-four large wooden idols overlaid with gold. Rods, stretching shoulder to shoulder between idols, supported hammocks which held offerings of gold.

At the time of the Spanish conquest, much of the region was divided into three domains, whose rulers were related to one another: Cenúfana, Pancenú, and Fincenú. Cenúfana, located along the banks of the Nechi River, was ruled by a power *cacique* named Nutibara and was the most important of the provinces. Its territories embraced the rich sources of gold of the lower Cauca and Nechi. Pancenú, surrounded by ancient rock formations, was located on grassy flatlands and had extensive canal systems for flood control. An effective system of agricultural ridges and land reclamation was employed. Canals, with as little as 33 feet of land between them, were built perpendicular to existing natural waterways. The remains of this intricate network often have a fishbone appearance when seen from the sky. The third province, called Fincenú, located along the banks of the Sinú River, was ruled by a female *cacica* or chieftainess, named Tota. Fincenú was especially important as a burial center for the elite of all three provinces.

The chroniclers observed that burial mounds were the prerogative of the elite, who were buried with male and female retainers, while commoners were interred in oval or rectangular tombs, with few if any offerings. Corpses were first covered with red earth. Friends and relatives of the deceased would then hold a funerary service, and the "mourners," if we may use such a culturocentric term, would intermittently cast dirt over the red earth while consuming large quantities of maize beer. The size of the mound reflected how many friends and relatives one had, their ardor, and the ability of the hosts to sustain the festivities.

Martin Fernandez de Enciso noted another burial custom, which consisted of removing the viscera from the body by melting away the body fat and then hanging the dessicated body in a hammock inside a hut. We do not know how long the body was kept therein, nor whether this custom was reserved for a specific class of people or merely reflected the custom and influence of a foreign ethnicity.

These domains were defended by well-organized militia. The basic armaments were the bow with poisoned arrows and the spear. Chieftains and warriors alike went into battle in full regalia, to the accompaniment of conch war trumpets and other martial and bellicose sounds. One can imagine the panoramic display of feathered, bejeweled, and painted warriors, brandishing arms and engaging in mortal combat to the wind-blown sounds of trumpets, flutes, and horns and the percussive beat of drums and trammeling feet. However resplendent the costuming and score, the stage of war is the battlefield, and the price of admission often death.

Under their leader, Nutibara, the Sinús put up a formidable resistance to the invading Spanish, abandoning their towns and villages and removing or destroying all provisions, leaving the Spaniards to starve or to return to their bases to the northeast. As in all such military engagements between Spanish and Indian, however, the former's superiority in arms and military technology inevitably led to the defeat of the indigenous forces.

CERAMIC RECORD

The ceramic record is without doubt incomplete. Even a basic chronological ordering of the material is lacking. Additionally, the designs are less iconographically definitive than those of most other prehistoric traditions in Colombia. This is partially due to the infrequency of painted designs and the prevalence of monochromatically slipped surfaces. Designs recorded on roller stamps offer the student a rudimentary basis for such a study.

Some investigators have suggested that we seek the antecedents of local Sinú culture in the south, probably in the Cauca River Valley. This suggestion is based on the supposed concurrence in physical type depicted on ceramics in both areas and the close similarities in goldwork. A comparison of the ceramics of the Sinú and Cauca River Valley regions reveals, however, significant differences far in excess of any similarities observed. Affinities between the two regions are strongest in adjacent areas and most likely reflect trade and a mutual exchange of ideas. More impressive homologues exist between the earlier culture of the lower San Jorge and the Valencia phase of the central coast of Venezuela. Both areas are typified by artificial habitation, mounds, raised agricultural ridges, and a similar treatment of ceramics. The commonalities observed, however, date to the 10th century A.D. in Venezuela and are too late to have been the source of influence for the Sinú, although the reverse would at least be plausible. According to Plazas de Nieto and Falchetti de Saenz, the similarities are better explained on the basis of independent local development than on any strong cultural link between the two regions (1979).

Modeled-Painted is one of the important ceramic traditions and is identified with the first group of occupation, along the Rio San Jorge. Modeled-Painted ware is found from Montelibano in the southwest to Montanita in the northeast. (Other type sites include El Japon, Carate, and Viloria.) These wares include globular and sub-globular effigy jars, modeled figurines, pedestaled vessels, cups, bowls, ceramic roller stamps, and other forms. They were fashioned from the 6th to the 10th centuries A.D. in the nuclear area studied, but continued in modified form at sites such as Montelibano.

The second group of occupation, which appeared around the 15th century A.D. in the northeast portion of the region formerly occupied by the first group, was an extension of a large, widespread tradition. The ceramics associated with this group are in the Incised-Polished Tradition. The wares, distributed on both sides of the lower Magdalena River, are found as far north as the the Cienaga de Santa Marta. Only a few of their sites fall within the zone of occupation of the first group. Of these, the most important are Las Palmas and Tiesto. Within the Incised-Polished Tradition are a number of defined ceramic complexes, such as the Las Palmas, a local variant. The Las Palmas complex is comprised of a number of ceramic wares: Las Palmas Red-slipped Ware, Las Palmas Hachured Ware, Las Palmas Plain Polished Ware, and Las Palmas Fine Incised Ware. Very typical of the Las Palmas Fine Incised wares are the distinctive pedestaled cups.

So as not to burden the reader with the innumerable incomplete designations for the many variations of local wares within the Sinú region, we shall simply refer, when possible, to the locale where similar forms have been found.

The ceramic art of the Sinú region reflects a cultural province quite distinct from those to the south in the Cauca Valley. Conspicuously absent are the *alcarrazas*, although a highly modified and distinctive form of double-tubular jar is known for certain friable, cream-colored wares (Plate XXII). Also absent is the use of negative painting. Additionally, there is an emphasis on female forms (#92). The traditions of the Sinú region either developed locally or derived from traditions east of the region, such as Zambrano (ca. 600–1200 A.D.), centered along the lower Magdalena. About 600 A.D., Zambrano was characterized by settlements in which large mounds served as house platforms. These communities, like those of the Sinú, had a mixed economy based on farming and fishing. The Zambrano region (not to be confused with the tradition) is rich in cultural remains, having an almost unbroken record of 4000 years of settlement, represented by the Puerto Hormiga (ca. 3000–2000 B.C.), Malambo (ca. 800–600 B.C.) (#90), Momil (ca. 600 B.C.–600 A.D.), Zambrano, and other phases (Plate XXIV).

Typical of the area around the Serrania de San Jacinto in the Sinú region, and also at Betanci and other sites in Córdoba, are the many finely modeled ceramic flutes characterized by four playing holes with cayman *adornos* (#99). The flutes are occasionally patterned in the form of a fish. Figurines depicting seated dignitaries (#92) were probably made from around 1000 A.D. to the Spanish conquest. The Sinú ceramicists exhibit a fine control over their media (#96). The sculptural tradition as a whole, however, lacks the variety of form and power of expression exhibited in the Cauca Valley or the Tumaco-La Tolita area.

Grater bowls (#95) with deeply incised lines are not unusual along the upper Sinú and other areas. Fine pedestaled cups (#97) are relatively common. Some of the the ocarinas (#100) show clear relations with cultures to the east, such as the Tairona, as do some motifs on roller stamps (#98 r.). A very typical design pattern, observed on vessels, figurines, and rollers (#98 l.), is the cross and rhomboid.

89

(Preceding page)

89
Human-effigy figure
Grayish-brown slip
h: 9½ in. (24.1 cm) × w: 7½ in. (19.1 cm)
Provenance unknown and dates undetermined
Probably from the lower Magdalena River region

This is a highly stylized depiction of the human form with incised tattoos. The arms and ear spools are stylized zoomorphs shown in profile.

90
Mask
Burnished variegated grayish-black slip
h: 4 in. (10.2 cm) × w: 4¾ in. (12.1 cm)
Malambo style (dates undetermined)
Lower Magdalena River region

91
Anthropomorphic figure
Burnished grayish-black slip
h: 8¼ in. (21 cm) × w: 4⅜ in. (11.1 cm)
(Dates undetermined)
Sinu-Magdalena River region

92
Seated female figure
Gray
h: 8 in. (20.3 cm) × w: 4 in. (10.2 cm)
(Dates undetermined, probably ca. 600 A.D.–1500 A.D.)
Sinu region

The wraparound skirt and the distinctive nipples support the interpretation that the figure is intended to be female, but it is highly unusual for a female to be seated on a bench. The bench is usually associated with male figures in prehispanic Colombian art as a symbol of authority.

93
Female figure – "Moon Deity" (see back cover)
Brownish-orange terracotta
h: 10½ in. (26.5 cm) × w: 7 in. (17.8 cm)
(Dates undetermined)
Sinu region

Powerful fertility symbolism is incorporated in the figural form of this exquisitely modeled representation of a moon goddess. The feet are modified to represent breasts when the figure is viewed horizontally, and the legs and torso are modeled as an abstraction of the male generative organ. The head, modeled in the form of a crescent moon, also symbolizes the female generative organ.

94
Colander
Buff terracotta
h: 11 in. (27.9 cm) × circum: 32¾ in. (83.2 cm)
(Dates undetermined, probably ca. 600 A.D.–1500 A.D.)
Sinu region

95
Ring-based pedestal grater-bowl
Burnished grayish-black slip
h: 5 in. (12.7 cm) × d: 10½ in. (26.7 cm)
(ca. 1400 A.D.–1600 A.D.)
Sinu region

96

96
Ring-based pedestal bowl
Buff terracotta
h: 5¾ in. (14.6 cm) × d: 6⅜ in. (16.2 cm)
(Dates undetermined,
probably ca. 600 A.D.–1500 A.D.)
Sinu region

97
Pedestal bowl
Brown slip, decorated with incised details
h: 10¾ in. (27.3 cm) × d: 8½ in. (21.6 cm)
(Dates undetermined, probably ca. 600 A.D.–1500 A.D.)
Sinu region

The vessel is decorated with classic Sinu cross-and-rhomboid incised patterns.

98
Roller stamps
Grayish-black
left: l: 2¾ in. (8.9 cm)
center: l: 3¾ in. (9.5 cm)
right: l: 3 in. (7.6 cm)
(Dates undetermined)
Sinu region

99
Flute with cayman adorno
Burnished grayish-black slip
l: 8 in. (20.3 cm)
(Dates undetermined)
Sinu region

100
Ocarinas
Gray, decorated with incised details
left: w: 1¾ in. (4.4 cm)
right: w: 1½ in. (3.8 cm)
(Dates undetermined)
Sinu region

This type of ocarina is also found in the neighboring lower Magdalena River region.

98

99

10

CHAPTER V

THE MAGDALENA RIVER REGION

Bones and Burial Urns — The Seeds of New Life

101
Zoomorphic flutes
Grayish-black
left: h: 3¾ in. (9.5 cm) × w: 2⅝ in. (6.7 cm)
center: h: 2¼ in. (5.7 cm) × w: 1¼ in. (3.2 cm)
right: h: 3¾ in. (9.5 cm) × w: 2½ in. (6.4 cm)
(Dates undetermined)
Sinu region

SANTA MARTA
BARANQUILLA
Tairona
Atlantic Ocean
CARTAGENA
Bajo Magdalena
SINCELEJO
MONTERIA
Sinú
Guané
Pacific Ocean
TUNJA
MANIZALES
"Quimbaya"
PEREIRA
Muisca
Middle Cauca
BOGOTÁ
ARMENIA
CALI
Calima
NEIVA
Tierradentro
POPAYAN
Tumaco-La Tolita
San Agustín
Nariño
FLORENCIA
PASTO

GEOGRAPHY

The great Magdalena River lies east of the Sinú Region and empties into the Caribbean Sea. This 1100-mile-long waterway, which flows north between the Eastern and Central Cordilleras, is geographically divided into upper, middle, and lower courses.

The lower Magdalena, characteristically a broad, marshy flood plain comprised of numerous channels, swamps, and lagoons, is joined by other great waterways, such as the Cauca and the San Jorge.

The source of the Magdalena is to be found far to the south in the region of San Agustín, visited by the Spanish friar Juan de Santa Gertrudis in 1757. Little is known concerning the prehistory of the Magdalena River Valley, which served as an important corridor for the movement of peoples.

ARCHAEOLOGY

Archaeological research, conducted in the mid-20th century by G. Reichel-Dolmatoff and others, revealed a number of important sites along the river, notably San Jacinto, Tamalameque, Ocana, Puerto Niño, Rio de la Miel, Rio Guarino, Honda, Giradot, Ricaurte, and Espinal.

Of particular interest are the numerous large cemeteries with shaft graves containing large numbers of burial urns. We know little concerning the origins of the burial urn custom, although it was practiced from Darien to the Guajira, along the Cauca and Magdalena rivers, and in other parts of Colombia.

At Tamalameque, along the lower Magdalena, are large cemeteries composed of shaft graves with side chambers containing groups of cylindrical urns. These urns are characterized by lids in the shape of large heads, with short, stubby arms and with hands raised in symbolic gesture (#102). Often the faces are painted with curvilinear designs, perhaps representing facial tattoos. The Moskito Burial Urn style, also found in the lower Magdalena region, is characterized by lids usually surmounted by a seated male or female figure, often with traces of black resinous paint on the body (#103). The base of the urn usually has four handles and is decorated with applied, modeled bird heads. Many sub-regional variations in urn style are known for the lower Magdalena (Plate XXVII).

Urns in a number of sub-styles commonly referred to as the "Chimila style" are found in the frontier region between the departments of Magdalena and Cesar. The body of these urns is egg-shaped, the lid forms the head of a stylized human figure; and the base is often footed. Arms fashioned from long fillets of clay are often decorated with sets of clay bangles. Necklaces of disc beads are sometimes indicated (front cover; #105).

Important burial sites have been found along the middle Magdalena, particularly in the region of Rio de la Miel and around the Palagua River. The urns are in a style different from those of the lower Magdalena. The form tends to be more globular than cylindrical. The shoulder and neck of the vessel are often decorated by means of incising, effecting a maze of rectilinear, scroll-like patterns (#105). Generally, the lids are either surmounted by a male figure seated on a bench (#104) or by opposing bird figures (Plate XXVIII). As both types of urn have been found in the same tomb, this may indicate that urns with male figures are specified for male burials and the other type for female burials. The binding of calves and upper arms of male figures has led some investigators to hypothesize that the urns were fashioned by Carib-speaking peoples.

Surveys and excavations in the 1970s by Luisa Fernanda Herrara de Turbay and Mauricio Londoño Paredes at Puerto Serviez in the middle Magdalena region have contributed important information on the context of these urns. The preferred location for burial sites was atop hills and hillocks that rise 90 or so feet above the otherwise flat topography. Graves are of the shaft-and-chamber variety. One of the excavated tombs contained a chamber already discovered and looted by *guaqueros*. The chamber was positioned to the side of the shaft, about seven feet below the surface. Continuing their dig to 20 feet, Turbay and Londoño discovered the entrances to two undisturbed chambers, positioned opposite one another, with the shaft inbetween. They found 63 funerary urns and 63 other vessels comprised of bowls, cups, and *ollas*. A cup, bowl, or *olla* had been placed beside each urn.

The urns contained badly decomposed bones of adults, adolescents, infants, and some animals such as deer and armadillos. The condition of the bone material led the excavators to hypothesize ritual cannibalism. Along the middle portion of the larger bones was a sizable cavity, which may have been made after death in order to extract and eat the marrow (Herrera de Turbay and Londoño Paredes, 1975) This would suggest Carib custom. Some urns contained a mélange of both adult and infant bones, with as many as three individuals found in the same urn.

The excavators reported that it was difficult to determine osteopathological patterns. Some bones showed signs of osteoporosis, and one lower mandible from an adolescent indicated pyorrhea. Unfortunately, no radiocarbon dates were obtained for this tomb.

ETHNOHISTORY

Surprisingly little information has been handed down concerning the Indians who lived along the middle Magdalena at the time of the Spanish Conquest. According to the accounts, one group, the Pantagoras, believed in an afterlife consisting of a carefree existence along the banks of the Magdalena, where game, fish, and other amenities abounded. Considering the nature of many Indian religions, such reports are highly suspect. The happy-hunting-ground paradises reported for Indian groups form North to South America are nowhere to be found when one penetrates the religious perspectives of extant Indian societies. Such accounts probably reflect the inability of the European observer to transcend the metaphoric and allegorical imagery of the native informant. We should also question whether the informant was privy to the esoteric truths of his own culture and did not simply reflect a layman's understanding of more profound principles. In any event, such cursory observations do not help interpret the archaeological evidence.

No mention is made of urn burials among the Pantagoras, although it is probable that it was practiced, given their geographical distribution and the archaeological evidence.

There are few references in the chronicles concerning urn burials. Pedro de Aguado informs us that the corpse of a chief was placed in a hollow tree trunk which was set aflame, reducing the corpse to ash and bone. The ash was placed in a clay vessel, later adorned with jewels and other finery. The bones were ground to a powder and placed in a second urn. Oviedo, in reference to the Indians of Cartagena, records that the bones were cleaned, painted red, placed in jars, and kept inside the houses.

Among the Desana, when a *kumu*, a man of wisdom, dies, he is buried in the center of his dwelling (the *maloca*) and abandoned for five years:

> After five years or more have passed, the members of the sib gather there and exhume the body. The bones of the toes and hands are burned and pulverized and the powder is then mixed with chicha, which the men drink to incorporate into themselves the wisdom of the dead kumu. The cranium and the rest of the bones are collected together with his personal ornaments and wooden figurines into a large earthen jar and then buried in a hidden place. (G. Reichel-Dolmatoff, *Amazonian Cosmos*, 1971, pp. 138–139)

Noteworthy is the fact that some bones are ground into powder, mixed with maize beer, and consumed in the belief that the wisdom of the deceased accrues to those who partake of the drink.

The urn burial custom is undoubtedly linked to specific concepts regarding bones and the afterlife. As noted in Chapter Two, the Desana metaphorically define the grave as a uterus to which the corporeal part of man returns. There is widespread belief among many Indians of both Middle and South America that bones are a form of seed, from which new life will spring. Recall the Mexican allegory of the personification of the dual lifeforce, Quetzalcoatl, descending to the underworld to retrieve the bones of mankind to resurrect them to new life. Within the Colombian context, the act of placing bones in cylindrical, phalliform urns, and placing these in the womb-like shaft-and-chamber tomb within the "Earth Mother," seems to be an enactment of such beliefs.

Ethnographic information gathered throughout northern South America informs us that bones were linked to concepts of power, fertility, and resurrection. There is a clear link between certain bone rituals and the idea of resurrection among the Makiritare, a Caribban group of Guiana (Otto Zerries, 1969). Among other groups, such as the Betoi of eastern Colombia, bones are felt to contain special power and energy when linked with the lifeforce of an individual. The Betoi, wounding themselves with a bone of the species of animal they wish to hunt, believe this will give them added prowess.

Such ethnographic insights must be employed in any valid interpretation of archaeological data if an accurate prehistory is to be formulated.

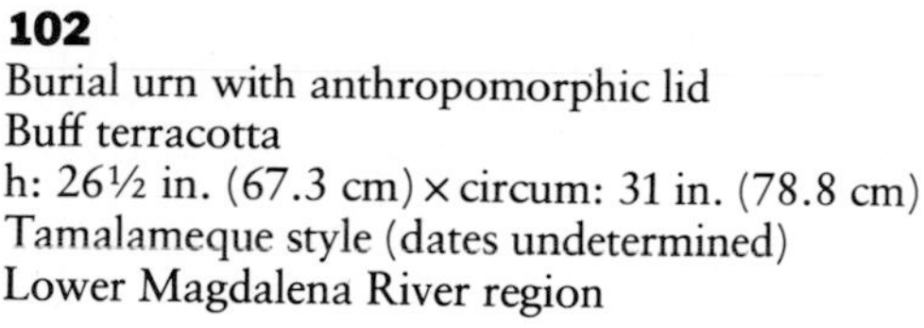

102
Burial urn with anthropomorphic lid
Buff terracotta
h: 26½ in. (67.3 cm) × circum: 31 in. (78.8 cm)
Tamalameque style (dates undetermined)
Lower Magdalena River region

103
Burial urn with a seated human figure on the lid
Buff terracotta
h: 25½ in. (64.8 cm) × circum: 26 in. (66 cm)
Moskito style (dates undetermined)
Lower Magdalena River region
The urn is decorated with modeled zoomorphic heads.

104
Burial urn with a seated anthropomorphic figure on the lid
Buff terracotta, decorated with appliquéd and incised details
h: 26 in. (66 cm) × circum: 50¾ in. (128.9 cm)
(Dates undetermined)
Middle Magdalena River region

Shell beads have been applied with a black, resinous substance to the male figure seated on a bench. The urn's lid, shoulder, and neck are incised with rectilinear geometric decoration.

105
Burial urn with two figures on the lid
Buff terracotta
h: 25¾ in. (65.4 cm) × circum: 38 in. (96.5 cm)
(Dates undetermined)
Middle Magdalena River region

106
Burial urn with seated human-effigy on the lid
Brownish-orange terracotta
h: 32 in. (81.3 cm) × circum: 50½ in. (128.3 cm)
Mixed style (dates undetermined)
Provenance unknown

This urn demonstrates both Chimila and Lower Magdalena stylistic traits. The figure is rendered in Chimila style, but the composition of a figure seated on a bench is a Lower Magdalena River characteristic.

107
Detail

108
Anthropomorphic burial urn with lid (see front cover)
Buff terracotta
h: 25¼ in. (64.1 cm) × circum: 53¾ in. (136.5 cm)
Chimila style (dates undetermined)
Provenance unknown

109
Anthropomorphic burial urns with lids
Buff terracotta
left: h: 25¾ in. (65.4 cm) × d: 48¼ in. (122.6 cm)
right: h: 24¼ in. (61.6 cm) × d: 48¾ in. (123.8 cm)
Chimila style (dates undetermined)
Provenance unknown

CHAPTER VI

SAN AGUSTÍN AND TIERRADENTRO

Vaults of Power and Transformation

SANTA MARTA
BARANQUILLA
Tairona
Atlantic Ocean
CARTAGENA
Bajo
Magdalena
SINCELEJO
MONTERIA
Sinú
Pacific Ocean
Guané
TUNJA
MANIZALES
"Quimbaya"
PEREIRA
Muisca
Middle Cauca
BOGOTÁ
ARMENIA
CALI
Calima
NEIVA
Tierradentro
POPAYAN
Tumaco-
La Tolita
San Agustín
Nariño
FLORENCIA
PASTO

GEOGRAPHY

Travelling south from the middle Magdalena River Region one crosses the departments of Tolima and Huila, ultimately reaching the area of Colombia where the southern part of the Eastern Cordillera fuses with the mass of the Andean chain. This marks the beginning of the Magdalena River Valley. Slightly to the east, at an elevation of 4,800–5,400 feet, lies the region of San Agustín. From here, one can discern the peaks of the Colombian Massif, approximately centered where the Andes branch off to become three distinct ranges: the Eastern, Central, and Western Cordilleras. This is a special place, a place of power, great beauty, beginnings, and creation. Here lie not only the pregnant, sometimes explosive energies of the Massif, the birthplace of three distinct, impressive ranges, but also the source of three of Colombia's most important rivers: the Cauca, Magdalena, and Caquetá. Here the country's most impressive archaeological remains are found: hundreds of sculptured monuments and stone-lined tombs, the lasting memories of people who lived and died, expressing their reality, perceived or imagined.

The San Agustín archaeological zone encompasses the towns of San Agustín, San Jose de Isnos, and Saladoblanco, an area demarcated by the basins of the Magdalena, Bordores, Mazamorras, and Sombrerillos rivers. The region is composed of variegated, verdured mountains, ravines, and spectacular waterfalls. Although modern man's activities have markedly altered the green canopy of trees once covering the hillsides, what remains of the magnificent melée of groves, ferns, mosses, and flowers stills excites a poetic note in those who have not altogether lost that vital link to their humanity.

[The first European to visit and describe the region was Fray Juan de Santa Gertrudis, a Franciscan friar who beheld its natural beauty in 1756 A.D. Santa Gertrudis noted his impressions in a book called *Maravillas de la Naturaleza (Marvels of Nature)*.]

ARCHAEOLOGY

The first scientific investigations were undertaken by Konrad T. Preuss, in 1914, which were followed by those of José Perez de Barradas and Gregorio Hernandez de Alba, in 1937. Between 1943 and 1960, San Agustín was the focus of serious study by Luis Duque Gómez, Eduardo Unda, and Tiberio Lopez, and it was later explored by Gerardo and Alicia Reichel-Dolmatoff in 1966. More recent investigations include the almost unbroken archaeological research conducted by Luis Duque Gómez and Julio Cesar Cubillos from 1970–77 and the ongoing work of Annabella Duran de Gómez and Hector Llanos.

One would imagine that the collective impact of research by such archaeologists would have resolved the enigmas of San Agustín. The truth is that much remains to be done.

We do know that this region was occupied from 3300 B.C. to the 16th century A.D., but there is disagreement as to how to interpret the archaeological data. G. Reichel-Dolmatoff proposed that

> [t]he geographical extensions, as well as the marked stylistic differences in sculptures and other artifacts, makes it evident that they are not the work of a single cultural occupation, and that prolonged periods must have been involved. We cannot speak of one and only one San Agustín culture, but must think in terms of a long sequence of different cultural phases, which in part evolved one from the other and in part represent successive occupations. (G. Reichel-Dolmatoff, *San Agustín: A Culture of Colombia*, 1972, p. 115)

He also felt that the burial sites, when compared with other aspects of culture, are a minor feature; and although impressive as works of art, they are not disproportionate to cultural activities in the normal cycles of life and death for any community over centuries of occupation.

Luis Duque Gómez, on the other hand, feels the evidence at San Agustin indicates that

> [t]he differences of style in the statuary, and particularly in the pottery, together with the succession of other elements, which brings to light several clearly defined periods in their process of integration, are more in conformity with the internal development of this cultural complex than with the influence of foreign elements. (Luis Duque Gómez, *San Agustín*, 1982).

More than 300 stone carvings, both of monumental and mundane proportion, and elaborate graves generally associated with the monuments constitute the most impressive remains.

Cist graves consisting of single supine burials placed in rectangular tombs were the most common. The tombs are lined with stone slabs positioned vertically and generally overlaid by other slabs. Reichel-Dolmatoff reports that at the Quinchana site, a large stone statue was discovered enclosed in a cist-like structure, with smaller cist graves nearby.

Shaft-and-chamber tombs, some with elaborate chambers formerly decorated with black, red, and yellow paint, have also been found.

An interesting grave type consists of burials in stone sarcophagi, almost always placed within stone cists. More than thirty stone sarcophagi have been noted in research reports. The sarcophagi are often overlaid by artificial mounds that rise to 15 or more feet and that may attain 100 feet in diameter. Certainly this uncommon form of burial was reserved for the most powerful or respected members of the community.

Shallow pit graves, sometimes overlaid with irregular circular slabs of stone, contain single or multiple burials, usually in a flexed position.

Urn burials containing bones are usually deposited in shaft-and-chamber tombs, as along the. middle and lower Magdalena.

Shaft tombs are believed to date from the 5th century A.D. at San Agustín (G. Reichel-Dolmatoff, 1972). Such a distinctive burial custom suggests the arrival of a new ethnicity in the area. Some of the differences in grave type undoubtedly reflect class structure..

According to Duque Gómez, the monumental necropolises reflect an established elite, which directed and organized the labor force. Cieza de León, speaking of other groups in western Colombia, informs us that special tombs were built for chieftains. The chieftains were accompanied by retainers, favorite wives and attendants, who were intoxicated and placed alive in the tomb along with the corpse. Cieza continues:

> . . . a tomb the size of a small hill is built, with the door facing the sun. Inside this large tomb, a vault larger than necessary is built with numerous stone slabs. Here the deceased is placed, covered with cotton fabrics, with his gold and weapons. . . . (Cieza de León, 1947)

Most of the gold funerary offerings are small items of jewelry, such as necklace beads, pendants, and nose and ear ornaments produced by lost-wax casting and cold hammering, techniques evident as early as the 7th century B.C. A few exquisite gold feline masks in the San Agustín style are also known.

An interesting burial custom was the placing of volcanic ash tuff and obsidian flakes as funerary offerings, undoubtedly of symbolic significance, perhaps pertaining to concepts of rebirth and renewal.

Bodies were sometimes extended, as in sarcophagus burials, large cist graves, and some pit burials. Flexed burials are usually associated with shaft tombs, or sometimes with cist graves. Occasionally, bodies were placed in niches at the base of a shaft, as in the Middle Cauca Region. The variety of burials may signify differences in status, occupation, clan, or ethnicity. Unfortunately, many of the tombs at San Agustín lack dates with which to identify changes through time.

The stone monuments, hewn from volcanic tuffs and andesites, and usually associated with tombs, have long fascinated the casual as well as the observant scientist. Statues vary greatly in size, some exceeding 12 feet in height and weighing several tons. Sculptures are generally anthropomorphic, although the eagle, monkey, frog, lizard, cayman, rat, serpent, squirrel, bat, and fish are also depicted singularly, in combination with one another, or with anthropomorphic figures. Thematic depictions include an eagle holding a serpent with its beak and talons and alter-ego representations of lizards surmounting fanged human personages. Interestingly, among the Waica of the upper Orinoco, the alter ego of a child is imaged as a brown lizard.

Human figures are often fanged, as are some zoomorphic representations, suggesting jaguars or other felines. G. Reichel-Dolmatoff has distinguished three basic categories of jaguar sculpture at San Agustín: realistic jaguars attacking human females, men transforming into jaguars, and fanged anthropomorphic beings with alter-ego representations. He links these categories to thematic concepts still prevalent today among the Paez, Kogi, and Tukano Indians:

> Zoologically speaking, the jaguar impresses the rainforest Indians I know, not so much because it is powerful, swift, or physically dangerous to the hunter, but rather because it can easily be associated with vital forces which act upon society. (G. Reichel-Domatoff, *The Shaman and the Jaguar*, 1975)

He also noted that among the same Indians, the jaguar represents essentially male characteristics (i.e., aggressiveness, cunning, and the fierceness of the predator; as opposed to the passive, more fearful stance of the herbivore, perceived to be characteristically female). The jaguar, therefore, symbolizes the feral lifeforce.

The Arawak Indians claim "everything has jaguar" (Roth 1915, 367). The term "jaguar" is used by the Arawaks in the same sense that *teotl* was used by Nahuatl-speaking Mexicans. It signifies an undifferentiated energy permeating all things, and it may be concentrated in certain persons, places, or things, thereby giving them more power (Labbé, 1982). This vital force, as raw, unbridled energy, must be harnessed and directed by the shaman for the benefit of the community, and thus brought under the civilizing laws of culture.

Even a superficial study of themes and icons depicted at San Agustín confront us with an elaborate and systematic presentation of myth and philosophy of a profound religious nature. These themes are not specific to San Agustín alone, but have influenced Indian civilization from the American Southwest to Argentina. The Shamanic iconography of San Agustín points once again to the tropical forest cultures of Amazonia for its source of inspiration. Additionally, many of the human figures are unclad save for penis strings, necklaces, and other jewelry, a condition appropriate to the tropical lowlands but not germane to the colder highlands.

Figures holding clubs, spears, or maces and placed at the entrance of tombs are also part of the shamanic complex and appear to be tomb guardian figures.

CERAMIC RECORD

Two classificatory systems are employed for San Agustín. The first is divided into a number of periods on the basis of settlement patterns, construction activity, and distinctions in pottery. The Horqueta Period is characterized by sedentary farmers living in scattered settlements at localities such as Las Mesitas, Cerro de los Idolos, the region of the Alto de las Piedras, and the Cerro de la Horqueta. The pottery type is generally monochromatic, dark brown to blackish, and decorated with incised and punctate designs often filled with a white paste (Plate XXX; #112). This period may have begun sometime in the early or mid-first millenium B.C., and it apparently ended around the close of the first century B.C.

The Primavera Period begins around the first century A.D. and was of notably short duration. According to Reichel-Dolmatoff, the pottery (#115) and stone implements of the Primavera are clearly derived from those of the Horqueta. During the Primavera Period, people continued to live on the sides and slopes of hills. They also built their settlements (not as widely dispersed or scattered as those of the previous period) on the hilltops.

The next sequence, the Isnos Period, begins toward the end of the first century A.D. Reichel-Dolmatoff (1972) felt that Isnos represents a major change in culture, signifying the advent in San Agustín of a new group of people who either replaced the previous population or assimilated their culture. Population density increased markedly during this period. Habitation sites are typified by large deposits of accumulated refuse thrown down the slopes of the hills. Agricultural terracing, the formation of embankments, and the leveling of hilltops increased markedly. New forms of ceramics were introduced, including *alcarrazas* (#113; Plate XXXI) and negative-painted bowls. The use of incising and punctation for designs is notably absent.

The typical Isnos decorated ceramics bear little resemblance either in form or surface decoration to those of the Horqueta. Does this signify the intrusion of new peoples, or simply new ideas and styles, or perhaps both?

The abrupt disappearance or change in form and decoration of ceramics has often signified that an older, established group was dominated and assimilated by a new and more powerful one, who either by force of arms or by ideological dominance persuaded the former group to abandon their symbols and adopt those of the conqueror.

The Isnos *alcarraza* is similar to that of the Tumaco-La Tolita region, Tierradentro, and the Yotoco phase of the Calima region, sharing such features as the dome-shaped protrusion between the actual stirrup handle and the main body of the vessel. Although Isnos persisted for several centuries at San Agustín, the precise end of this period remains undetermined.

The next sequence is called the Sombrerillos Period, which, according to Reichel-Dolmatoff (1972), represented yet another cultural group present at San Agustín by 1410 A.D. and occupying the area until historic times. Population density increased, and the cultural remains of this period are to be found throughout the area, with settlements composed of groups of huts with circular floor plans. The economy, based on maize cultivation combined with root-crop growing, was similar to that of previous periods.

Typical of this period are distinctive tripod vessels with solid conical supports and small cups decorated with triangles painted in a black-on-red scheme.

Duque Gómez, however, perceives more continuity of culture at San Agustín. Certain motifs, the ancestral forms of which appear as early as the 7th century B.C.,

> . . . persist, side by side with other more recent forms, until the 16th century A.D., as is shown by the results achieved during excavations in the Alto de las Piedras and at La Estacion. (L. Duque Gómez and J. C. Cubillos, 1981)

This perspective formulates grand scheme divisions, embracing cohesive regional cultural developments. Duque Gómez and Cubillos have divided these long-term developments at San Agustín into the following periods:

1. ARCHAIC PERIOD:	3300 B.C.–1000 B.C.
2. FORMATIVE PERIOD:	1000 B.C.–300 A.D.
a. Lower:	1000 B.C.–200 B.C.
b. Upper:	200 B.C.–300 A.D.
3. REGIONAL CLASSICAL:	300 A.D.–800 A.D.
4. RECENT:	800 A.D.–16th century A.D.

[Each system used to classify culture at San Agustín has advantages and disadvantages, being simply a model to be used, then discarded when no longer useful or when contradicted by data.]

San Agustín is comprised of a number of prominent sites located on both sides of the Magdalena River. Among the better known are San Agustín Archaeological Park, including the various Mesitas and other monuments; Alto de los Idolos; Alto de las Piedras; Alto de las Guacas; El Tablon; El Jabon; Quebradillas; and La Parada.

Following are some of the dates obtained at some of these sites.

RADIOCARBON DATES OBTAINED AT SAN AGUSTÍN PRIOR TO 1972

*B.P. Date**	*Date*	*Site and Associations*
320 ± 90	1630 A.D.	Mesitas, NE end of plateau, middle layer of midden
540 ± 110	1410 A.D.	Mesitas, NE end of plateau, bottom layer of midden
770 ± 120	1180 A.D.	Potrero de Lavapatas, charcoal from house site
1525 ± 150	420 A.D.	Mesita B, NW Barrow, burial beneath mound
1620 ± 100	330 A.D.	Alto de los Idolos, midden
1800 ± 100	150 A.D.	Mesita B, NW Barrow, midden beneath mound
1810 ± 100	140 A.D.	Alto de los Idolos, midden
1840 ± 110	110 A.D.	Mesitas, W edge, midden
1850 ± 100	100 A.D.	Mesitas, W edge, midden
1900 ± 140	50 A.D.	Mesitas, W edge, midden
1910 ± 110	40 A.D.	Mesitas, W edge, midden
1930 ± 120	20 A.D.	Alto de los Idolos, midden
1930 ± 50	20 A.D.	Mesita B, NW Barrow, midden beneath mound
1960 ± 50	10 B.C.	Mesitas, W edge, midden
2505 ± 50	555 B.C.	Alto de Lavapatas, coffin

*Before Present

SOME ADDITIONAL DATES DETERMINED SINCE 1972

* 7th century B.C. for Chief tomb of monticule #1 at Alto de Los Piedras, San Jose de Isnos.
* 4th century A.D. –(?) for tombs of Mesita C of the Archaeological Park.
* 5th century A.D. for northwest monticule of Mesita B.
* 3rd century A.D. for tombs opposite the tumulus of the western monticule of Mesita A.
* 1st century B.C. (?) for tomb at monticule 1 at Mesita A in Alto de los Idolos, San José de Janos.
* 1st–3rd centuries A.D. for chamber of monticule 3 of Mesita A, Alto de los Idolos contouring monolithic sarcophagus.

TIERRADENTRO

To the north of San Agustín lie the rugged lands of Tierradentro, a place of steep slopes and deep canyons carved out of the living mountain formations. Tierradentro, located in the Department of Cauca, encompasses a fertile land nestled deep within the mountains.

In the 16th century, the Spanish conquistador Sebastian de Belalcazar passed through Tierradentro seeking the fabled lands of El Dorado, only to later discover that he would have to share his vision with others, such as Gonzalo Jimenez de Quesada, also in search of the same dream.

The ubiquitous friar Juan de Santa Gertrudis visited the region in 1756. The first archaeological expeditions, however, were those of George Burg, the German who investigated the sites of Loma de Segovia, Loma del Aguacate, and San Andres in 1936; and the Spaniard José Perez de Barradas, who undertook a descriptive comparative analysis of the cultures of Tierradentro with those of San Agustín in 1937. In the same year, the Colombian Gregorio Hernandez de Alba studied the tombs, attending to differences in form and decoration.

At the time of the Spanish incursion in the 16th century, this area was inhabited by the Paez Indians, a Chibcha-speaking group, who today still number about 25,000. According to the Paez, however, the region was formerly inhabited by the Pijaos, their traditional enemies.

Tierradentro is particularly noted for the elaborate burial chambers found along the mountains and ridges of sites such as Loma del Aguacate, Alto de San Andrés, Loma de Segovia, San Adres de Psimbala, El Tablon, and Alto del Duende.

Entrance to the tombs, or *hypogea*, were intentionally hidden under dirt and overgrown by surrounding verdure. The funerary vaults are typically entered by a straight, spiral, or zigzag stairway descending to a chamber hewn from the semi-soft, living rock. Burial vaults vary greatly in size. Some of the largest chambers are located as far as 21 feet below the level of the entrance. Chambers differ as to size, the number of pillars, niches, and decoration of the walls. The walls of the most elaborate tombs are decorated with geometric forms, such as concentric rhomboids painted with white, red, and black vegetal and mineral paints. The concentric rhomboids are usually arranged in contiguous, repeating rows or in panels flanked by rows of concentric triangles. Other painted decoration includes anthropomorphic and zoomorphic forms.

These chambers were the repository of large secondary burial urns decorated with white-filled incised and punctate patterns alternating rows of dots with rows of dashes. Other vessel decor consists of animal figures, such as lizards, centipedes, and serpents, in relief or in the form of *adornos*. As many as thirty to forty urns have been found in one tomb.

Although no stone statues carved in the round have been found within the *hypogea*, a few tombs contain large figures in relief on pillars and walls. The region of Tierradentro abounds in stone statues varying from three to seven feet high and carved in a style different from those at San Agustín, but also evincing fanged feline mouths. At present, however, no direct link has been established between the stone sculptures and the *hypogean* tombs.

At Loma de Segovia, the tombs are grouped together on the basis of size and elaboration. At some other sites, large tombs are found next to smaller ones.

Other work carried out at Tierradentro include the excavations of Eliecer Silva Celis in 1942, Horst Nachtigall in 1955, Stanley Long and Juan Yanguez in 1967, and Ana Maria Groot in 1973, as well as the ongoing investigation by Alvaro Chaves Mendoza and Mauricio Puerta Restrepo that began in 1973.

Additional studies of Tierradentro cultural remains include architectural studies of the tombs by Luis Raul Rodriguez Lamus and Leonardo Ayala and other research focusing on the classification of Tierradentro ceramics.

Other types of burials are found in the region, including primary interments in shafts and shaft-and-chamber tombs in association with ceramics seemingly unrelated to those found in the *hypogea*. The ceramics associated with some of the shaft and shaft-and-chamber tombs include tripods, double-spouted *alcarrazas*, bowls, plates, and *ollas*.

Research efforts at Tierradentro have been hampered by the lack of firm radiocarbon dates which could be used to chronologically order the material. Two radiocarbon dates have been obtained, one for a primary burial at Santa Rosa dating to 630 A.D., and the other for a secondary burial in a *hypogeum* at Loma del Aguacate, dating to 850 A.D.

Between 1976–77, Chaves and Puerta excavated 24 tombs. Sixteen (some simple shafts and some with chambers) were uncovered at San Francisco, and eight (three simple shafts, and five shaft-and-chamber) were excavated at Santa Rosa. Much of the recovered offerings were forms also encountered at San Agustín, such as globular *ollas*, plates, bowls, double-spouted *alcarrazas*, and tripods.

Chaves and Puerta have divided the ceramics associated

with burials in shaft or shaft-and-chamber tombs into two groups: those monochromatically decorated (with red or brown slips), consisting of bowls, dishes, globular and semi-globular *ollas, alcarrazas,* and tripod vessels; and those consisting of urns with wide mouths and hemispherical bowls in a bichromatic black-on-red scheme. An analysis of their excavations at San Francisco during 1976, which accounted for nine of the 16 tombs excavated, yielded the following contextual associations:

Tomb 1. Bones with monochromatic pottery.
Tomb 2. Bones with a grinding stone.
Tomb 3. Bones and a bichromatic urn, which contained black dirt but no bones.
Tomb 4. A solitary skeleton.
Tomb 5. No bones, but two stones and two stone *manos*.
Tomb 6. No bones, but one monochrome ceramic vessel and one bichrome plate.
Tomb 7. No bones, but a monochrome plate.
Tomb 8. No bones, but a monochrome plate.
Tomb 9. No bones, but various bichrome urns, a monochrome *olla*, a stone, and a stone *mano*.

It is apparent from this analysis that monochrome and bichrome wares are sometimes found together in the same tomb, as exemplified by numbers 6 and 9. The excavators feel that the evidence strongly suggests two stages in the burial of an individual. The first consisted of a primary interment accompanied by funerary offerings of monochrome pottery. Following the full decomposition of the flesh, the bones were gathered and placed in urns for a second burial, this time accompanied by other offerings of monochrome and bichrome wares. Those tombs without bones, containing only a ceramic or stone oblation, were likely for primary burials.

The evidence at Santa Rosa suggests a similar pattern. Additionally, some of the primary burials at Santa Rosa may have been re-interred in secondary burial urns within some of the vaulted *hypogea* of neighboring cemeteries at Aguacate and Alto de El Duende.

Ethnographically, the custom of two separate burials within two distinct graves may derive from ideas similar to those of the Desana. Among the Desana, the corporeal part of man is returned to the grave, the uterus of the Earth-Mother. Thus the first burial at Tierradentro may symbolize the return of the individual's material aspect to the Earth-Mother. The bones, however, contributed by the male, symbolize the spiritual essence of the individual, which must return to the uterus of Ahpikondia, the paradisic and etheric source of being. It is possible that the secondary burial represented the return of this spiritual essence to a spiritual uterus, similar to the Ahpikondia of the Desana. In such a case, the second grave, whether simple shaft-and-chamber or elaborate *hypogeum*, would signify a spiritual uterus, rather than the uterus of the Earth-Mother.

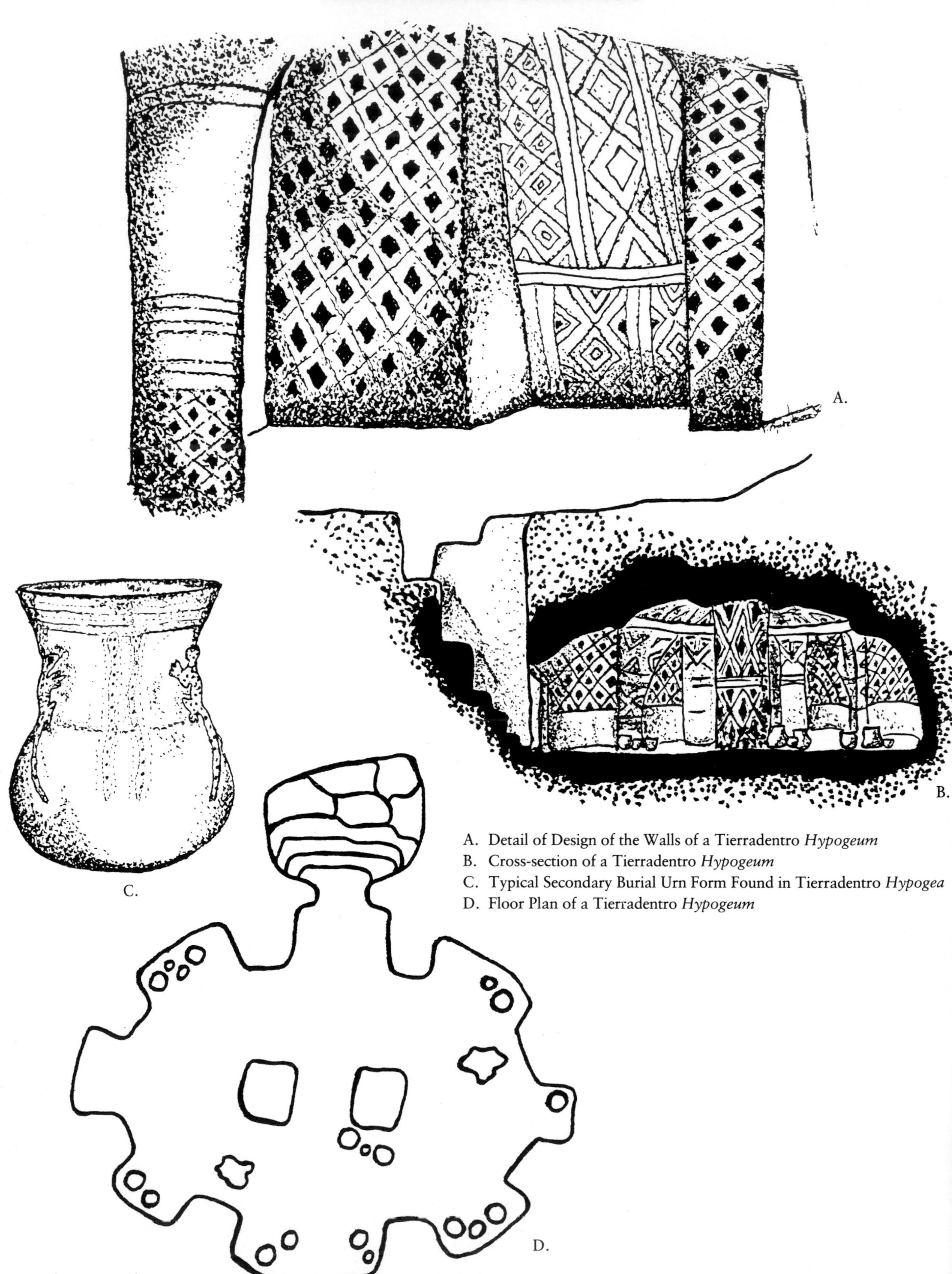

A. Detail of Design of the Walls of a Tierradentro *Hypogeum*
B. Cross-section of a Tierradentro *Hypogeum*
C. Typical Secondary Burial Urn Form Found in Tierradentro *Hypogea*
D. Floor Plan of a Tierradentro *Hypogeum*

110
Carinated jar with elliptical rim
Dark-brown slip
h: 5 in. (12.7 cm) × d: 6 in. (15.2 cm)
Horqueta period (ca. 600 B.C.–100 B.C.)
San Agustin cultural tradition
San Agustin archaeological zone

111
Carinated bowl with modeled figures
Burnished brown slip, decorated with modeled details
h: 4 in. (10.2 cm) × w: 8¼ in. (21 cm)
Horqueta-Primavera periods (ca. 200 B.C.–100 A.D.)
San Agustin cultural tradition
San Agustin archaeological zone

112
Carinated vessels
Burnished dark-brown slip, decorated with punctate design
left: h: 4 in. (10.2 cm) × d: 7½ in. (19.1 cm)
right: h: 3 in. (8.9 cm) × d: 6½ in. (16.5 cm)
Horqueta period (ca. 600 B.C.–100 B.C.)
San Agustin cultural tradition
San Agustin archaeological zone

113
Tripod *alcarraza*
Reddish-brown slip
h: 8½ in. (21.6 cm) × w: 7½ in. (19.1 cm)
Isnos period (ca. 100 A.D.–700 A.D.?)
San Agustin cultural tradition
San Agustin archaeological zone

114
Alcarraza with coiled serpent
Reddish-brown slip
h: 3½ in. (8.9 cm) × d: 4 in. (10.2 cm)
Isnos period (ca. 100 A.D.–700 A.D.?)
San Agustin cultural tradition
San Agustin archaeological zone

115
Carinated anthropomorphic-effigy vessels
Burnished dark-brown slip
left: h: 4½ in. (11.4 cm) × circum: 19¾ in. (50.2 cm)
right: h: 5¼ in. (13.3 cm) × w: 4½ in. (11.4 cm)
Horqueta-Primavera periods (ca. 200 B.C.–100 A.D.)
San Agustin cultural tradition
San Agustin archaeological zone

CHAPTER VII

THE NARIÑO REGION

Shaft-tombs of the Southern Highlands

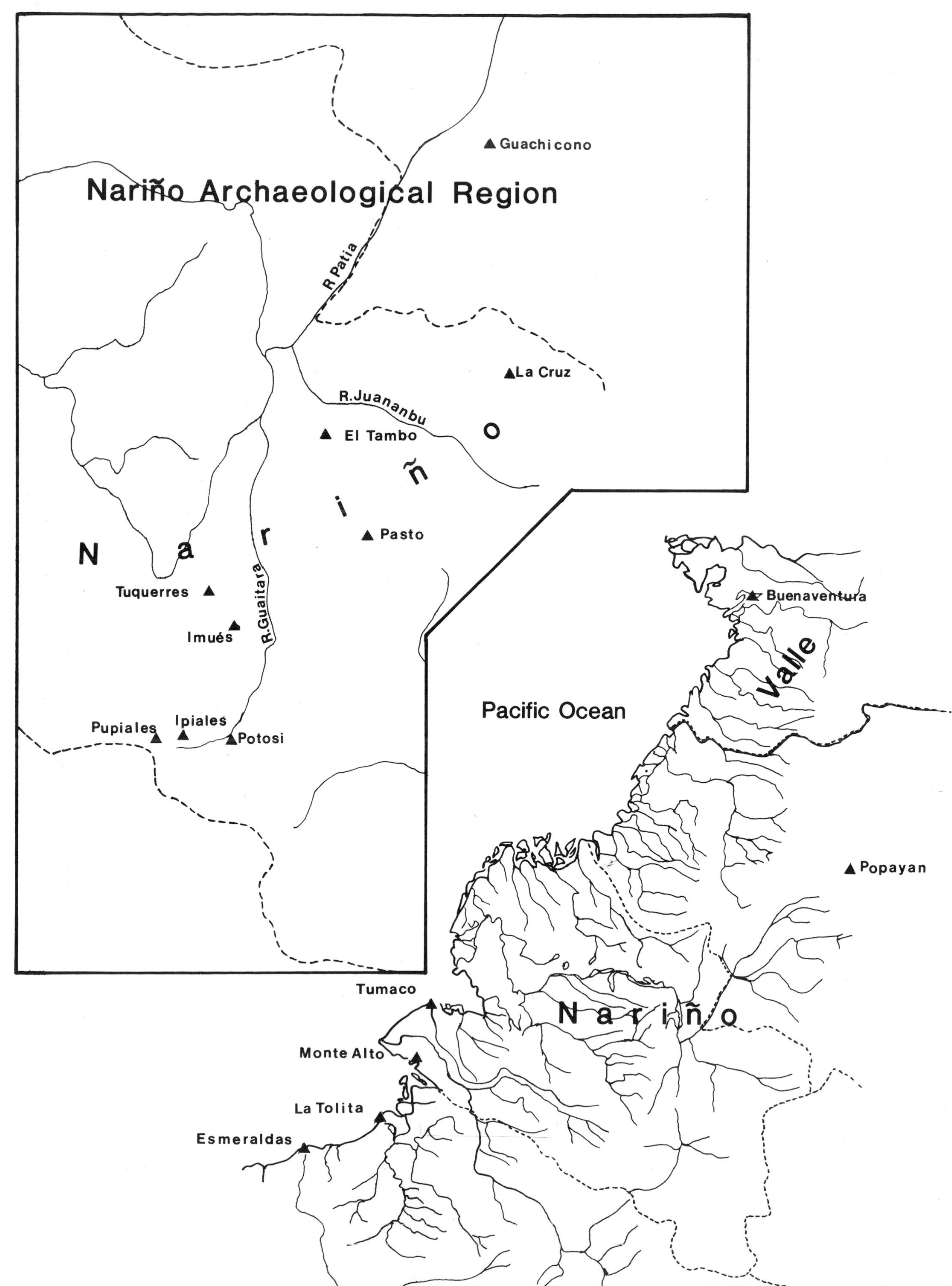

Nariño Archaeological Region
Guachicono
R. Patia
La Cruz
R. Juananbu
El Tambo
Nariño
Pasto
Tuquerres
Imués
R. Guaitara
Pupiales
Ipiales
Potosi
Buenaventura
Valle
Pacific Ocean
Popayan
Tumaco
Nariño
Monte Alto
La Tolita
Esmeraldas

GEOGRAPHY

The Department of Nariño, which lies southwest of San Agustín, is divided into three distinct geographic zones: the Pacific coastal lowlands, the Andean highlands, and the Eastern tropical lowlands.

The Andean highlands of Nariño are separated into a number of sub-regions: the Tuquerres-Ipiales *altiplano*, a region of high, fertile flat-lands; the central region, composed of a rugged topography with contrasting majestic peaks, flat plains, and picturesque valleys; and the northern region, which blends soft hills with rugged slopes.

The Department of Nariño is the home of many active and inactive volcanoes, the most prominent of which are El Galeras, El Cumbal, El Azufral, El Donna Juana, and El Chiles. These volcanoes, in part, are responsible for many of the igneous rocks, such as andesites and basalts, found in the highlands.

Andean Nariño also spawns numerous lagoons and rivers which course toward the Pacific lowlands in the west and the tropical lowlands in the east.

ETHNOHISTORY

While focusing attention on the cultures that flourished in the Andean highlands of Nariño, we should bear in mind that they did not develop in isolation, but were in contact with peoples to the north, south, east, and west, as indicated by items of trade found in highland tombs and in peculiar art motifs representing exotic species of fauna not found in the highlands.

At the time of the Spanish contact, Highland Nariño was the home of a number of distinct tribes noted by chroniclers such as Cieza de Léon: the Masteles, Chipancitas, Abades, Pastos, and Quillacingas. This was a time of expanding empires, not only those of the Aztecs of Mexico and the Incas of Peru, but also of the various European states encroaching on native America on all fronts. By the 16th century, the Incas had established strongholds in northern Ecuador and were impinging on southern Colombia. Moreover, population pressures were high throughout the most fertile lands within Colombia, and bellicose relations with one's neighbors was the rule rather than the exception.

The Pastos, a Tukanoan tribe, and the Quillacingas, possibly a Kamsa-speaking tribe, were both numerous and noteworthy. The Pastos may have been in the Nariño highlands for many centuries, while the Quillacingas were most likely relative newcomers. Both cultivated crops such as corn, fruits, and various tubers (*guinoa* or pigweed, potatoes, *oca* or wood sorrel, and *ulluco*, a climbing plant with tuberous roots), supplemented by hunting and fishing. However, the tribes differed in that the Quillacingas were ferocious cannibal warriors, while the Pastos were a peaceful, more sedentary people who did not practice anthropophagia, the eating of human flesh.

The Pastos were dispersed over a wide area in large settlements, such as Ascual, Mallama, Tucures, Zapuys, Piales, Pupiales, Turca, and Cumbal. Relatively highly organized, they were governed by a powerful chieftain assisted by lesser *caciques*. Their society was clearly divided into classes of elite and commoners.

The peasantry, like all peoples inured to the inequities forced upon them by entrenched privilege, impressed Cieza as simple folk harboring their pain deep within, with little show of external malice, their faces ever downcast.

Among the class of ruling elite, the chieftainship was inherited from the father's lineage, and exogamy was the rule of marriage. Among commoners, both exogamy and endogamy were practiced and descent was bilateral, i.e., males inherited the familial name of their father, while females inherited that of their mother (a practice noted for other groups within Colombia with exogamous clans).

Nothing is known concerning the religion of the peoples, but archaeological evidence and fragments of surviving ethnography suggest a strong shamanic base, probably organized into a rudimentary priesthood.

The Pastos practiced shaft-and-chamber tomb burials, at least for the elite. Cieza noted that upon the passing away of a man of distinction, a period of mourning was initiated, lasting many days. The deceased was sometimes accompanied to the grave by a number of wives and servants ritually intoxicated with *chicha* beer and possibly with potent narcotics, such as datura.

The Pastos had an influential merchant class who obtained some raw and manufactured goods from the Pacific lowlands, including gold, cotton, coca leaf, and shell beads. Pasto ceramics were an important trade item.

Pasto clothing was often made of tree bark, although cotton was also used. Tree-bark clothing (more typical among tropical forest tribes) was sometimes worn in Mexica Mesoamerica on ceremonial occasions.

By the 16th century, although still powerful and numerous, the Pastos, armed with stones, crook-headed wooden war clubs, and spears, were losing ground to more aggressive, cannibalistic neighbors (located along the Patia River), who persistently encroached on their lands. Other hostile groups, such as the Adabes, were centered along the Pasqual River. To the east of the Guaitara River were the numerous, combative Quillacingas.

The Quillacingas appear to have been a Carib-related group. Entering the Highlands shortly before the Spanish contact, they were neither as culturally developed nor as highly organized as the Pastos, from whom they nevertheless borrowed the superficial trappings of civilization, i.e., clothing, ceramics, burial customs, and subsistence patterns. Fierce, experienced warriors, the Quillacingas firmly resisted sporadic incursions by the Incas, who by the 16th century had established military outposts in northern Ecuador, from which they exerted cultural and political influence over the Indians of southern Nariño.

ARCHAEOLOGY

Many of the artifacts found in highland Nariño from the 8th century A.D. are in styles common to Nariño in Colombia and the provinces of Carchi and Imbadura in Ecuador. In the popular literature, much of this material is erroneously ascribed to the historical Quillacinga tribe.

On the Colombian side of the border, archaeological remains consist of habitation sites; agricultural terraces and ramparts; funerary architecture (in the form of shaft and shaft-and-chamber tombs); middens; large quantities of sherds; and ceramic, gold, copper, silver, stone, wood, and textile artifacts deposited with the dead as offerings.

Archaeology in Nariño is of relatively recent vintage. [Lucia Perdomo and Luisa Fernanda Turbay published their field work on Nariño in 1974. Investigations undertaken by Ana Maria Groot, Luz Correa, and Eva Hooykos were published in 1976. More recent findings and investigations by Maria Victoria Uribe were reported in 1977–78.]

Groot and Correa (1976) investigated 32 cemeteries located in flatlands, on hilltops, and along slopes in the Andean Nariño region. Tombs consist of shaft-and-chamber graves, as well as simple shafts without chambers. The depth and diameter of the shafts vary markedly. Some are as shallow as 5 feet, while others easily exceed 60 feet. The shaft's diameter generally increases in proportion to its depth, while varying in width from 3 to 9 feet. The deepest tombs generally contain the richest burials, and the material recovered from them has been classified into a number of cultural complexes, noted only as styles by researchers in the early 1970s.

Alice Francisco (1969) defined an integrated temporal sequence of three distinct ceramic styles for the province of Carchi in Equador. Capuli, believed to be the earliest, was followed by Piartal and Tuza. This sequence was based on observable changes in style believed to reflect temporal developmental changes—not correlated, however, with firm radiocarbon dates. Since identical styles were also found on the Colombian side of the border in Nariño, Francisco's nomenclature was soon adopted by Colombian investigators.

The Capuli style has been found at a number of sites in Colombia, notably Ipiales, Pupiales, Potosi, Cumbal, and Pasto. The Piartal style has been found at Cumbal, Pupiales, Guachucal, Catambuco, Pasto, and Chachaqui; and the Tuza style, at Pasto, Pupiales, Ipiales, Iles, Buesaco, and other locales.

Radiocarbon dates obtained for Colombian sites during the 1970s, however, did not corroborate Francisco's temporal sequence. Consequently, a new series of hypotheses was formulated by Uribe (1977–78), who retained Francisco's nomenclature (Capuli, Piartal, and Tuza) but preferred to view the three classifications as ceramic complexes rather than styles. Uribe felt that the Capuli material was of a different ethnicity than that of Piartal and Tuza, which she considered but two phases of the same complex. Radiocarbon dates indicate that Capuli began sometime around 850 A.D. and continued to 1500 A.D. The radiocarbon dates obtained for the Piartal complex indicate that it began about 750 A.D. and continued until about 1250 A.D. Radiocarbon dates for Tuza (as noted by Uribe) supported a beginning date of about 1250 A.D. and an ending period sometime around 1500 A.D.

A tomb, interpreted as transitional between Piartal and Tuza, was excavated by Francisco to the south of San Gabriel in Carchi. Uribe proposed that Piartal and Tuza were but two phases of the same complex. She based this on the fact that Piartal and Tuza ceramics are found together at the same habitation sites and the pattern of settlement is similar for both. Certain forms, such as the ceramic ocarinas shaped like seashells, are common to both Piartal and Tuza, but are absent in Capuli. The following are other supporting observations made by Uribe:

- Amphoras are present in both Piartal and Tuza but not in Capuli. The Piartal forms have conical bases that narrow at the neck, while Tuza have flat, truncated bases and widen towards the mouth.
- Both Piartal and Tuza stress the interior painting of annular-based dishes.
- Both emphasize the painting of zoomorphic motifs such as monkeys, deer, birds, and felines.
- In Capuli, there is a continued presence of a tradition of modeled anthropomorphic vessels, sculpture, and certain zoomorphic forms, nonexistent in Piartal-Tuza (Uribe, 1977). Another form uniquely Capuli is the pedestal-based cup.

From the evidence presented by Uribe, it can be observed that Capuli is contemporary, in certain stages, with both Piartal and Tuza. It should also be noted that Capuli habitation sites have not as yet been identified.

Before commenting on Uribe's hypothesis, we should perhaps examine the ceramics of each proposed complex from a definitive and comparative point of view.

Capuli

The basic Capuli scheme is a black-on-red resist pattern of rectilinear geometrics in parallel lines, concentric rhomboids, cross-net patterns, crosses, stepped frets, and zoomorphic figures as negative design. Other decorative attributes of Capuli ceramics include anthropomorphic and zoomorphic figures modeled in the round, free-standing sculpture, modeled *adornos*, and sculptural modification of basic vessel forms. Certain forms found exclusively or predominantly in Capuli are absent or only rarely represented in Piartal or Tuza.

Typical of Capuli, but rare or absent in Piartal or Tuza, are annular-based, stemmed cups (#118); bowls supported by either anthropomorphic or zoomorphic atlantean figures

(#119); single or joined jars with strap handles (#120); and modeled zoomorphic and anthropomorphic vessels (#116); Plate XXXV), including male figures seated on a bench. The latter are usually depicted with a bulge on one side of the face, indicating a quid of coca leaf (Plate XXXVII). Female figures, in styles similar to the male-on-a-bench genre, are depicted seated on the ground (#125).

Capuli is also noted for a variety of eccentric forms: gourd-shaped vessels; rectangular jars; drum-shaped pedestaled vessels; lime flasks or *poporos* used to contain lime (mixed with coca leaves to extract alkaloids) (#126); and the so-called *gritón* jar, with a rim modified to represent a human or animal head with mouth agape (#122). These figures stare toward the sky. The *gritón* motif is a stock theme found widely in precolumbian America, as far north as the Casas Grandes culture (Chihuahua, Mexico). Among the tropical-forest cultures of South America, this genre is ethnographically related in imagery to ritual petitions for rain.

In addition to the basic negative-painted black-on-red wares, a number of vessels, related to the Capuli complex in both form and modeled decoration, have a completely black surface finish. Of excellent manufacture, all of the specimens examined by the writer were relatively small, under 6 inches in diameter. The most common form is the short-necked modeled jar (#129; 130).

Piartal

The basic Piartal ceramic decorative scheme is a black-on-cream resist design with added red. This color scheme is identical to that used on some Middle Cauca complex three-color-resist vessels. Piartal, however, lacks modeled anthropomorphic and zoomorphic ceramic forms. If we are to trust the available radiocarbon dates obtained for both Piartal and the Middle Cauca, it would appear that the Piartal resist scheme is earlier than the Middle Cauca one. There are, however, similarities between Capuli resist anthropomorphic jar forms and certain resist wares from the Middle Cauca. The problem of possible cross-cultural influences between the two regions is far from resolved.

Typical Piartal forms include footed dishes painted generally on both inner and outer vessel surfaces (using a resist decorative scheme); carinated jars (Plate XLI); and conical-based, long-necked amphoras (Plate XL).

Tuza

The basic Tuza ceramic decorative scheme is a two-or-more color, positive design generally employing black, brown, red, or combinations of these colors on a light cream-colored ground. (Some negative painting in Tuza style is also known.) Incising is usually restricted to modeled shell ocarinas. A very common Tuza form is the footed, concave dish (Plate XLIV). These dishes are generally decorated with geometric designs arranged in bands around a central tondo or covering the inner vessel surface. Also common are stylized bird forms, deer, monkeys, felines, and stylized anthropomorphic figures. A relatively common Tuza form, also found in Piartal, is the modeled ceramic shell ocarina, often embellished with modeled monkeys and human figures (Plate XLVII). An unusual Tuza ceramic flute is shaped like a bone, with modeled monkeys in relief.

Another rare artifact is a ceramic hollow tubular device, open at both ends (#138). These instruments, both in form and function, appear to be ceremonial clyster tubes, perhaps used for ritual enemas. Among groups in the western Amazon, adolescent males were given anal infusions of *Datura*, a potent hallucinogen, during coming-of-age rituals. Although the ethnographic data on hallucinogenic plant use by indigenous groups in Nariño is meager, it is known that the Kamsa and Ingano tribes, in the southern Colombian highlands, not only used datura for ritual purposes, but also hybridized certain species of tree datura by infecting them with viral strains. (W. Emboden, 1979, 118)

COMMENTARY

Although the annular-based footed bowls are common in both Piartal and Tuza, there are notable differences. Piartal forms are decorated through a negative resist technique, while those of Tuza are generally painted using a positive schema. In Piartal, it is quite common to find both the outside and the inside decorated; in Tuza, the design is almost exclusively restricted to the interior. Moreover, the designs of Piartal are very different from those of Tuza, not only with respect to the number and kind of design elements used, but also in the way the elements are integrated with one another and the manner in which the design is laid out. Tuza designs are often arranged in bands, divided from one another by framing lines, with a negative tondo at the center of the bowl. This would be a highly unusual decorative pattern for Piartal.

Uribe (1977–78) felt that Tuza amphoras were an outgrowth of Piartal forms. However, there are striking dissimilarities between the two. The Piartal resist-decorated amphoras are characterized by conical bases, medium to long necks, and flaring rims. The Tuza amphoras are truncated and flat-based and are painted in a positive schema employing typical Tuza designs such as lug handles, a trait absent or extremely rare on Piartal specimens. The neck of a Tuza specimen is not clearly distinguished from the body of the vessel, as it is in Piartal.

Another weakness in Uribe's argument lies in using similarities in form to determine affinity between Piartal and Tuza. Capuli, Piartal, and Tuza share at least five basic forms in common: carinated jars, tripod and globular *ollas*, moccasin-shaped vessels, and footed annular-based bowls. However, the specific shape and decoration of these forms differ distinctively among the three styles. Piartal and Capuli have in common two additional forms not shared with Tuza, namely the shouldered globular jar with small, pointed, podal supports and the footless bowl. Finally, Piartal and Tuza have four forms not shared with Capuli: annular-based vases; the annular-based jar; the rectangular, annular-based bowl; and shell ocarinas. As previously noted, Capuli has a developed ceramic sculptural tradition lacking in either Piartal or Tuza.

An examination of the geographic distribution of Capuli, Piartal, and Tuza ceramics is also revealing. Uribe argued that cultural continuity between Piartal and Tuza was indicated by the fact that their ceramics are found together at the same habitation sites. However, the available data suggests otherwise. That Piartal and Tuza ceramics are found together at habitation sites is simply raw data: mere association does not prove affinity. Regionally, Piartal ceramics are found alone and unassociated with Tuza at Chapal, Esnambu, and Patapamba. Furthermore, at San Isidro, Piartal ceramics are present in areas overlapping Capuli sites. Finally, Tuza ceramics are found in several areas, such as La Victoria, Casafria, Pilcuan, and Gualmatan, where Capuli is also found, although Piartal is not.

If Tuza is a simple outgrowth of Piartal, how do we explain the apparent rapid increase in population from Piartal to Tuza? Piartal sites are relatively few and far apart. If population increased due to a southward movement of Piartal people from areas such as Paltapamba and Esnambu, which show no signs of Tuza occupation, then why is there such a relative paucity of ceramics in a Piartal style for the Nariño region as a whole, vis-a-vis Tuza or Capuli? In contrast, the evidence and dates from the Middle Cauca Region for a three-color resist decorative scheme very similar to Piartal would support a movement of Piartal people or ideas from Nariño to the Middle Cauca, but not vice versa.

What the available data suggest is that Tuza represents an intrusive people with a symbolic artistic tradition different from that of either Piartal or Capuli. They may, however, have adapted their iconography to the traditional ceramic forms found in the Nariño, Carchi, and Imbadura regions of Colombia and Ecuador. We have already observed how a relatively recent group, the Quillacingas, appear to have borrowed many customs (e.g., styles of dress and clothing, burial rites, subsistence patterns, and ceramic forms and styles) from a culturally and linguistically distinct group, the Pastos.

In conclusion, the evidence supports Uribe's hypothesis that Tuza probably represents the material cultural remains of the historically noted Pastos, but does not support the hypothesis that Tuza and Piartal reflect one ethnicity, expressing different art styles through time. Thus, Tuza should be viewed as a distinct cultural complex, at least until more conclusive evidence has been uncovered.

A number of radiocarbon dates (listed below) have been obtained for each of the complexes. At Miraflores, a tomb dated at 860 A.D. contained gold, silver, and both Piartal and Tuza ceramics (Perdomo, 1985), thus suggesting that Tuza indeed may be earlier than previously believed. Rather than an outgrowth of Piartal, in places it may actually have been contemporary. [The fact that ceramics of two apparently distinct complexes are found together in the same tomb does not necessarily imply that they were made by the same cultural group. Objects of trade were sometimes included as funerary offerings elsewhere in Colombia (Middle Cauca tombs, among others) and in other regions of prehispanic America.]

RADIOCARBON DATES OBTAINED FROM SITES IN COLOMBIA CORRELATED WITH CAPULI, PIARTAL, OR TUZA CULTURAL MATERIAL

Cultural Complex	*Date Obtained (Avg.)*	*Investigator*
Capuli	ca. 1100 A.D.	M.V. Uribe and Macias
Capuli	ca. 1460 A.D.	M.V. Uribe
Piartal	ca. 745 A.D.	Parra
Piartal-Tuza	ca. 860 A.D.	G. Correal
Piartal	ca. 1030 A.D.	L. F. de Turbay
Piartal	ca. 1080 A.D.	L. F. de Turbay
Piartal	ca. 1120 A.D.	G. Rojas
Tuza	ca. 1410 A.D.	Groot and Correa

TONDO DESIGN

BAND OR LAYOUT DESIGN

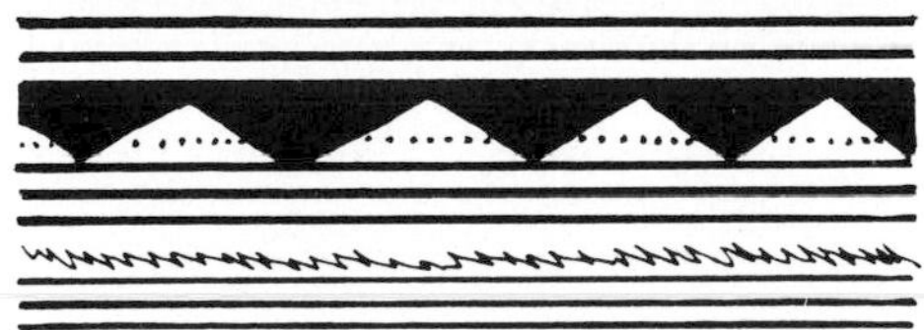

Bowl A:
There is no design in the center of the tondo. The design, which forms a band encircling the inner surface of the bowl, consists of interfacing and interlocking bands of solid and dotted triangles. Identical patterns found on prehistoric pottery from the American Southwest signify the union of positive–male and negative–female forces, hence fertility. The individual triangular elements arranged in this fashion are sometimes called cloud bands. Dotted triangles signify "pregnant clouds," i.e., rain clouds. In the prehistoric and contemporary Southwest American context, the zigzag pattern symbolizes lightning. It should be noted that similar symbolic meaning is given to downward- and upward-pointing triangular elements among the Kogi Indians of the Sierra Nevada de Santa Marta, as well as the Tukano Indians of the northwest Amazon, both Colombian Indian groups.

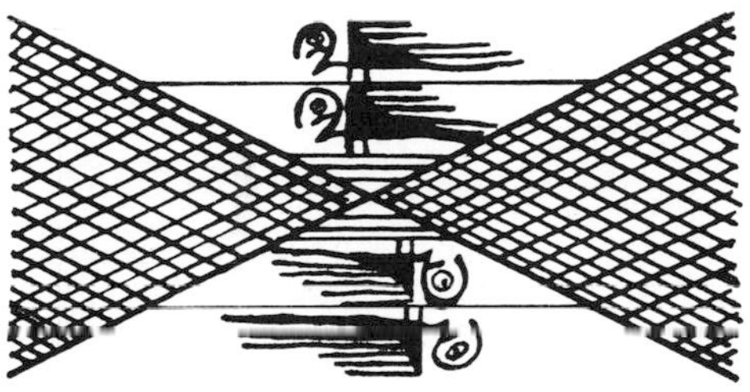

Bowl B:
There is no design in the center of the tondo. The design is distributed over the entire inner surface of the bowl. It consists of joined and opposing pairs of birds and triangular net elements. The net arranged in the form of a butterfly pattern can have several hypothetical meanings. Among Southwest American Pueblo Indians, the butterfly pattern is a clan symbol for the Butterfly clan. It has fertility–transformational meaning. The wings formed by the two joined triangular elements would signify the union of male and female principles, hence fertility. Among many Indian groups, the net was used as a symbol for the Milky Way, which was metaphorically described as a net in which the stars were caught and concentrated. The opposing geometric birds also seem to emphasize complementary or opposing positive–male and negative–female forces.

Bowl C:
There is no design in the center of the tondo. The design is distributed over the entire surface of the bowl. Its symbolic intent seems clearly related to that of Bowl B. On Bowl C, paired human figures have been substituted for the paired bird figures. One should also note that in addition to the net form of the butterfly motif is a smaller butterfly pattern at the center formed by parallel lines, with the human figures perpendicular to its wings.

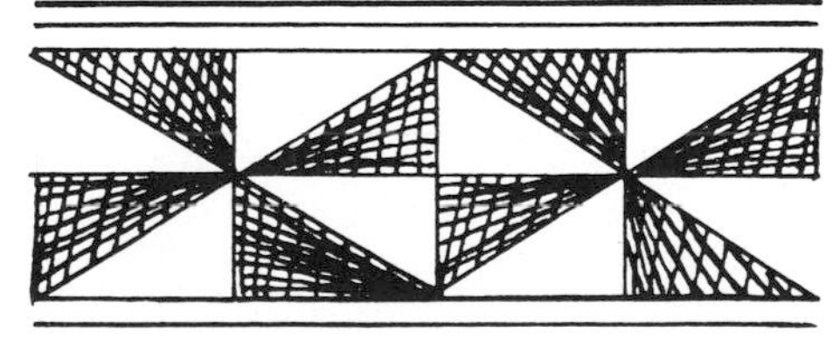

Bowl D:
The design in the center of the tondo consists of an eight-pronged star with paired lines and concentric rectangles at the center. It is possible that in many instances, the tondo is reserved for a clan insignia. This particular eight-pronged star form is common in both the American West and Southwest, where it is identified as representing the planet Venus. The rationale for using this as a Venus symbol is thus: In Mexico, as well as the American Southwest, a star is often simply designated by a cross, as it is among the Pawnee. The two-pronged arm of the cross (eight prongs constituting four arms) is used to indicate that Venus is no ordinary star, but has a mornig and an evening aspect, hence its use as a symbol of duality by prehispanic Mesoamericans. This symbol is very common on Tuza bowls and is often used on the headgear of geometric anthropomorphic figures. The remaining design consists of stylized maltese cross forms with net patterns, arranged in a band around the inner surface of the vessel.

Bowl E:
There is no design in the center of the tondo. The design elements consist of opposing stepped geometrics with crooks. This form is also common on prehistoric pottery of the American Southwest, where studies have indicated it to be a stylized version of the geometric bird form, probably representing a superimposition of geometric rainbird elements over a butterfly pattern. Whether it had similar significance for the Tuza artist is unknown.

TONDO DESIGN — BAND OR LAYOUT DESIGN

Bowl F:
The center of the tondo is decorated with an eight-pronged star element, possibly representing Venus. The center of this element has only one dash. The center of the "Venus" symbol may have been reserved to designate the numerical insignia of sub-clans within the Venus Clan. I must emphasize that these interpretations are purely hypothetical and based on familiarity with clan insignia patterns for Indian groups within the American Southwest.

Bowl G:
The center of the tondo is decorated with a stylized bird form, possibly representing a clan insignia. The design elements consist of stepped geometrics affected as both positive and negative design. Identical designs are also found on prehistoric American Southwest Indian pottery bowls. Within that context, the zigzag design represents lightning, hence fertility. The design on Bowl G forms a band encircling the inner bowl.

Bowl H:
The center of the tondo is decorated with a highly stylized bird form, probably representing a clan insignia. The repeating scroll pattern and stepped geometric pattern are arranged as a band encircling the interior of the bowl. This pattern is also very common on American Southwest Indian pottery.

Bowl I:
The center of the tondo is decorated with markings which were probably used as a clan insignia. The geometric design of this bowl forms a band encircling the interior. This design is also identical to designs found on prehistoric American Southwest Indian pottery.

Note:
There are interesting parallels between the geometric art tradition of the prehistoric Southwest Indians, such as the Anasazi and Mogollon, and the Tuza geometric art tradition of the highland Nariño. I must emphasize that at this point, I am not interested in developing hypotheses concerning migrations and contacts between the two areas, but merely noting observable similarities. The pottery forms on which the designs were laid were quite different in the two areas. The geometric design elements used, however, show a high degree of correspondence not only with respect to the identity of individual design elements, but also in the way these elements were integrated with one another within the design. The designs, moreover, are often laid out in a similar fashion, with framing lines above and below the bands, which are often arranged about a central tondo. Geometric figures representing anthropomorphic and zoomorphic beings are also executed in a similar manner in both areas. There are other correspondences, such as depictions of stylized human figures shown holding hands in a circle. Geometric figures with curved canes in their hands are also common to both areas. Among the Pueblo Indians of the American Southwest, these canes were associated with itinerant "teachers." The canes themselves became a symbol of authority. Science does not progress by denying the data, but at the same time must exercise great care in interpreting it. At this point, it is sufficient to note some of the similarities between the two regions, which, although contemporary in some of their sequences, were separated by enormous distances. Only additional significant data can ascertain whether the observable similarities are merely fortuitous or are meaningful correlations.

116
Anthropomorphic-zoomorphic-effigy jar
Black-on-red resist painted
h: 13½ in. (34.3 cm) × circum: 26 in. (66 cm)
Capuli cultural complex (ca. 850 A.D.–1500 A.D.)
Highland Narino region

117
Bowl supported by jaguar
Black-on-red resist painted
h: 5½ in. (14 cm) × l: 7½ in. (19.1 cm)
Capuli cultural complex (ca. 850 A.D.–1500 A.D.)
Highland Narino region

118
Annular-based cup
Black-on-red resist painted
h: 5¼ in. (13.3 cm) × d: 7 in. (17.8 cm)
Capuli cultural complex (ca. 850 A.D.–1500 A.D.)
Highland Narino region

119

120
Joined jars with strap handle
Black-on-red resist painted
h: 5½ in. (14 cm) × w: 6½ in. (16.5 cm)
Capuli cultural complex
(ca. 850 A.D.–1500 A.D.)
Highland Narino region

119
Bowls supported by Atlantean figures
Black-on-red resist painted
left: h: 7 in. (17.8 cm) × d: 7¼ in. (18.4 cm)
right: h: 8 in. (20.3 cm) × d: 5½ in. (14 cm)
Capuli cultural complex (ca. 850 A.D.–1500 A.D.)
Highland Narino region

121
Strap-handled jars
Black-on-red resist painted
left: h: 4½ in. (11.4 cm) × w: 5½ in. (14 cm)
right: h: 5¼ in. (13.3 cm) × w: 4¼ in. (10.8 cm)
Capuli cultural complex (ca. 850 A.D.–1500 A.D.)
Highland Narino region

122
Gritones
left: Black-on-red
h: 3½ in. (8.9 cm) × circum: 11 in. (29 cm)
Capuli cultural complex (ca. 850 A.D.–1500 A.D.)
center: Black-on-red resist painted
h: 6 in. (15.2 cm) × d: 4½ in. (11.4 cm)
Piartal cultural complex (ca. 750 A.D.–1250 A.D.)
right: Red-on-tan
h: 5 in. (12.7 cm) × w: 3 in. (7.6 cm)
Piartal cultural complex (ca. 750 A.D.–1250 A.D.)
Highland Narino region

This is a common genre in the Americas. Ethnographic evidence based on the cultures of Indians from the forests of South America suggests that these figures may be petitioning the heavens for rain.

123
Assorted jars
Black-on-red resist painted
upper row, left: h: 5 in. (12.7 cm) × d: 8 in. (20.3 cm)
upper row, right: h: 6¼ in. (15.9 cm) × w: 5½ in. (13.9 cm)
upper row, center: h: 6 in. (15.2 cm) × circum: 19⅜ (49.2 cm)
lower row, left: h: 4 in. (10.2 cm) × circum: 20½ in. (52.1 cm)
lower row, right: h: 3 in. (7.6 cm) × w: 4 in. (10.2 cm)
Capuli cultural complex (ca. 850 A.D.–1500 A.D.)
Highland Narino region

(Overleaf)

124
Coqueros
Black-on-red resist painted
left: h: 6½ in. (16.5 cm) × w: 4¾ in. (12.1 cm)
right: h: 7¼ in. (18.4 cm) × w: 5¼ in. (13.3 cm)
Capuli cultural complex (ca. 850 A.D.–1500 A.D.)
Highland Narino region

For a definition of *coquero*, see Plate XXXVII.

125
Coqueras
Black-on-red-and-cream resist painted
left: h: 6½ in. (16.5 cm) × w: 4¾ in. (12.1 cm)
right: h: 6¼ in. (15.9 cm) × w: 4½ in. (11.4 cm)
Capuli cultural complex (ca. 850 A.D.–1500 A.D.)
Highland Narino region

The femalè version of the *coquero* genre is depicted sitting on the ground rather than on a bench.

For a definition of *coquero*, see Plate XXXVII.

126
Poporos
left: Red slip
h: 4⅜ in. (11.1 cm) × circum: 12½ in. (31.8 cm)
center: Black-on-red resist painted
h: 3¼ in. (8.3 cm) × circum: 10⅛ in. (25.7 cm)
right: Black-on-red resist painted
h: 4¼ in. (10.3 cm) × circum: 13 in. (33 cm)
Capuli cultural complex (ca. 850 A.D.–1500 A.D.)
Highland Narino region

For a description of *poporos*, see item 14.

127
Quadrangular pedestal bowls
left: Black-on-red resist painted
h: 5½ in. (14 cm) × w: 6 in. (15.2 cm)
right: Red slip
h: 6 in. (15.2 cm) × w: 6⅜ in. (16.2 cm)
Capuli cultural complex (ca. 850 A.D.–1500 A.D.)
Highland Narino region

128
Black jars with modeled monkey adornos
Burnished dark-brown slip
(Note: The variance from black to brown tones is due to differences in the firing of the clay. Full reduction firing results in a black surface; incomplete reduction firing results in lighter, browner tones.)
left: h: 3¼ in. (8.3 cm) × circum: 15 in. (38.1 cm)
center: h: 4⅞ in. (12.4 cm) × circum: 19 in. (48.3 cm)
right: h: 4¼ in. (10.8 cm) × circum: 14¼ in. (36.2 cm)
Capuli cultural complex (ca. 850 A.D.–1500 A.D.)
Highland Narino region

The fact that the monkeys always look in opposite directions is indicative of dimorphic, complementary duality.

129
Blackware jars with snail figures
Burnished black slip, decorated with modeled details
left: h: 5¾ in. (14.6 cm) × d: 5 in. (12.7 cm)
right: h: 3¾ in. (9.5 cm) × d: 4½ in. (11.4 cm)
Capuli cultural complex (ca. 850 A.D.–1500 A.D.)
Highland Narino region

129

131
Phytomorphic blackware jars
Burnished dark-brown-to-black slip
left: h: 4½ in. (11.4 cm) × circum: 17¼ in. (43.8 cm)
right: h: 4 in. (10.2 cm) × circum: 14¾ in. (37.5 cm)
Capuli cultural complex (ca. 850 A.D.–1500 A.D.)
Highland Narino region

130
Armadillo-effigy blackware jar
Burnished dark-brown-to-black slip, decorated with incised details
h: 3¾ in. (9.5 cm) × d: 5 in. (12 cm)
Capuli cultural complex (ca. 850 A.D.–1500 A.D.)
Provenance unknown

130
Detail showing the incised bottom of the jar

131

132
Footed bowls
Black-on-white
left: h: 4 in. (10.2 cm) × d: 7⅛ in. (18.1 cm)
right: h: 4 in. (10.2 cm) × d: 7½ in. (18.7 cm)
Tuza cultural complex (ca. 1250 A.D.–1500 A.D.)
Highland Narino region

133
Footed bowls
Black-on-white
left: h: 4 in. (10.2 cm) × d: 7¾ in. (19.7 cm)
right: h: 3¾ in. (9.5 cm) × d: 7¼ in. (18.4 cm)
Tuza cultural complex (ca. 1250 A.D.–1500 A.D.)
Highland Narino region

134
Footed bowls
Black-on-white
left: h: 4¼ in. (10.8 cm) × d: 7½ in. (19.1 cm)
right: h: 3½ in. (8.9 cm) × d: 7¼ in. (18.4 cm)
Tuza cultural complex (ca. 1250 A.D.–1500 A.D.)
Highland Narino region

135
Whistles in the form of shells
Brown-on-cream
left: l: 3¼ in. (8.3 cm)
right: l: 3¾ in. (9.5 cm)
Tuza cultural complex (ca. 1250 A.D.–1500 A.D.)
Highland Narino region

136
Ocarinas modeled in the form of shells
left: Tan with red paint
l: 5½ in. (14.0 cm)
right: Grayish-black
l: 5¾ in. (14.6 cm)
Tuza cultural complex (ca. 1250 A.D.–1500 A.D.)
Highland Narino region

137
Snail-effigy ocarina
Red and tan
l: 6¼ in. (15.9 cm) × w: 2½ in. (6.4 cm)
Tuza cultural complex (ca. 1250 A.D.–1500 A.d.)
Highland Narino region

138
Ceremonial clyster tubes
left: Red paint
l: 19 in. (48.3 cm)
Tuza cultural complex (ca. 1250 A.D.–1500 A.D.)
right: Black-on-red resist painted
l: 13¼ in. (33.7 cm)
Capuli cultural complex (ca. 850 A.D.–1500 A.D.)
Highland Narino region
See glossary

139
Amphora
Black-on-cream-and-buff terracotta
h: 21¾ in (55.2 cm) × circum: 22 in. (55.9 cm)
Tuza cultural complex (ca. 1250 A.D.–1500 A.D.)
Highland Narino region

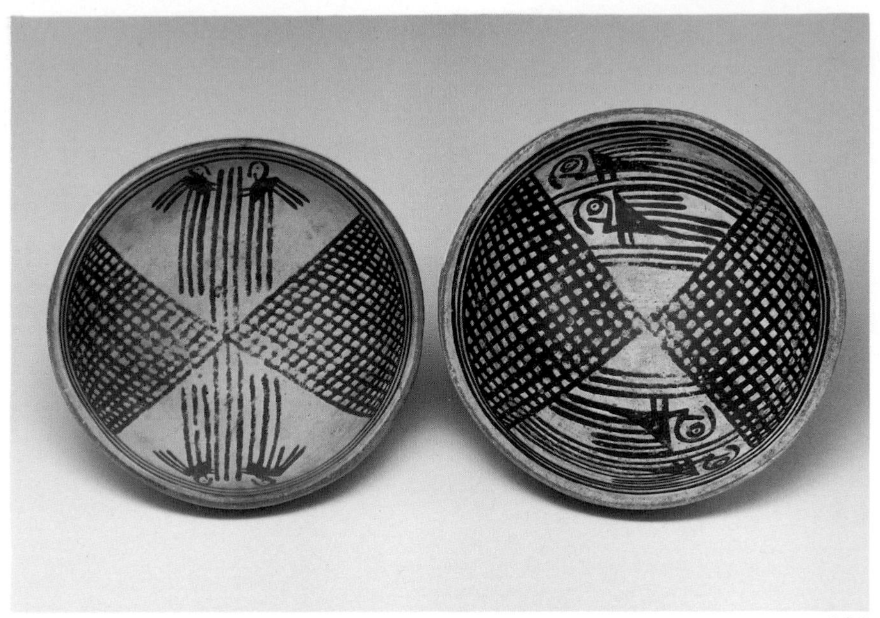

132

133

134

135

136

137

138

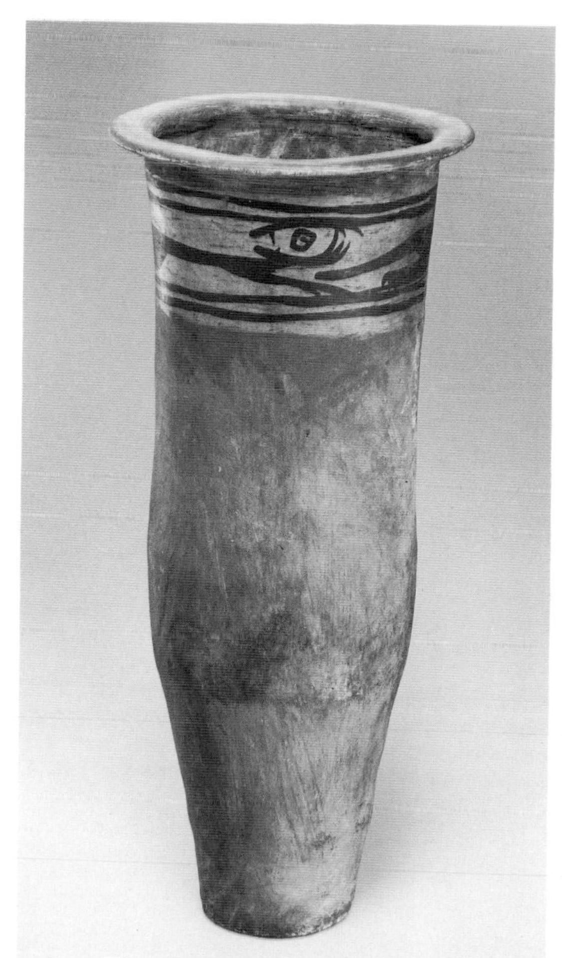

139

CHAPTER VIII

THE MUISCA

The Chibcha Federation of "El Dorado"

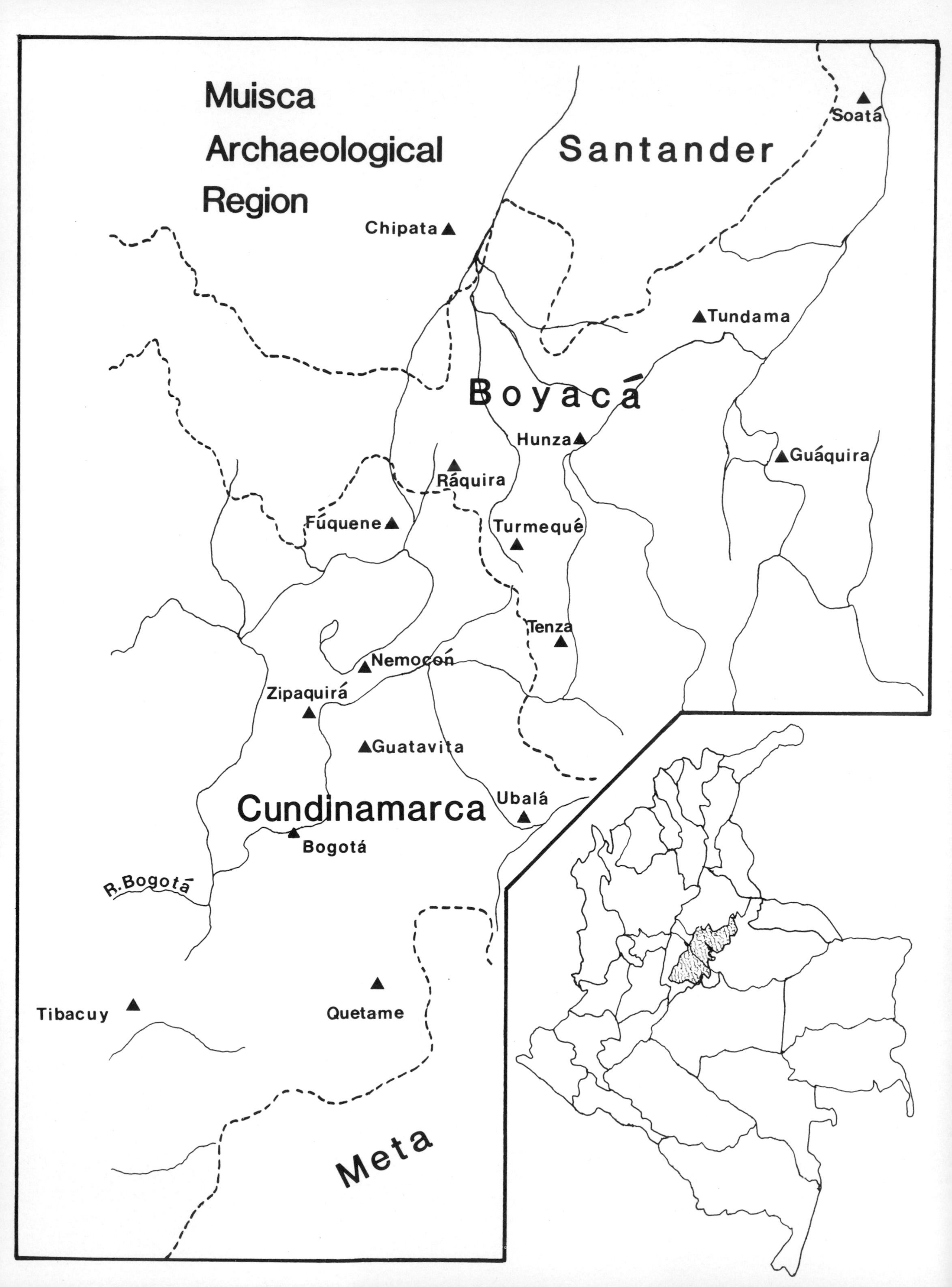

Muisca
Archaeological
Region
Santander
Soatá
Chipata
Tundama
Boyacá
Hunza
Guáquira
Ráquira
Fúquene
Turmequé
Tenza
Nemocón
Zipaquirá
Guatavita
Cundinamarca
Ubalá
Bogotá
R. Bogotá
Tibacuy
Quetame
Meta

GEOGRAPHY

Far to the northeast of Nariño lay the Muisca homelands, the lands of El Dorado, nestled in the fertile highland basins of Bogotá and Tunja in the modern departments of Cundinamarca and Boyacá. Much of the native vegetation and natural fauna has disappeared, replaced by species introduced since the Spanish Conquest. The contours of the natural topography, however, remain.

Boyacá, noted for its emerald-bearing geologic formations, is crossed by many rivers and dotted with lagoons. Here the Muisca were centered, in the valleys of Chiquinquirá, Sogamoso, Tenza, Ramirigui, and the *altiplano* of Tunja.

The Muisca of Cundinamarca inhabited Bacatá (modern Bogotá), as well as places like Nemocón and Zipaquirá, noted for their salt mines.

Other areas, such as Muzo (within the Panches territory), Somondoco, and Ubala, were important regions of emerald mining. Muisca lands were also rich in coal and copper, and this mineral wealth was the foundation of their mercantile power.

ARCHAEOLOGY

Muisca is derived from the Chibcha term *muexa*, as they called themselves. As is true of so many Amerindian names applied by Indians to themselves, *muexa* simply means "the people," or "the human beings."

Relatively little Muisca material culture has survived. A few postholes and, occasionally, stone columns are all that remain of buildings, as much was of a perishable nature and has been reabsorbed by the earth. What has survived are the ceramics and artifacts of gold, copper, and tumbaga, an alloy of gold and copper.

The middens and habitation sites are composed of shallow deposits and are not indicative of high population density, such as that reported by the Spanish for the Muisca of the 16th century.

More recently acquired radiocarbon dates support a Muisca presence in the area around 300 A.D., but also possibly as early as the 6th century B.C., a date obtained at Tequendama in Cundinamarca (Correal and Van der Hammen). Other radiocarbon dates for the Muisca include 600 A.D. at Buenavista in Boyacá; 850 A.D. for Cogua in Cundinamarca; 1000 A.D., also at Buenavista in Boyacá; 1000 A.D. for Sutamarchan in Boyacá; and 1300 A.D. for Guatavita in Cundinamarca. These dates are interesting in that they confirm a time depth for the Muisca, but they are puzzling in that given such a depth, so little evidence of Muisca presence should have survived archaeologically. It is probable that the Muisca population was greatly augmented by groups displaced by Carib conquests of the Magdalena Valley after 1000 A.D.

ETHNOHISTORY

The Muisca have often been portrayed as the most advanced of all of the Colombian cultures—an overstatement, particularly if technological criteria is employed. Certainly, many other groups exhibited a superior level of craftsmanship in goldworking and ceramics. Muisca goldwork lacks the originality, technological virtuosity, and power of expression exhibited by the goldsmiths of the Sierra Nevada de Santa Marta or those of the Cauca Valley. Muisca ceramics are almost devoid of sculpted forms. Although some vessels display a certain elegance, they are unimaginative when compared to the finer works of many groups.

The only dimensions in which the Muisca truly exceeded their neighbors were the vastness of the territories over which a relatively homogenous expression of their culture could be found and the extent and cohesiveness of their trade relationships. The basis of Muisca mercantile power lay in the veritable mountains of salt found within their territories, the huge deposits of copper they cast into bars for trade, and the large deposits of emerald-bearing minerals.

Because the Muisca generally lived at elevations over 7,500 feet above sea level, they grew neither cotton, tobacco, nor coca leaves, all of which had to be obtained from the warmer lands at lower elevations. Gold was probably obtained from lands to the west along the highly aurific Cauca River Valley tributaries. From the northern coastal people, the Muisca obtained conch shells for fashioning trumpets and other artifacts. Certain kinds of fish were traded from the north and from groups along the Magdalena River.

The Muisca excelled at weaving, and their *mantas* were highly prized, providing a staple of trade over wide areas of Colombia. A single *manta* would buy enough cotton to weave three additional ones. This may seem like a good profit margin, but considering the time required to spin fiber into thread using a simple spindle stick and whorl, and the time needed for weaving and applying the painted design, it appears that the cotton supplier got the better deal. *Mantas* were decorated with hand-painted light or dark red-and-black designs or with the imprints of clay stamp rollers.

Gold was cold hammered, cast by means of the lost-wax technique, or embossed over stones, with relief carvings. Small, thin, slab-like votive figurines with appendages composed of attenuated fillets of applied metal were common.

Muisca houses were constructed of upright posts set directly on the ground and had a circular floor plan (ceremonial structures and communal houses were sometimes rectangular or elliptical in shape) and thatched roofs. Beds were raised rectangular rack-like structures built of cane, over which the hides of animals such as deer and tapir were thrown. The house of the elite differed from that of the commoner only in size and embellishment. The Spaniards reported that some chieftain's houses had large plates of sheet gold covering the entrance.

The Muisca kitchen consisted of a fire pit lined with stones. Cooking was done in clay pots. Many of the utensils were made of wood or split cane.

Like other Colombian Indians, the Muisca made *chicha*, a maize beer, which they kept in large earthen jars.

Muisca kinship was matrilineal. Men of rank and means often had more than one wife, while the common man was of necessity generally monogamous.

Caciques, or leaders, adorned with gold jewelry and diadems, were carried about on litters, often faced with sheet gold. As in Peru, servants swept the ground before the advancing potentate.

Muisca society was divided into a number of distinct classes: a ruling elite, composed of chieftains and their extended families; the priest-shamans, who also exerted considerable power; warriors of rank and distinction, who seem to have formed a special strata of Muisca society; artisans and merchants; and at the base of Muisca society, the common farmer, who was also a part-time warrior. Another group were prisoners of war, destined to be sacrificed or used to supplement the work force.

The Muisca farmer grew a variety of crops: corn, two kinds of potatoes, sweet potatoes, *guinoa*, *oca*, red beans, kidney beans, lima beans, red peppers, squash, tomatoes, avocados, papaya, guava, and soursop. Pineapples were obtained from the lower valleys. Although the variety of foodstuffs is impressive, crop diversity should not be equated with crop yield. The Muisca diet contained little meat protein, which is not required if the vegetal diet contains a balance of cereal grains eaten with legumes, such as beans. A fire-hardened digging stick was used to plant seeds, while clods of earth were broken with heavy wooden clubs.

Muisca clothing was simple. Men wore a wraparound garment about the waist, extending to the knees; a thick cotton manta, tied over one shoulder in a manner similar to the Mexica-Aztecs of Mexico; and a thick cap woven from the fibers of the *cabuya* plant, a species of sisal hemp. Women wore a wraparound skirt similar to that of the men and a cotton blanket draped about their shoulders like a shawl, which they fastened with a metal pin. They wore their hair long and sometimes braided in various styles.

The Muisca maintained amicable relationships with most of their neighbors. The belligerent Panches who lived to the west, however, insisted on harassing them, forcing the Muisca to station garrisons along the western border. To the north and slightly east lived the Guane, renowned as merchants and skillful weavers, who shared many cultural traits in common with the Muisca. To the south were the Sutagaos and the Buayupes, and to the east, the Laches, Tunebos, and Achaquas.

At the time of the Spanish contact, the Muisca were divided into three principal political factions: those allied with the Zipa of Bacatá (or Bogotá); those allied with the Zaque of Hunsa or Tunja; and those following the Iraca, the religious leader of Sogomoso.

Tisquesusa, the Zipa of Bogotá, was portrayed by Castellanos as a man of dignified demeanor who commanded respect by his presence.

Quemuenchatocha, the Zaque of Tunja, was described in less favorable terms by the Spaniards. Thick-set and corpulent, with large, flaring nostrils set on a broad, somewhat contorted face, Quemuenchatocha could hardly be said to exude an aura of refined dignity.

Political differences centered around the control of certain trade routes. The balance of power rested with the Zipa, and things would perhaps have gone his way if the Europeans had not come upon the scene.

Unknown to the Muisca and the Europeans, three separate armies of conquest were converging upon the Muisca homeland, lured by tales of El Dorado and other fables of gold. From the east, in what is now Venezuela, an army under Nicolaus Federmann had marched through 1000 treacherous miles of jungle, *llanos*, and brutally cold mountains. Environment and Indians had decimated Federmann's army and when he arrived in the Muisca homeland, it numbered little more than 200 weak, starved, emaciated men.

At the same time, another army under Sebastian de Belalcazar, who had recently assisted Pizarro in the Conquest of Peru and had been appointed governor of Quito in Ecuador, arrived in the Muisca highlands with 166 well-fed, well-dressed, and well-equipped men of arms.

A third army of about 800 men under Gonzalo Jimenez de Quesada had begun its long trek far to the north at Santa Marta in 1536. When all three armies met in the fateful year of 1539, Quesada, like Belalcazar, had precisely 166 men. Quesada's journey had taken him 900 miles; Belalcazar's, 800; and Federmann's, 1000.

By the time Belalcazar and Federmann arrived, Quesada had already systematically pillaged the richest of the Muisca towns, routed their armies, and destroyed their power. Gold and emeralds had fueled his soldiers' fanatical zeal.

Strangers in a foreign land, the three European armies now stood facing one another. No one was willing to leave empty-handed. But to engage amongst themselves in mortal combat, surrounded as they were by hostile enemies, would have assured the demise of all. They agreed, therefore, to split the booty three ways, though not evenly, and later plead their respective claims before the crown.

On April 29, 1539, Gonzalo Jimenez de Quesada, Nicolaus Federmann, and Sebastian Belalcazar joined together in a public ceremony and proclaimed the founding of Santa Fe de Bogotá, which became the capital of New Granada and later, the capital of the Republic of Colombia.

And of the Muisca, what can be said? Muisca glory was reduced to ash and tears; their language is heard no more, and they were destined to enter history as an extinct people. Their blood, however, mixed with that of their conquerors, still flows in many who today call Bogotá home. In purer form they are still to be found in the surrounding countryside, rooted and bound to the hills, plateaus, and valleys, as were their ancestors, centuries before the tale of El Dorado altered their faith and destiny.

MUISCA RELIGION

According to the Muisca, before the beginning there was no light, for it was enclosed within the creative force called Chiminigagua. The beginning of creation was the shining forth of Chiminigagua.

In some versions of the cosmogonic myth, Chiminigagua is said to have first created enormous black birds which flew forth over the mountains, releasing his light. Obviously, the black birds are a poetic metaphor for some esoteric truth lost in the translation from Chibcha, the language of the Muisca, into Spanish, the language of Pedro Simon, who recorded the myth.

Profound esoteric truths such as Chiminigagua are usually reposited within the minds of priests. The common man requires a more tangible symbol of creation, and in the daily lives of the people, Zuhe, the Sun, and Chía, the Moon, were of more immediate significance.

Bochica, sometimes identified with the invisible aspect of the Sun, was occasionally personified as Nemquetheba, a culture hero said to have taught the arts and sciences of civilization to the Muisca. Nemquetheba was also identified with Chiminizagagua, Messenger of Chiminigagua, the light giver. Bochica-Nemquetheba, as an old man who came from the east and taught civilization to the Muisca, is a metaphor in the same tradition as the allegorical legends of Quetzalcoatl in Mexico. As noted previously, old age was sometimes used as an icon of divinity. The image of the old man from the east dispensing wisdom as he journeyed westward was most likely a metaphor for the Sun defined as Nemquetheba. As with other Colombian Indians like the Desana, the Sun is considered the source of all creative energies.

In Muisca legend, the Sun represented light, wisdom, and civilization; while the Moon, Chía, signified darkness, sorcery, instinct, and the sinister side of human nature. Mythologically, Bochica-Nemquetheba is frequently depicted as a hero, while Chía, Bochica-Nemquetheba's wife before he changed her into the moon, is said to be villain. Her crime was to preach doctrines contrary to those of Nemquetheba. In another version, Chiminizagagua changed her into an owl, symbol for darkness, sorcery, and the moon, condemning her to walk the night. This rendition suggests an allegory for the apparent conflict between solar and lunar cults.

In another allegory recorded by Piedrahita, we are again confronted with Bochica as hero and Chía as villain. Chía, as was her nature, enticed the people of Bogotá to murmur against their tutelary deity, Chibchachum, who in revenge sent a flood. The people, however, appealed to Bochica for help, who appeared upon a rainbow striking the mountains with his staff, thereby opening a passage for the waters to subside. He then punished Chibchachum by placing him beneath the earth where he holds the world together. His weariness is said to be the cause of earthquakes. Chibchachum, angered at his punishment, cursed the rainbow, Chuchaviva (symbol of the covenant between Bochica and humankind), saying that when it should appear, many would perish. For this reason, the rainbow was said to be a mixed blessing, bringing joy and fear.

According to some traditions, mankind was born of two forces: Bachue, also called Turachoque, the Good Woman, and her infant son, both of whom were said to have emerged from the depths of Lake Iquaque (near Tunja) following the creation of light. After the youth matured, Bachue coupled with him and brought forth mankind, thereby peopling the earth. Later, the aquatic couple returned to the waters in the guise of serpents. Two coupling serpents, representing the positive and negative, male-female polar energies from which life is created, was a widespread icon in antiquity imbued with deep esoteric significance. Thus, lagoons and lakes were held sacred by the Muisca and the serpent, as symbol, was closely associated with such bodies of water.

As was the custom in prehispanic Mexico and Peru, the Muisca personified and honored the different forces of nature governing their lives and everyday activities. In addition to his role as the force sustaining the earth, Chibchachum was also revered as patron of commerce and industry. In like manner, Bachue, the mother of mankind, was also patron of springs and agriculture; and Chuchaviva, the rainbow, was patron of those suffering from fevers and of women in childbirth. Another personification was Chuken, patron of footraces. Nemcatacom, portrayed as a bear, was patron of drunkards, weavers, and cloth dyers.

Very little is known about Muisca rituals and ceremonials. The Muisca practiced human sacrifice, including child sacrifice, but certainly not on the scale of the Mexica-Aztecs of Mexico.

Sacrifices, usually captives obtained through warfare, were made to the sun. As in Mexico, the victim's heart was extracted from the chest and offered up. Entrails were removed, and the blood was often sprinkled over sacred spots. Children, usually purchased from other tribes, were sacrificed to promote rain. Prisoners of war to be sacrificed were sometimes tied atop a pole and riddled with arrows shot from below. Parrots, purchased and taught to speak, were sometimes sacrificed in place of human victims.

Masks were an important part of ritual dances. Tears indicated on masks used in certain solar dances represented a petition to the sun for pity.

A ritual performed at Tunja, consisting of twelve red-painted men dancing about a central figure painted blue, may have represented the twelve lunar months encircling the annual sun, or sky.

The best known of Muisca rituals was that of "El Dorado," performed at a sacred lagoon which, according to legend, was formed many years before the arrival of the Spanish when a huge meteor fell from the sky and imbedded itself on the *paramo* of Guatavita. The crater formed by the meteor impact eventually filled with water, forming the lagoon. Accordingly, when a new *cacique* came to power, he was brought to Guatavita and covered with gold dust. He was then placed on a raft and conducted to the center of the lagoon. People along the shores tossed small offerings of gold trinkets and figurines into the water, while regal attendants cast forth large gold oblations. Meanwhile, the *cacique* jumped into the water, disencumbering himself of his golden burden, as the heavy, glistening particles settled to the bottom of the sacred lagoon. According to local Muisca history, the ritual came to an end when Guatavita was conquered by the Zipa of Bogotá. Whatever the historical accuracy of this legend, it appears to have been based on fact, for a gold model of such a raft was found, replete with small figures representing the *cacique* and his attendants.

In another legend related to Guatavita, the Zipa's wife had a secret lover. When this clandestine relationship became known to the Zipa, who in typical husbandly fashion became enraged, he had the lover slain and dismembered. The slain man's privates were served at dinner to the cuckolding wife, who not only had to partake in this undesired communion with her former lover, but also had to listen to songs the Zipa contrived for the occasion. Distraught and shocked, she is said to have plunged into Guatavita with her daughter, nevermore to be seen.

The ritual life of the Muiscas was directed by an established priesthood. Candidates for priesthnood had to undergo several years of training, including years of seclusion in a temple, where they practiced celibacy and fasting and learned religious oral histories and arcane sciences.

Rituals centered around rites of passage, such as puberty rites. Girls coming of age were secluded in a special hut for a certain period of time, as is common among many tropical-forest Indians. Later, the girl was bathed in a river and was officially transformed into a woman, an adult member of the community. Although little detail is given about the boy's puberty ceremony, it is known that the occasion was marked by great festivity. Like puberty ceremonies everywhere, the ritual marked a change in the psychological orientation of the young personality, which must now relinquish the irresponsible, less fixed role of the child and become an adult member of the community. His relationships extended from the immediate and familial to those of the community and the larger world beyond. Failure to incorporate the emerging adult into the larger society was to arrest his development and risk his becoming a burden or a danger.

Muisca temples were constructed mainly of wood and thatch. Some were said to have been quite large, although this has not been confirmed archaeologically. The remains of a few modest enclosures found near Tunja consist of post holes and roughly hewn columns of stone set in a circle or an elliptical pattern.

The most famous of the Muisca temples was that dedicated to the Sun, at Sogamoso, an important Muisca trading center. According to the Spanish, it was constructed of wood and contained a row of mummies adorned with parrot feathers and with emeralds set as eyes. An old, bearded priest, its custodian, fought desperately to protect the mummies from the marauding Spaniards, equally desperate to deprive the mummies of their emerald eyes. The Spaniards managed to loot the temple of emeralds and gold. The temple burned to the ground, set aflame by the lighted embers of a temple torch knocked down in the scuffle of priest and soldiers.

The Muisca had great respect for nature, and they established shrines throughout their territories at mountains, lagoons, and caves considered sacred because they were perceived as places endowed with power or were significant in Muisca myth, religious history, or legend.

The Muisca had an intimate and extensive knowledge of the medicinal and mind-altering properties of plants. Plants were used for healing and to bring the practitioner, usually the shaman-priest, into direct relationship with other perceived or imagined dimensions of reality. Oviedo noted that the Muisca used both *yop* and *osca* for purposes of divination:

> ... two herbs which they consume, called *yop* and *osca* which, when taken separately and after a certain time span and interval, reveal to them, in answer to their inquiries, what it is the Sun wants them to do on these occasions. And having asked them how the Sun makes this known, once they have taken the herbs, they answer that there will be a twitching in a certain joint, after they have taken the herbs, which denotes that their wish and enterprise will be granted, while if other joints are twitching, it means that it will not be successful but to the contrary; and for the purpose of this extraordinary vagary they have classified, named, and observed all the joints of the body, some for good and some for evil. (Gonzalo Fernandez de Oviedo y Valdes, *Historia General y Natural de las Indias, Islas y Tierra Firme de la Mar Oceano*, 1851–55, Madrid)

The *yop* (or *yopo*) referred to by Oviedo was likely the seeds of the leguminous tree *Anadenanthera peregrina*, which contains powerful mind-altering chemicals. (We cannot be sure to which plant *osca* referred.) According to Oviedo, *yop* and *osca* were taken separately.

The usual manner of ingesting *yopo* was to grind it into a fine powder which was then blown up the nose by a second individual using a tubular apparatus. Typically, mind-altering substances were used in Colombia to gain insight into the inner working of things and to obtain personal power or energy with which to influence or manipulate the immediate environment. Hallucinogens were also used for divination and healing, and as an aid in effecting psychological transformations in young minds during rites of passage. With the possible exception of *chicha* (maize beer), apparently used for recreational purposes at group functions, mood- or mind-altering substances were societally controlled, and their use was culturally restricted to priests, shamans, or initiates. When employed by others, it was for a specific time or occasion, such as the initiation and training of candidates to shamanhood and priesthood, during rite-of-passage ceremonies, or during healing rituals.

Fasting, emetics, and induced vomiting usually preceded the ingesting of mind-altering substances. Modifying the external environment could enhance the effectiveness of the psychomimetic substance. This might include designating a specific place or dwelling as the "sacred space" for the occasion; designating a specific time of day or night as the auspicious time for the rite; and using certain ritual objects—drums, flutes, whistles, rattles, amulets, fetishes, and other artifacts—to modify the natural effects of the ingested substances.

MUISCA CERAMICS

Certain centers, such as Tinjaca, Raquira, Tunja, Soacha, and Tocamcipa, were noted for their superior ceramics; but in general, Muisca workmanship is crude and ill-finished by prehispanic Colombian standards. Sculpted forms are relatively few, and most of these are static and inflexible. The head is generally very large compared to the rest of the body, which tends to be rigidly rendered, with little attention placed on arms and legs. Facial features such as the mouth and eyes are usually indicated by straight, grooved lines (Plate XLIX).

The greatest care seems to have been devoted to the fashioning of the *múcura*, a pitcher characterized by a globular body, a low, flaring shoulder, and long, attenuated spout (#141, 143). The spouts are often modeled as a stylized human face and head, and many have a delightful charm and elegance lacking in other forms. Painted decoration, composed of geometrics, is usually effected in brownish-red and restricted to the shoulder and spout. Many of these geometric forms and the manner in which they are integrated to effect motifs, are linked to a common prehispanic geometric symbol tradition shared by indigenous groups from the American Southwest to Argentina. This tradition spread from some as yet undetermined center and diffused across the great Cordilleras that form the backbone of the American continents. Cross-cultural studies of the iconography associated with these forms by widely dispersed native informants would indicate that these symbolic geometric elements constitute a common and widespread tradition, which transcended linguistic and political boundaries. (A comprehensive study of these geometric symbols will be included in a subsequent publication by the author.)

The geometric design elements on many of these vessels are motifs consistently identified with water, the life force, and fertility in many contemporary North and South American Indian ethnographies. The face-effigy *múcuras*, used for liquids, may portray Bachue, the female aspect of the creative lifeforce, mother of mankind and patron of agriculture, lagoons, and the spring of life.

The *múcura*, undoubtedly the most elegant of Muisca ceramic forms, had a number of variations (including double jars) evincing differences in the globularity of the vessel body and in the neck and handle form. Generally, the body of these vessels was painted an orange-tan color.

Some *múcuras* have spouts in the form of a seated figure, apparently male (Plate LI). Icons, such as ear spools, necklace, and seated posture, indicate an important personage of elevated status. Painted lines extending downward from the eyes most probably represent tears. As tears on masks were said to signify a petition to the Sun for pity (probably for rain), it is possible that this rendition portrays the lord Zuhe interceding on behalf of mankind in his aspect as Bochica.

The *múcura* clearly derives from another common Muisca ceramic form, the shouldered, short-necked, wide-mouthed spouted jar. Painted bowls generally emphasize interior bowl painting, while pedestaled cups are often painted on the inside and along the upper vessel exterior (Plate L). There are few known examples of Muisca effigy jars and other figural forms. However, some show clear influence from groups to the north.

Few tripodal offertory bowls have survived archaeologically. Small votive figurines in gold, copper, and tumbaga were placed within the bowl. The rim of the bowl is sometimes modified into anthropomorphic figures and decorated additionally with added bird *adornos* (Plate LIII).

Muisca ceramics are relatively scarce in public or private collections. The Colombian archaeologist Lucia Rojas de Perdomo reported that in one survey of Muisca pottery in public and private collections (including those of the Museo Nacional, the Museo del Oro, and the Museo del Banco Popular), 950 intact vessels were identified as Muisca (Perdomo, 1985). This is a remarkably small number considering the collections of these prestigious institutions. The survey and subsequent analysis of this pottery, however, enabled the researchers to divide the ceramics into identifiable typologies labeled after place names such as Tequendama, Guatavita, Guasca, Sutamarchan, Tenza, and Buenavista. These typologies need to be correlated to specific time periods which would allow researchers to reconstruct developmental histories and determine variations and other changes through time. Dated ceramics could then be used to determine the period or age of other related cultural developments.

140
Globular vessel
Red-on-orange-buff terracotta
h: 15½ in. (39.4 cm) × circum: 46 in. (116.8 cm)
Specific culture uncertain (ca. 1000 A.D.–1500 A.D.)
Muisca-Guane archaeological zone

141
Jar with spout modeled as a face
Buff terracotta, decorated with red, black, and cream painted design
h: 16¾ in. (42.6 cm) × circum: 39 in. (99.1 cm)
Muisca culture (ca. 1000 A.D.–1540 A.D.)
Muisca archaeological zone

141

142
Carinated vessel with lugs
Red-and-white-on-orange-buff terracotta painted and incised designs
h: 8¼ in. (21 cm) × d: 8¼ in. (21 cm)
Muisca-Guane culture (ca. 1000 A.D.–1540 A.D.)
Muisca-Guane archaeological zone

143
Jar with spout *(mucura)* modeled as a human face
Cream, decorated with red and orange painted design
h: 7 in. (17.8 cm) × d: 6 in. (15.2 cm)
Muisca culture (ca. 1000 A.D.–1540 A.D.)
Muisca archaeological zone

143

144
Bowl
Red-on-cream
h: 2¾ in. (7 cm) × d: 5¼ in. (13.3 cm)
Muisca-Guane culture (ca. 1000 A.D.–1540 A.D.)
Muisca-Guane archaeological zone

145
Pedestal bowl
Buff terracotta, decorated with black paint
h: 5¼ in. (13.3 cm) × d: 10 in. (25.4 cm)
Muisca-Guane culture (ca. 1000 A.D.–1540 A.D.)
Muisca-Guane archaeological zone

145

146
Double vessel
Black-and-white-on-orange-buff terracotta
h: 4 in. (10.2 cm) × l: 9½ in. (24.1 cm)
Muisca-Guane culture (ca. 1000 A.D.–1540 A.D.)
Muisca-Guane archaeological zone

(Opposite)

Plate XXXII
Male figure
Black-on-red resist painted
h: 17⅝ in. (44.5 cm) × w: 10¼ in. (26 cm)
Capuli cultural complex (ca. 850 A.D.–1500 A.D.)
Highland Narino region

This representation of a male figure masturbating may be linked to agricultural, field-fertility rites. Many early agricultural societies in the old world as well as in the new practiced fertility rites during the spring planting season, during which young male virgins masturbated on the soil to symbolize copulation with the earth mother. This practice has been reported among the peoples of the American Southwest and of southern Colombia. The figure depicted is chewing coca leaves, indicated by the bulge in the cheek. (as seen in *Precolumbian Ceramics* by Jesus Arango Cano, 1979, Plate 79)

Plate XXXIII
Globular jar
Black-on-red resist painted
h: 14¾ in. (37.5 cm) × circum: 37⅞ in. (96.2 cm)
Capuli cultural complex (ca. 850 A.D.–1500 A.D.)
Highland Narino region

Plate XXXIV
Gourd-shaped vessel
Black-on-red resist painted
h: 11 in. (27.9 cm) × d: 8 in. (20.3 cm)
Capuli cultural complex (ca. 850 A.D.–1500 A.D.)
Highland Narino region

Plate XXXV
Anthropomorphic-effigy jar
Black-on-red resist painted
h: 7¼ in. (18.4 cm) × w: 5⅝ in. (14.4 cm)
Capuli cultural complex (ca. 850 A.D.–1500 A.D.)
Highland Narino region

XXXIII

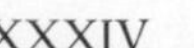

XXXIV

XXXV

XXXVI

Plate XXXVI
Male figure seated on a bench with a child
Black-and-red-on-cream resist painted
h: 8 in. (20.3 cm) × w: 4¾ in. (12.1 cm)
Capuli cultural complex (ca. 850 A.D.–1500 A.D.)
Highland Narino region

Plate XXXVII
Coqueros
Black-and-red-on-cream resist painted
left: h: 7¾ in. (19.7 cm) × w: 4¼ in. (10.8 cm)
right: h: 7¾ in. (19.7 cm) × w: 4¼ in. (10.8 cm)
Capuli cultural complex (ca. 850 A.D.–1500 A.D.)

A *coquero* is a male figure, usually seated on a bench, who is depicted chewing coca leaves, which is indicated by a bulge in the cheek.

Plate XXXVIII
Coquero
Brown and tan
h: 7 in. (17.8 cm) × w: 4 in. (10.2 cm)
Capuli cultural complex (ca. 850 A.D.–1500 A.D.)
Highland Narino region

For a definition of a *coquero*, see Plate XXXVII.

XXXVII

XXXVIII

Plate XXXIX
Amphora
Black-on-cream resist painted, with added red paint
h: 18½ in. (47 cm) × circum: 25 in. (63.5 cm)
Piartal cultural complex (ca. 750 A.D.–1250 A.D.)
Highland Narino region

The neck of the *amphora* is decorated with a painted, anthropomorphic face, and the body is decorated with geometric patterns.

XL

XLI

Plate XL
Amphoras
Black-on-cream resist painted, with added red paint
left: h: 33 in. (83.8 cm) × circum: 36 in. (91.4 cm)
right: h: 30½ in. (77.5 cm) × circum: 35 in. (88.9 cm)
Piartal cultural complex (ca. 750 A.D.–1250 A.D.)
Highland Narino region

Plate XLI
Carinated jars
Black-on-red-and-cream resist painted
left: h: 8½ in. (21.6 cm) × d: 10½ in. (26.7 cm)
right: h: 10½ in. (26.7 cm) × d: 13½ in. (34.3 cm)
Piartal cultural complex (ca. 750 A.D.–1250 A.D.)
Highland Narino region

Plate XLII
Pedestal bowls with bird design
Black-on-red-and-cream resist painted
left: h: 3¾ in. (9.5 cm) × d: 8 in. (20.3 cm)
right: h: 4 in. (10.2 cm) × d: 8½ in. (21.6 cm)
Piartal cultural complex (ca. 750 A.D.–1250 A.D.)
Highland Narino region

Plate XLIII
Footed bowls with a solar motif
Black-on-white
left: h: 3½ in. (8.9 cm) × d: 6⅜ in. (16.2 cm)
right: h: 3¾ in. (9.5 cm) × d: 7½ in. (19.1 cm)
Tuza cultural complex (ca. 1250 A.D.–1500 A.D.
Highland Narino region

Plate XLIV
Footed bowl
Red-on-cream
h: 3¾ in. (9.5 cm) × d: 7½ in. (19.1 cm)
Tuza cultural complex (ca. 1250 A.D.–1500 A.D.)
Highland Narino region

The stylized, geometrically-formed figure wears the symbol of Venus on his chest and a butterfly pattern, the symbol of fertility and duality, on his lower body.

Plate XLV
Footed bowls
Black-on-white
left: h: 3¼ in. (8.3 cm) × d: 7⅜ in. (18.7 cm)
right: h: 3½ in. (8.9 cm) × d: 7½ in. (19.1 cm)
Tuza cultural complex (ca. 1250 A.D.–1500 A.D.)
Highland Narino region

The geometric forms on these vessels probably represent stylized birds. The body of the bird is formed by black serrated patterns that interface with white serrated elements representing clouds. Both the "clouds-coming-together" motif, which is common in Colombian imagery, and the zigzag border between the black-and-white elements signifying lightning symbolize fertility. Identical design elements and patterns were used in the prehistoric art of the Anasazi Indians of the American Southwest.

Plate XLVI
Human-effigy ceremonial clyster tube
Black-on-tan
l: 14½ in. (36.8 cm)
Tuza cultural complex (ca. 1250 A.D.–1500 A.D.)
Highland Narino region

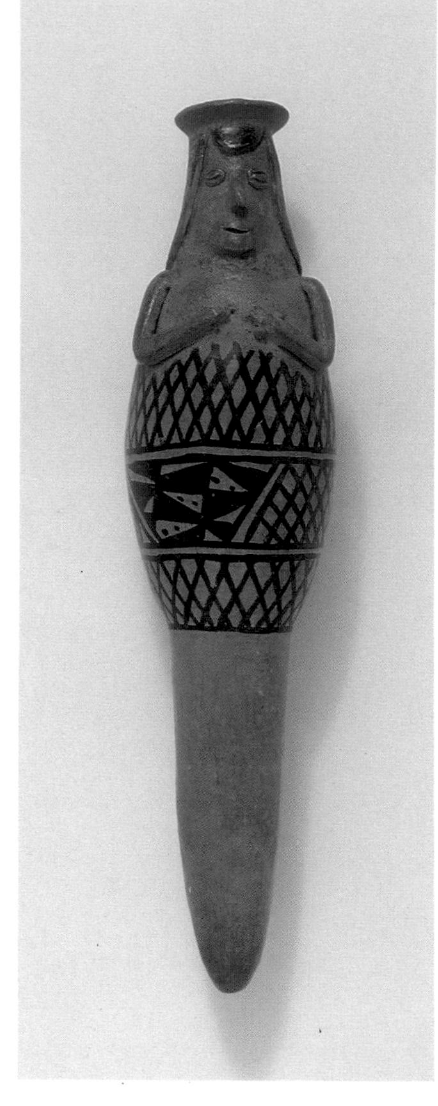

Plate XLVIII
Coquero mask
Cream
h: 7½ in. (19 cm) × w: 5½ in. (14 cm)
Tuza cultural complex (ca. 1250 A.D.–1500 A.D.)
Highland Narino region
These masks are extremely rare.

Plate XLVII
Ocarinas in the form of conch shells with monkey figures
left: Grayish-black
l: 5½ in. (14 cm) × w: 2¾ in. (7 cm)
center: Red and tan
l: 5¼ in. (13.3 cm) × w: 2½ in. (6.4 cm)
right: Red and tan
l: 7 in. (17.8 cm) × w: 2⅝ in. (6.7 cm)
Tuza cultural complex (ca. 1250 A.D.–1500 A.D.)
Highland Narino region

L

(Opposite)

Plate XLIX
Anthropomorphic figure
Variegated gray slip
h: 11 in. (28 cm) × w: 6 in. (15.2 cm)
Muisca culture (ca. 1000 A.D.–1540 A.D.)
Muisca archaeological zone

The figure was originally attached to a base, probably an offertory vessel lid.

Plate L
Pedestal bowls with modeled anthropomorphic serpentiforms adornos
Red-on-cream
left: h: 5 in. (12 cm) × d: 7 in. (17.8 cm)
right: h: 4½ in. (11.4 cm) × d: 6⅝ in. (16.8 cm)
Muisca-Guane culture (ca. 1000 A.D.–1540 A.D.)
Muisca-Guane archaeological zone

Plate LI
Jar with spout in the form of a human figure
Red, tan, and white
h: 15½ in. (39.4 cm) × d: 9 in. (22.9 cm)
Muisca culture (ca. 1000 A.D.–1540 A.D.)
Muisca archaeological zone

LII

LIII

LIV

LV

LVI

Plate LII
Pedestal bowl
Red-on-cream
h: 5 in. (12 cm) × d: 7½ in. (19.1 cm)
Muisca-Guane culture (ca. 1000 A.D.–1540 A.D.)
Muisca-Guane archaeological zone

Plate LIII
Tripod offertory bowl with mold-cast figurines
Red-on-cream
h: 4¾ in. (12.1 cm) × w: 4¼ in. (10.8 cm)
Muisca culture
Muisca archaeological zone

The rim of the vessel has been modified and extended to form two figures, who hold the bowl that contains small copper figurines.

Plate LIV
Figural jar
Buff terracotta
h: 6¾ in. (17.2 cm) × d: 8⅞ in. (22.6 cm)
Tairona culture (ca. 1000 A.D.–1550 A.D.?)
Tairona region

The figures depicted are taking part in a ritual ceremony. There are four primary and two secondary officiates, two attendant figures, and two seated figures holding a child.

Plate LVII
Zoomorphic-effigy vessel
Brownware
h: 8⅜ in. (21.4 cm) × w: 11¾ in. (29.8 cm)
Tairona culture (ca. 1000 A.D.–1550 A.D.)
Tairona region

Plate LVIII
Figural whistle
Fine brownware
h: 3⅜ in. (9.5 cm) × w: 2⅛ in. (5.4 cm)
Tairona culture (ca. 1000 A.D.–1550 A.D.)
Tairona region

The figure, wearing a jaguar mask, probably represents a priest impersonating the sun as culture hero.

(Preceding page)

Plate LV
Serpentiform jar
Fine brownware
h: 3 in. (7.6 cm) × w: 4¼ in. (10.8 cm)
Tairona culture (ca. 1000 A.D.–1550 A.D.)
Tairona region)

The jar is composed of four double-headed and two single-headed serpents. Within the context of pre-Columbian iconography, the double-headed serpent is the "precious twin," the dual-natured lifeforce. These double-headed serpents are decorated with incised zigzag parallel lines and small punctated dots. The zigzag pattern represents lightning, another common icon for the life force, and the small dots may represent seeds of potential life.

Plate LVI
Serpent-effigy jars
Fine brownware
left: h: 4⅜ in. (11.2 cm) × d: 3⅞ in. (9.9 cm)
right: h: 2¾ in. (7 cm) × w: 4 in. (10.2 cm)
Tairona culture (ca. 1000 A.D.–1550 A.D.)
Tairona region

Plate LIX
Figural ocarina
Fine brownware
H: 3½ in. (8.9 cm) × w: 3¼ in. (8.3 cm)
Tairona culture (ca. 1000 A.D.–1550 A.D.)
Tairona region

The figure's elaborate headdress, ear spools, and costume, its protruding tongue, and the double-cayman bench on which it is seated support the interpretation that it represents an aspect of the solar deity.

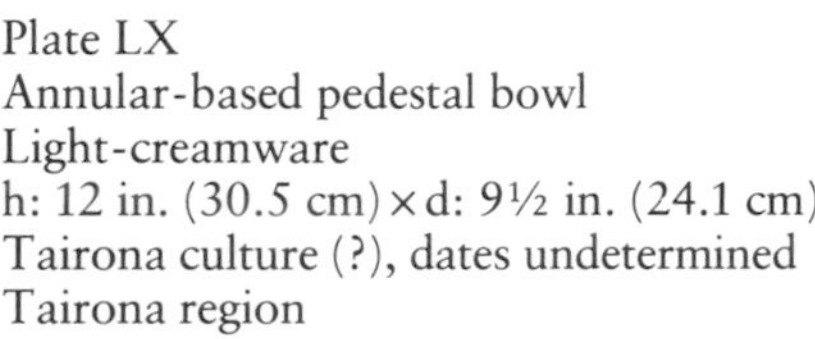

Plate LX
Annular-based pedestal bowl
Light-creamware
h: 12 in. (30.5 cm) × d: 9½ in. (24.1 cm)
Tairona culture (?), dates undetermined
Tairona region

Plate LXI
Anthropomorphic-zoomorphic-"Janus" figures supporting jars
Light cream
h: 5¾ in. (14.6 cm) × l: 11¾ in. (29.8 cm)
Tairona culture (?), dates undetermined
Tairona region

CHAPTER IX

THE TAIRONA

Guardians of Fertility and Lords of thc Sierra Nevada de Santa Marta

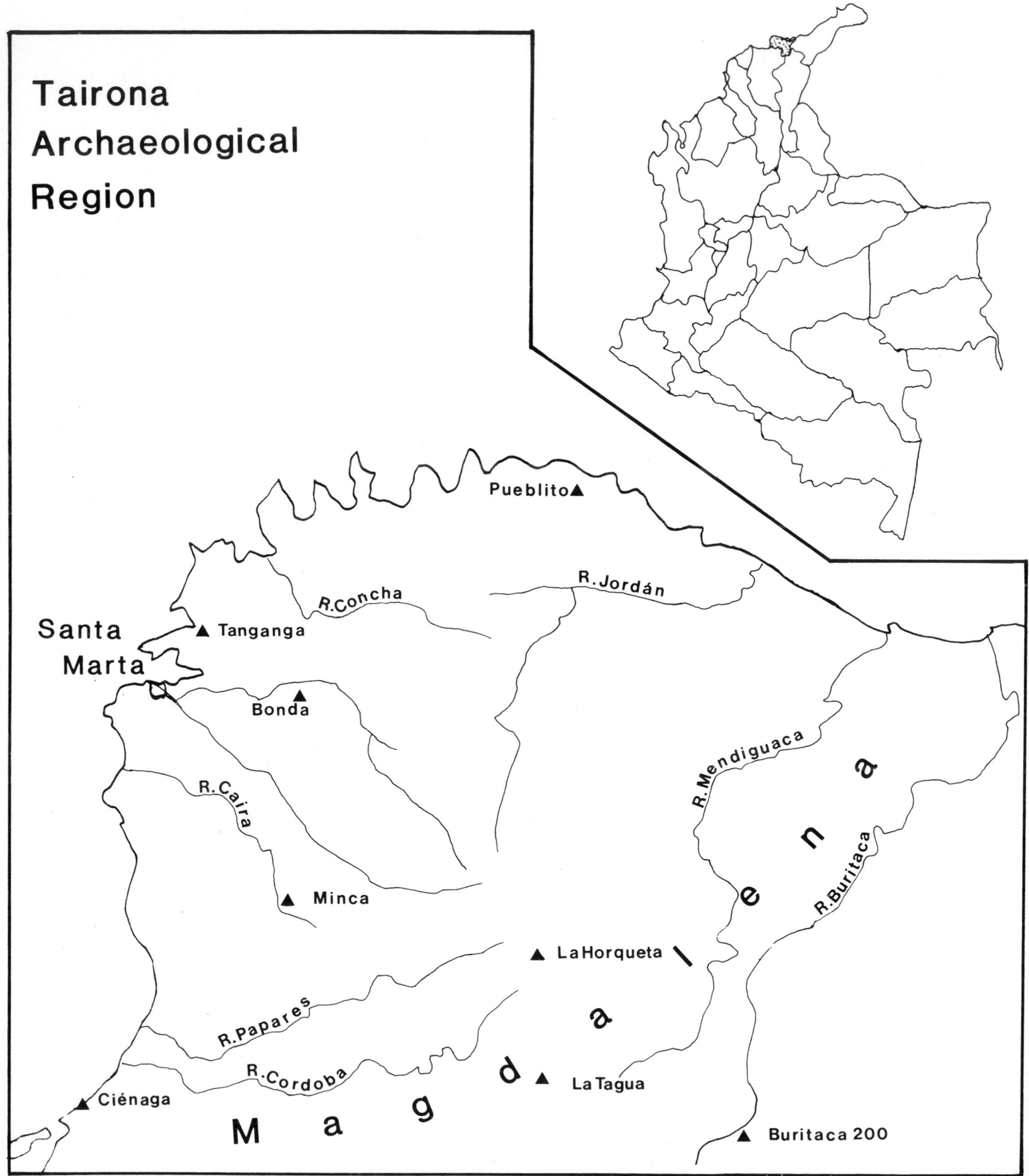
Tairona
Archaeological
Region
Pueblito
R.Concha
R.Jordán
Santa
Marta
Tanganga
Bonda
R.Caira
R.Mendiguaca
Minca
R.Buritaca
LaHorqueta
R.Papares
R.Cordoba
LaTagua
Ciénaga
Buritaca 200
Magdalena

GEOGRAPHY

The lands of the great Tairona culture lay far to the north of the Muisca homeland, in what is today the modern Department of Magdalena, east of the Magdalena River and west of the departments of La Guajira and Cesar.

The Sierra Nevada de Santa Marta, an isolated, massive rock formation containing snow-capped peaks, some of which peer over 17,000 feet above sea level, is the most prominent geological and topographical feature of this region. Below the cold, sharp, craggy peaks lie a number of diverse ecological zones. Ranging from rain forests to semi-desert lands, these zones change as one descends from the frigid peaks to the warmer climes of the coast. The amount of annual rainfall in the Sierra Nevada is directly correlated to the cardinal direction of the mountain slope; the north and west slopes are generally wetter than those of the east and south. Tairona culture was centered in the lower elevations, generally below 3,000 feet above sea level.

ARCHAEOLOGY

Over 200 Tairona sites have been recorded in archaeological surveys conducted by Colombians Luisa Fernanda de Turbay and Gilberto Cadavid in the 1970s. Of these, only two have been excavated systematically.

The first of these, Pueblito, extending over 10 square miles of ridges and valleys, was still occupied at the time of the Spanish Conquest. Pueblito was studied by James Mason (1931–39), by Gerardo Reichel-Dolmatoff (1954), and by Reichel-Dolmatoff and his wife, Alicia (1955).

The second major site studied and excavated to date is Buritaca 200, also commonly called the Ciudad Perdida, or "Lost City." This major site, located along the Buritaca River, was brought to the attention of the archaeological community by *guaqueros* in 1976. A team of investigators headed by Alvaro Soto, Director of the Instituto Colombiano de Anthropología, have been conducting research there since 1976.

The circular house platforms discovered at sites such as Pueblito indicate that the houses were between 18 and 22 feet in diameter. Those at Buritaca were somewhat smaller, due to the restricting nature of the natural topography, and contained artifacts whose distribution indicates that dwellings were divided into distinct sections for men and women. The men's section contained stone axes and chisels, fishnet weights, ceremonial pottery, and other ritual objects of stone, such as forked staffs and rectangular, wing-shaped, bat-wing pendants. The bat-wing pendants were used as chimes and dangled from the arms of ritual dancers during specific ceremonies, just as they are used today by the Kogi (G. Reichel-Dolmatoff, 1965). The women's section included water jars, grinding stones, utilitarian cooking vessels, and small burnishing stones used in finishing the surface of pottery prior to firing.

Large quantities of finished and unfinished stone necklace beads of agate, carnelian, and quartz have also been found at Tairona sites and were widely traded in prehispanic times. Although the Tairona were excellent workers of polished stone implements, ritual objects, and beads, they do not appear to have carved significant stone sculptural monuments. Their skill in using stone for engineering projects, however, is unquestioned.

ETHNOHISTORY

In the 16th century, the specific group known as Tairona, occupying the foothills of the north slope of the Sierra Nevada de Santa Marta, lived along the Don Diego, Buritaca, and Guachaca Rivers. The Spanish distinguished them from neighboring groups living in the Manzanares River Valley, the Jordan and Piedras River Valley, and the coastal area, and even from groups living at Betoma or Bonda. The aforementioned groups, however, shared many cultural traits which differentiated their tradition from neighboring groups living further west and east. Thus, the term *Tairona* as used in this chapter will be employed to designate the Tairona Cultural Tradition, and not simply the ethnic group referred to as Tairona in the chronicles and 17th-century histories.

Tairona villages were often quite large, consisting of hundreds of—and sometimes over a thousand—dwellings. Villages were well ordered and were connected with one another by an elaborate network of stone, slab-paved roads. The typical house had a circular floor plan with a stone foundation, while the walls and support beams were made of wood. The roof, as was common all over Colombia, was thatched.

In many houses, a pottery vessel containing small pebbles was kept buried beneath the floor or door. According to Kogi ethnographic data, these pebbles represent the occupants of the household:

> At the birth of a child, the pot is dug up and a new pebble is added; in this manner all the inhabitants are identified and taken under the protection of the spirits which are the guardians of the dwelling. (G. Reichel-Dolmatoff, 1965, p. 149)

Tairona towns, particularly the more developed settlements, were distinguished by large temples and expansive, stone-faced and paved ceremonial plazas. Stone stairways connected the lower areas with the agricultural terraces located at higher elevations. Bridges of stone slabs layered in rows, one above the other and resting on pilasters of smaller stones, were constructed where needed to cross over gulleys and ditches. The surrounding countryside was terraced for farming, and elaborate stone retaining walls prevented erosion. Irrigation water was channeled to the terraces and fields by means of stone-lined ditches and small canals. Rock-lined channels and conduits directed excess rain water to lower elevations, preventing flooding of the fields and settlements.

Tairona engineers integrated their buildings and structures with the surrounding environment. Many of the towns appear to be outgrowths of the natural landscape. The modern Kogi still reflect a close bond between human and natural ecology.

Corn and manioc farming provided the economic base of Tairona society. This was supplemented by a variety of cultivated foodstuffs, such as beans, sweet potatoes, chili peppers, plantains, avocados, guavas, pineapples, and cacao. Cotton was also grown. Agricultural implements, like all Tairona tools, were of stone and wood, and they appear to have been kept in communal storage houses, as was the case with weapons.

Powerful secular chieftains governed the Tairona towns, though priests also exerted great influence over the communities. Political organization usually did not extend beyond a central town, which exercised authority over a number of satellite villages. By the 16th century, however, the Tairona were well on their way to statehood. Two large confederations vied with one another for control of the region: Bonda, centered in the foothills above the modern city of Santa Marta, and Pociqueica (location not known).

Culture and society were defended by the Tairona warrior, sometimes a professional captain of war, but more often a farmer-turned-soldier as the occasion required. The Tairona warrior was a valiant adversary, but according to the Spanish who engaged him in combat, those living along the coast were not as warlike as those in the mountains.

The basic Tairona armaments were the war club and the bow and arrow. Some of the arrows were tipped with stingray spines, while others were dipped in poison, possibly from the leaves of the tree *Hippomane mancinella*.

According to chroniclers and historians, such as Oviedo and Castellanos, the ruling class was held in high esteem by other members of Tairona society. Both men and women took pride in their appearance and adorned themselves with feathers and with gold, tumbaga, stone, and shell jewelry such as nose ornaments, labrets, and necklaces. Tairona metalsmiths were skilled artists and artisans. The better Tairona work is among the finest produced anywhere in the New World.

People living in the colder, mountainous areas wore more clothing than those living along the coast. Among some of the coastal groups, the men went about naked save for penis sheaths of shell, gold, or tumbaga. Judging from the chronicles, as well as from gold and ceramic art, ceremonial attire was often elaborate.

Tairona society was divided into a number of exogamous clans. Although polygamy was practiced, monogamy seems to have been the norm. According to Simon, incest and homosexuality were not uncommon and apparently were not looked upon as aberrant by the society at large.

RELIGION

Undoubtedly much of the old Tairona religion survives in that of the Kogi, their modern descendants, who currently number about 6,000. Kogi life is regulated by the movement of the sun, moon, stars, and planets, and the ideal community is one which is in harmony with the natural order of things: Men are admonished to pattern their lives after the model of the sun; women are counseled to follow that of the moon.

There is a clear perception of the dimorphic dual nature of reality. There are male structures, forms, and norms, just as there are those that are female. According to the Kogi, before the beginning there was nothing material: there was only the spirit of "that-which-was-to-be" and darkness everywhere. The spirit of that-which-was-to-be is sometimes imagined as a spiritual, immaterial sea called the Mother and ultimate source of all things.

The esoteric truths of every culture are hidden behind colorful allegorical and metaphoric imagery which forms the exotic camouflage of meaning behind the myth. According to an exotic Kogi myth, Sintana, the messenger-son of the Mother of creation, searched for a young boy and girl. He asked them if they wished to become father and mother of the earth, to which they answered affirmatively. Sintana then dressed them in golden raiments, after which they rose to the sky to become the Sun and Moon. Their first-born child was a girl, the planet Venus.

The Sun is metaphorically described as dwelling in a house whose roof is the sky. There he sits on a bench and chews coca. It is probable that some Tairona art objects depicting personages seated on a bench (many chewing coca) may in fact be icons representing the sun. Some of these figures are portrayed with their tongues fully extended (an icon also used by the Mexica-Aztecs in some of their portrayals of the sun, most notably on the so-called Aztec calendar stone).

According to G. Reichel-Dolmatoff, the Kogi personified the sun as a jaguar, while the moon is represented as a mountain lion. Jaguar imagery is closely associated with concepts of fertility:

> The jaguar sun god is thus a very ambivalent being, part progenitor and creator, part aggressive devourer. The Kogi see in this ambivalence the image of Man, of the individual torn between matter and spirit, and the essence of Kogi religion refers to the need for finding a balance between the conditions necessary for physical survival—food, sex, and dominance—and the equally necessary satisfaction of spiritual and psychological needs. (G. Reichel-Dolmatoff, *Sweat of the Sun, Tears of the Moon*, 1981, p.27)

An exquisitely modeled figuring whistle portrays a priest dressed in rich ceremonial attire (Plate LVIII). He is wearing a fanged jaguar headdress. At his right side is a *mochila*, a woven bag used to contain coca leaves. Lines extending from the eyes may represent tears, which, as noted for the Muisca, are iconographically associated with personifications of the sun as culture hero. The combination of anthropomorphic form, jaguar headdress, tears, and coca bag strongly suggests that this figurine represents a personification of the jaguar sun deity.

In the Kogi model of the universe, stars are personified as children of the sun. The world, or universe, is said to be shaped like an egg composed of nine dimensions of being, described as nine worlds. The present humanity is said to be living in the fifth, or middle, world. Accordingly, the four worlds above the middle are benevolent, while the four below are malevolent.

The world is described as having seven cardinal points: the four directions, the zenith, the nadir, and the center. Each point is presided over by male and female totemic animals, paired so that the male is the predator (such as a jaguar, a puma, or an owl), while the corresponding female represents the prey. This reflects the pattern followed for designating the exogamous clans of the Kogi, where male clans are named after predatory animals and female clans after herbivores, the prey of the predators.

The cardinal directions play a practical role in the lives of the Kogi, as they assuredly did among the ancient Tairona. All agricultural societies developed a means of determining the most favorable time to plant and harvest, noting the regular and sometimes irregular patterns created by the movement of sun, moon, planets, and stars as they rise and set on the horizons.

The observation of the heavens was entrusted to certain individuals, usually a shaman or a priest. In the more complex civilizations of prehispanic America, elaborate and sophisticated calendars were developed based on the observation of the heavens.

The cardinal directions were used to mark the movement of the sun in its diurnal and annual cycles. The sun rose in the east, reached its zenith in the south, and set in the west. Continuing its journey through the night, it reached its nadir in the north. But the sun did not rise at the same point in the east every day of the year: It moved south to north and then north to south along the eastern horizon. The furthest point south marked the solstice, or place where the sun stands still, as did the furthest point north. In like manner, the point where it set on the western horizon shifted with the time of year. Twice a year the sun rose due east and set due west, marking the equinox when daylight is about equal to the night. Among Indians from the American Southwest to South America, the symbol used to depict the diurnal and annual movement of the sun marking the four directions, the rising and setting points at the solstices, and the points of the equinoxes, was the equilateral cross with an *X* superimposed on it. [The cross represents the four directions, and the east-west axis also represents the equinoxes. The *X* represents the solstices. The extreme eastern side of the *X* represents the rising points of the winter and summer solstices, while the western points represent the setting points.]

[In ancient Mexico, many of the temple platforms were aligned with the solstices, equinoxes, or other movements in the sky. Every 52 years, the Mexica-Aztecs would extinguish all fires to allow the priests to observe the approach of the star Aldabaran. As it moved overhead directly above the temple, a fire priest kindled a spark which set a new fire, ushering in a new 52-year cycle. The observation of the movements of the planet Venus and many constellations were also considered of great importance.]

Little is known concerning the astronomy of prehispanic Colombian Indians. The many references to the sun, the moon, Venus, and the stars in surviving ethnographies certainly demonstrate the important role they played in the lives of the people, but they tell us little concerning how or why they were observed. Elsewhere in the Americas, observations of the solstices and equinoxes were made either by means of direct or indirect observation. Direct observation involved watching the progression of sunrise or sunset from a fixed point and noting the position of the sun on the horizon with respect to a prominent geologic feature, such as a mountain peak. In indirect observation, a beam of sunlight from the rising or setting sun interacts with an artistic device, such as a spiral painted on a cave wall or rock, a series of marks cut into a tree, or marks made on the wall of a house. How and where the sunlight intersects with the motif or marks designates the time of year.

It is known that the Kogi Indians observe the solstices and equinoxes and that they possess a calendar. G. Reichel-Dolmatoff notes that the Kogi formerly kept records of the passing of time on mnemonic devices, such as sticks on which a groove or other mark, perhaps representing a month or year, was made. Their astronomy, however, is but a pale vestige of that of the ancient Tairona before the Spanish systematically executed all of the principal lords, priests, and shamans.

The Kogi year is divided into eighteen months consisting of twenty days each (G. Reichel-Dolmatoff, 1985). The additional five days of the year are those of the solstices, when the sun seemingly stops and rises at the same point on two or more consecutive days. The Kogi priest-astronomer made allowances for this, and he later determined the exact day when the movement began anew.

The Kogi realize that the planet Venus is both the Morning and Evening Star. This is reflected in a Kogi myth which relates that Venus was originally the son of the Sun, but was later secretly transformed into a woman. The unsuspecting Sun-father copulates with her, thereby committing incest. (It is interesting that the Kogi do not emphasize that this constituted a quasi-homosexual act.) The significance of the myth is linked to the exogamous clan structure of the Kogi. It is possible that at some time in the distant past, when Venus Morning Star and Venus Evening Star may have been perceived as two separate celestial bodies, there were two separate exogamous clans identified with what was thought to be two distinct entities. The realization that Venus Morning Star and Evening Star were one and the same would have caused certain embarassment because of the implication of incest. Thus, the Kogi allegory may have developed as a mythic rationale for earlier confusion created by the deceptive aspects of planet Venus as Morning and Evening Star.

In addition to their role as astronomers and keepers of time, Tairona priests coordinated the ritual life of the people by developing ceremonies around specific calendrical events, as was true everywhere in the Americas where agriculture was practiced. The priests also functioned as healers and psychopomps.

As is true of all societies having a clan structure, each clan is usually entrusted with specific knowledge, a part of the group myth. Among the Kogi, for example, the *kurcha*, a priestly lineage, are designated as the "Owners and Keepers of the Rock Crystal." Crystals and other stones are believed to possess certain powers which can be directed by a knowledgeable priest to cure specific maladies. Both Castellanos and Simon noted that the Tairona used natural as well as worked stones, such as quartz, carnelian, and agate, to cure colic and diseases of the blood and urine, among other illnesses. Many stones were worked into necklace beads, some of which were later ground and used as medicine or as part of certain rites. G. Reichel-Dolmatoff (1981, pp. 27–29) observed that Kogi priests

> . . . distinguish between some fifty or more different types of beads (Kuitsi), some of which may belong to a particular person or lineage. . . . Some of these beads represent permanent permission to carry out an activity or occupation, for instance, marriage, coca chewing, or to protect owners against aggressions and accidents.

We know from portrayals in the ceramic art that coca leaves were chewed by the ancient Tairona, as they are by the Kogi today. Other mood- and mind-altering substances were also used by the Tairona, but little specific information has survived. In Kogi mythology, shamans are said to be able to transform themselves into jaguars by placing a "blue ball" in their mouth. The "blue ball" is called *nebbi Kuai*, which means "jaguar's testicle" or "jaguar's sperm." G. Reichel-Dolmatoff states that it is highly probable that the "blue ball" refers to a poisonous, hallucinogenic mushroom (1975). The white portion of the mushroom would give it seminal significance on the basis of color classification. It is also likely that the energy released by the hallucinogenic plant alkaloid might suggest an analogy with sexual energy, closely identified with jaguar symbolism in the Kogi mind.

Our intention in placing emphasis on groups such as the Kogi is that they give the best perspective available to us with which to understand the nature of their Tairona ancestors. However rich the inner life of the modern Kogi, it constitutes but a faint expression of the rich philosophical, intellectual, and metaphysical life that flourished among the Tairona. When the Spanish killed the ruling families, priests, and shamans of the Tairona, they also extinguished, forever, the knowledge that had been entrusted to specific individuals among them.

In 1599 the Tairona, under their leader Cuchacique, staged their final rebellion against the Spanish invaders, almost one hundred years from their first meeting late in the 15th century. The battles were fierce, but superior armaments and military organization prevailed over valor and courage. Tairona defeat was inevitable. Cuchacique was captured and quartered, his head severed from his body and placed in a cage. The order was given for the army to gather all the chieftains and priests, as well as their families and relatives. All who could not escape into the mountains were killed. Chieftains were ordered hanged by the neck, their bodies burnt to ash and allowed to blow as dust upon the winds. The memory of the great Tairona was to be erased from the earth. The earth, however, did not forget, preserving their memory in the form of ruins and artifacts of gold, stone, and clay and nurturing their descendants, the Kogi of the Sierra Nevada de Santa Marta.

THE CERAMIC RECORD

Few radiocarbon dates have been obtained from any Tairona sites. Those by Louisa Herrara de Turbay and Ana Maria de Mohecha at Buritaca 200 indicate that the site was occupied somewhere between 1200 A.D. and 1520 A.D. Occupation may have continued somewhat later. These dates establish chronological parameters for ceramics found at Buritaca 200, affording us a means of estimating the age of similar ceramics found at other sites in the Tairona region. Most of the objects documented in this chapter were manufactured after 1000 A.D.

Researchers have established different schemes for classifying Tairona ceramics. James Mason (1936) divided Tairona decorated ceramics into (a) Red Ware, (b) Black Ware, (c) Fine Brown Ware, and (d) Light-colored Ware. Mason considered the Light-colored Ware exotic, possibly imported from along the Magdalena River outside the Tairona region, though it shares characteristics with ceramic wares found to the east in Venezuela.

Lucia Rojas de Perdomo (1985) distinguishes three primary wares: (a) Red, (b) Black, and (c) Fine Brown. No mention is made of the light cream-colored ware.

For the purposes of this publication, we will employ the classifications used by Perdomo. The cream-colored ware, although found within Tairona territory, perhaps represents either a different ethnicity within Tairona territory or an import. Tairona lacks painted wares. A few painted vessels were uncovered at one site, Nahuange, in Tairona territory, but these are now believed to have been manufactured by another cultural group.

BLACK WARE

The most common form of Black Ware vessels is the ring-based vessel, which may be *olla*-shaped, carinated, or quasi-cylindrical. Very often the body of these vessels has been modified to represent an anthropomorphic or zoomorphic effigy (Plate LVII). A separate genre within the ring-based anthropomorphic *ollas* are the so-called *cacique*, or chieftain, jars (#147), the spout of which forms the head. The figure is typically portrayed wearing a large nose plaque and often a cylindrical lip-plug, or labret. Arms and hands are generally in relief and only alluded to by the artist. Legs are not indicated on this genre.

A variation of the chieftain jar is the double-chieftain jar (#152). The individual vessels are often joined at the sides and also again by a strap handle. Ithyphallic genitalia are often depicted on such vessels.

Another relatively common Black Ware form is the ring-based, double-spouted vessel, with an elliptically shaped base and body and large cylindrical spouts. Variations of this type exist in which one or both spouts have been partially or completely modified to form the head of a zoomorph. (#156). Other Black Ware ring-based forms include bowls and some lidded treasure jars.

Zoomorphic and anthropomorphic whistles (#167), ocarinas (Plate LIX), and tetrapod vessels come in a variety of forms: bowls, *ollas*, and effigies (#157).

FINE BROWN WARE

Although Tairona pottery in general is well made and the sculptural lines are well defined, Fine Brown Ware tends to be the best executed and evinces the most detail with respect to incised decoration and distinction of form and features. Fine Brown Ware forms are typically smaller objects, such as figurine whistles (#163), anthropomorphic and zoomorphic ocarinas (#165), anthropomorphic flutes (#166), and small tetrapod vessels such as jars modeled as a figure seated on a double-headed cayman bench (#161) or as multiple serpents (Plate LV). Fine Brown Ware ceramics are often profusely incised and decorated with small circles (Plate LVI) and numerous punctated dots. Within the Fine Brown Ware ceramic styles are to be found some of the finest expressions of Tairona art (Plate VII).

RED WARE

Red Ware ceramics are characterized by thicker vessel walls, coarser paste, and rough surfaces. Decoration is usually sparing and applied as design in relief.

The execution of anthropomorphic features is sparse and impressionistic rather than realistic. Arms are applied as short, thin fillets of clay; legs are generally not depicted on effigy vessels. Red Ware vessels are often utilitarian, including forms such as plates, saucers, trays, bowls, globular and ring-based jars, carinated jars, cylindrical jars, treasure boxes, burial urns, and ladles, which often have handles modeled in highly stylized and abstract anthropomorphic and zoomorphic forms.

One unusual vessel is a double-handled bowl depicting a ritual enactment scene, at the center of which is a circular pit with two figures standing opposite one another, apparently holding rattles and officiating (Plate LIV). A large appendage extending from between their legs appears to be a bifurcated phallus resting on the edge of the ring. At opposite sides of the ring are two serpentiform, phallic elements (unbirfurcated and unattached to any figure) flanked by two standing figures with rattles. On either side of the main officiate is a seated figure holding a child. Opposite, a guardian figure stands on each side of a second officiate.

Kogi ethnography gives us insight into the possible meaning of this scene. The *kurcha*, an important Kogi priestly lineage said to be the keepers of the secret of fertility, are associated with iconographic concepts—large, powerful eyes, huge bifurcate phalli, and twins—present in this ritual scene. Indeed, the term *kurcha* means "seed, sperm, and origin," while a related word, *kurchaua*, means "eye." The Kogis closely associate the eye with concepts of supernatural shamanic impregnation and the *kurcha* are said to descend from a mythic progenitor, *kuncha vitabueya* (literally, "seed-half-span-long"), translated as "penis" by Kogi informants (ibid.), but probably signifying a huge phallus or copious sperm.

Note that in the ritual scene in question, great emphasis is placed on the eyes of the officiates, as well as on the phalli of the two central officiating figures, signifying complementary dualism. Additionally, there are two officiates with bifurcated phalli; two officiates without visible phalli; two phallic serpent forms, with heads that are not bifurcated; two guardian figures; and two seated personages, each holding a child. Significantly, the *Kurcha* identify themselves with the opossum, an animal with a bifurcate penis. The Kogi claim that if a man eats opossum meat, his wife will bear him twins. Are the two seated figures holding twins? Is this the significance of the bifurcate phalli of the officiates? Is this ritual scene depicting a fertility ceremony involving the birth of twins, officiated by priests of a lineage similar to the *kurcha* of the Kogi? All of these iconographic elements tend to support such an interpretation, although we must allow for other meanings.

The origins of Tairona iconography and culture are unclear. G. Reichel-Dolmatoff (1965) noted that some sherds found within Tairona territory are related to late Momil developments, but that Tairona pottery is most closely related to wares from the Zambrano region of the lower Magdalena. It is clear that some characteristics of the Fine Brown Ware, such as incised rectilinear decoration in combination with the incised circle and punctation, are to be found at Monsu as early as the Turbana Period (3350 B.C.). Other attributes of Tairona culture, such as the stone "bat-wing" chime pendants, are also found among contemporary (ca. 1000 A.D.–1500 A.D.) Venezuelan Andean groups at the same time horizon. Certain aspects of the Light-colored (Cream) Ware found in Tairona territory are related in style and form to certain ceramic complexes of the Valencoid Series (ca. 1000 A.D.–1500 A.D.) in Venezuela. It is impossible at present to determine the area of origin and diffusion of traits. The evidence is still too fragmentary, and there are insufficient radiocarbon dates to make such determinations.

Whatever its origins, Tairona stands at the pinnacle of cultural development in Colombia, and although of limited expression in terms of its territorial manifestation, it must be numbered among the high cultures of the Americas.

147
Anthropomorphic-effigy jar (Chieftain jar)
Blackware
h: 10½ in. (26.7 cm) × d: 8½ in. (21.6 cm)
Tairona culture (ca. 1000 A.D.–1550 A.D.)
Tairona region

Undoubtedly this effigy represents an important personage within the Tairona mythic world. The figure wears a large nose plaque and cylindrical labret (lip plug). A large eagle pendant hangs about his neck. In many pre-Columbian cultures, the eagle is a solar symbol.

148
Anthropomorphic-effigy jar
Blackware
h: 7⅞ in. (20 cm) × d: 7¾ in. (19.7 cm)
Tairona culture (ca. 1000 A.D.–1550 A.D.)
Tairona region

149
Anthropomorphic-effigy jar
Blackware
h: 7½ in. (19.1 cm) × w: 9½ in. (24.1 cm)
Tairona culture (ca. 1000 A.D.–1550 A.D.)
Tairona region, Magdalena
Armbands and leg bands are indicated by incised lines.

150
Anthropomorphic-effigy jars
Blackware
left: h: 11¼ in. (29.6 cm) × w: 6¾ in. (17.2 cm)
right: h: 8 in. (20.3 cm) × Circum: 19 in. (48.3 cm)
Tairona culture (ca. 1000 A.D.–1550 A.D.)
Tairona region

151
Joined ithyphallic male-effigy jars
Blackware
h: 9 in. (28.8 cm) × w: 9⅜ in. (24.8 cm)
Tairona culture (ca. 1000 A.D.–1550 A.D.)
Tairona region

The figures, with erect phalli, are depicted chewing coca leaves. Figures chewing coca are often represented with erect phalli in prehispanic Colombian art. It is possible that coca chewing was associated with male potency and fertility.

152
Joined anthropomorphic-effigy jars
Blackware
h: 6 in. (15.2 cm) × w: 9¼ in. (23.5 cm)
Tairona culture (ca. 1000 A.D.–1550 A.D.)
Tairona region

153
Double-spouted vessel with feline faces
Blackware
l: 10¼ in. (26 cm) × h: 7½ in. (19.1 cm)
Tairona culture (ca. 1000 A.D.–1550 A.D.)
Tairona region

154
Double-spouted vessels
Blackware
left: h: 9¼ in. (23.5 cm) × w: 11¼ in. (28.6 cm)
right: h: 9¼ in. (23.5 cm) × w: 11½ in. (29.2 cm)
Tairona culture (ca. 1000 A.D.–1550 A.D.)
Tairona region

155
Spouted zoomorphic-effigy vessel
Blackware
h: 8¾ in. (22.2 cm) × l: 11 in. (28 cm)
Tairona culture (ca. 1000 A.D.–1550 A.D.)
Tairona region

156
Spouted zoomorphic-effigy vessels
Blackware
left: h: 8¾ in. (22.3 cm) × l: 9½ in. (24.2 cm)
right: h: 9¾ in. (25.7 cm) × l: 9¾ in. (25.7 cm)
Tairona culture (ca. 1000 A.D.–1550 A.D.)
Tairona region

There can be little doubt that these vessels were fashioned by the same hand. The head of the effigy on the vessel on the left resembles an opossum. The Kurcha lineage of the Kogi Indians, who inhabit the Tairona region today, associate the opossum with twins and fertility. The curled cockscomb is a common Tairona culture art motif that is usually depicted on smaller works.

157

158

157
Tetrapod cayman-effigy vessels ("Janus"-type vessels)
Fine brownware
left: h: 6 in. (15.2 cm) × l: 6½ in. (16.5 cm)
right: h: 3⅜ in. (8.6 cm) × l: 3¾ in. (9.5 cm)
Tairona culture (ca. 1000 A.D.–1550 A.D.)
Tairona region

A study of all representations of the cayman motif in Tairona art and iconography indicates that the cayman symbolizes duality, the lifeforce, and fertility. Double-cayman iconography corresponds with the double-headed serpent iconography in ancient Mexican art. The two distinct ribs on the handle are common to this genre, reinforcing the symbolism of the overall motif.

158
Strap-handled, annular-based vessel with avian head
Blackware
h: 8¾ in. (22.2 cm) × d: 8½ in. (21.6 cm)
Tairona culture (ca. 1000 A.D.–1550 A.D.)
Tairona region

159
Zoomorphic-effigy vessel
Fine brownware, decorated with incised geometric designs
h: 5¾ in. (14.6 cm) × w: 12½ in. (31.8 cm)
Tairona culture (ca. 1000 A.D.–1550 A.D.)
Tairona region

160
Zoomorphic figure on a bench
Blackware
h: 4⅞ in. (12.4 cm) × w: 2½ in. (6.2 cm)
Tairona culture (ca. 1000 A.D.–1550 A.D.)
Tairona region

161
Jar with figure seated on a tetrapod double-cayman bench
Fine brownware
h: 3¾ in. (9.5 cm) × w: 3¾ in. (9.5 cm)
Tairona culture (ca. 1000 A.D.–1550 A.D.)
Tairona region

162

162
Standing figures
Blackware
left: h: 5¾ in. (14.6 cm) × w: 4¼ in. (10.8 cm)
right: h: 6 in. (15.2 cm) × w: 3½ in. (8.9 cm)
Tairona culture
Tairona region

163
Anthropomorphic-figural whistle
Fine brownware, decorated with incised details
h: 6⅛ in. (15.6 cm) × w: 4¼ in. (10.8 cm)
Tairona culture (ca. 1000 A.D.–1550 A.D.)
Tairona region

164

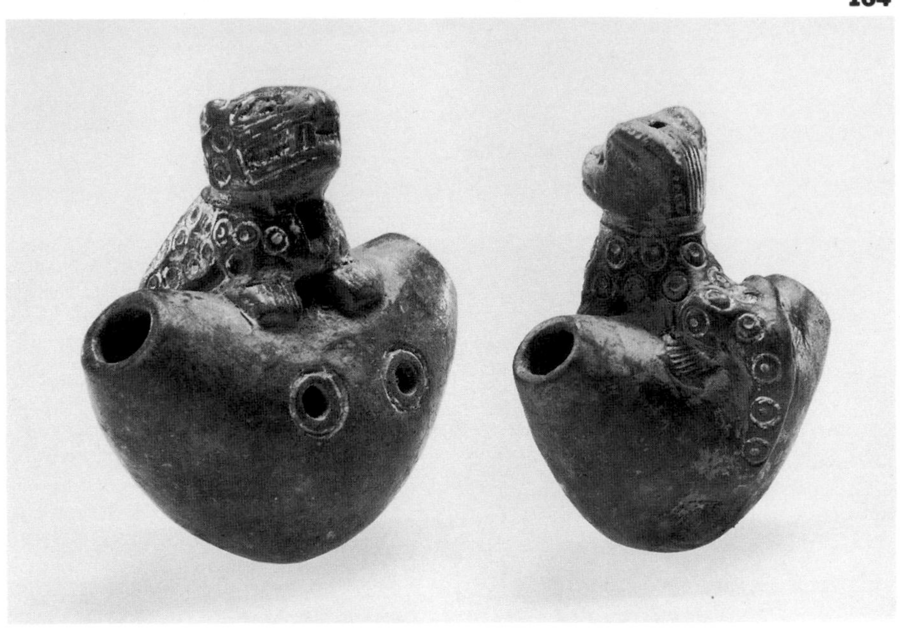

164
Avian ocarinas with double-headed caymans as tails
left: Blackware
h: 1⅞ in. (4.7 cm) × w: 1¾ in. (4.4 cm)
center: Fine brownware
h: 2½ in. (6.3 cm) × w: 2½ in. (6.3 cm)
right: Blackware
h: 1½ in. (3.7 cm) × w: 2 in. (5.1 cm)
Tairona culture (ca. 1000 A.D.–1550 A.D.)
Tairona region

165
Phalliform ocarinas surmounted by fanged felines
Fine brownware
left: h: 2½ in. (6.4 cm) × w: 2⅛ in. (5.4 cm)
right: h: 2 in. (5.1 cm) × w: 2 in. (5.1 cm)
Tairona culture (ca. 1000 A.D.–1550 A.D.)
Tairona region

This form of ocarina is frequently and clearly modeled as male genitalia. The jaguar is often associated with male potency, virility, and sexuality. Many of these small ocarinas have incised decoration filled with white powder or pigment, which in the color symbolism of the Kogi suggests seminal power.

166
Anthropomorphic-figural flute
Blackware
h: 5½ in. (13.9 cm) × circum: 4¼ in. (10.8 cm)
Tairona culture (ca. 1000 A.D.–1550 A.D.)
Tairona region

167
Anthropomorphic-figural flute
Fine brownware, decorated with details in relief
l: 4¾ in. (12.1 cm)
Tairona culture (ca. 1000 A.D.–1550 A.D.)
Tairona region

168
Anthropomorphic-effigy jar
Light-creamware
h: 8 in. (20.3 cm) × d: 7¾ in. (19.7 cm)
Tairona culture (?), dates undetermined
Tairona region

169
Treasure jar with lid
Blackware
h: 17½ in. (44.5 cm) × d: 10 in. (25.4 cm)
Tairona culture (ca. 1000 A.D.–1550 A.D.)
Tairona region

Vessels such as this, which are archaeologically associated with burial and ceremonial sites, contained ritual objects such as stone beads, stones, bat-wing pendants, and monolithic axes.

170
Treasure jars with lids
Redware
left: h: 10 in. (25.4 cm) × d: 11 in. (27.9 cm)
right: h: 14½ in. (36.8 cm) × d: 8¼ in. (21 cm)
Tairona culture (ca. 1000 A.D.–1550 A.D.)
Tairona region

170

171
Anthropomorphic burial urn
Redware
h: 29½ in. (74.9 cm) × circum: 27 in. (68.6 cm)
Tairona style (dates undetermined)
Tairona region

Fillets of clay were added to form the figure's facial features and arms and the necklace it wears. The nose plaque represents a gold nose ornament that was commonly worn by peoples of the Tairona region.

GLOSSARY

acromegaly: enlargement of the extremities and face as a result of an overactive pituitary.

***adornos*:** small figures or ornaments cast or modeled individually and attached as decoration to a vessel or other form.

***alcarraza*:** a basic jar form characterized by two vertical attenuated spouts joined by a strap, or bridge handle.

amphora: a basic vessel form characterized by an ovoid body and a distinct neck. The bases of such vessels are often conical, and the necks are often long and cylindrical.

analogue: a similar form.

annular-based: having a ring-shaped base.

anthropomorphic: having human-like characteristics.

anthropophagia: the practice of eating human flesh.

appliquéd: decorated through the application of fillets or other adornments first modeled or formed separately.

atlantean: a term describing figures portrayed supporting other forms.

***cacica*:** a female leader or ruler.

***cacique*:** a leader or ruler; a chieftain.

***canastero*:** a genre found in the Calima region characterized by an anthropomorphic or zoomorphic figure in crouched position, with a hollow receptacle at the back.

carinated: having a characteristic ridge formed by the point of contact of two sloping or inclined surfaces.

cayman: a South American crocodilian similar to alligators, but also resembling crocodiles.

ceramic tradition: a classificatory category embracing a number of related ceramic wares.

ceramic type: usually a regional or local variant and subdivision of a ceramic ware.

ceramic ware: a classificatory category that is a sub-division of a tradition embracing a number of related ceramic forms, characterized by similarities in surface treatment, core type, and techniques of manufacture.

***chicha*:** an alcoholic beverage made from fermented corn.

clyster tubes: tubular vessels used in administering anal infusions of emetic or hallucinatory substances.

datura: a genus of the nightshade family containing strong mind-altering alkaloids.

dimorphic: having two distinct forms for one class of objects or species of life.

endogamy: the practice of marrying within a specific group, such as a clan.

exogamy: the practice of marrying outside a specific group, such as a clan.

footed: characterized by a short supporting disc or other structural element.

geometrics: rectilinear or curvilinear design elements in the form of straight lines, triangles, squares, rectangles, circles, and / or combinations of the above.

***guaqueros*:** individuals who locate and excavate antiquities for the purpose of personal and financial gain, without regard to archaeological methodology or accepted procedures for information retrieval.

hachured: decorated with parallel lines used as filler.

homologue: an identical form.

***incensario*:** a vessel used to contain burning incense.

incised: effected as line detail by means of a sharp instrument cutting into the material.

in situ: in place (archaeologically, in context, at a site).

ithyphallic: characterized by an erect phallus.

labret: an ornament placed in a specially prepared hole in the lower lip.

lifeway: a subdivision of a cultural tradition incorporating specific patterns of behavior and subsistence.

***llano(s)*:** open grassy plain.

Mesoamerica: that part of Mexico and Central America which manifested a high level of civilization in antiquity, such as that of the Olmec, the Nahuatl cultures of the Valley of Mexico, the Zapotec, and the Maya.

midden: the accumulated refuse of people who once inhabited a site.

***múcura*:** a basic Muisca vessel form characterized by a globular body, a relatively tall, narrow, cylindrical spout, and a handle connecting the spout to the vessel body.

ocarina: as found in Colombia, it is a wind instrument with multiple holes used to vary pitch and tone, differing from a flute in shape and by the fact that the player usually blows across the blowhole rather than into it, as with a flute.

***olla*:** a basic vessel form characterized by a globular or subglobular body and a wide mouth.

pedestaled: having a supporting element characterized by a base and stem.

phytomorphic: having a plant-like form.

***poporo*:** a vessel used to contain lime, used in chewing coca leaf.

primitive agriculture: the casual planting of seed with little regard to support systems such as irrigation, ridges, or terracing.

psychopomp: a conductor of souls to the afterworld. *One who engineers or orchestrates the orientation and experiences of the mind and psyche. (author's definition)*

punctate: decorated with impressed points.

shouldered: having a distinct structural form curving outward from the base of the neck toward the middle of the body of a vessel.

sib: a group of persons unilaterally descended from a common ancestor.

stemmed: having a supporting column which attenuates away from a wide base.

tondo: a distinctly demarcated circular area found at the center of the inner surface of decorated bowls or cups.

tumbaga: an alloy of copper and gold.

zoomorphic: having an animal-like form.

BIBLIOGRAPHY

Acosta, Joaquin

1848 *Compendio historico del descubrimiento y colonizacion de la Nueva Granada en el siglo decimo sexto.* Paris.

1942 *Historia de la Nueva Granada.* Bogota.

Agreda, Manul

1954 "Dacion de tierras en Pasto al Capitan Rodrigo de Ocampo." *Revista de Historia*, vol. 5, no. 28/29. Pasto.

Aguado, Fray Pedro de

1956 *Recopilacion historial resolutoria de Sancta Marta y Nuevo Reino de Granada de las Indias del mar océano.* Biblioteca de la Presidencia de Colombia. Bogota.

1930 *Recopilacion historial resolutoria de Santa Marta y Nuevo Reino de Granada de las Indias del Mar Océano.* 3 vols. Espansa-Calpe.

1956 *Recopilacion historial.* 4 vols. Biblioteca de la Presidencia de Colombia. Bogota.

Alcina Franch, J.

1965 *Manual de argueología americana.* Madrid.

Allen, Paul H.

1947 "Indians of Southeastern Colombia." *Geographical Review*, vol. 37, no. 4, pp. 567–82. New York.

Andagoya, Pascual de

1865 *Narrative of the Proceedings of Pedrarias Davila in the Provinces of Tierra Firme or Castilla del Oro, and of the Discovery of the South Sea and the Coasts of Peru and Nicaragua* (ed., C. R. Markham). Hakluyt Society, vol. 34. London.

Angulo Valdés, C.

1962 "Evidencias de la serie barrancoide en el norte de Colombia." *Revista Colombiana de Antropología*, vol. 11. Bogota.

1962 "Cultural development in Colombia." *Aboriginal Cultural Development in Latin America. An Interpretative Review, S.M.C.* vol. 146, no. 1, pp. 55–56.

1934 "Investigaciones linguisticas y etnograficas en la Mision del Caqueta." *Senderos*, Biblioteca Nacional, vol. 1, no. 6, pp. 315–21. Bogota.

Anuncibay, Francisco de

1592 "Informe sobre la poblacion indigena de la Gobernacion de Popayan y sobre la necesidad de importar negros. . . ." Archivo Central del Cauca, Asig. Co. 12069. Popayan.

Arango, C. Luis

1924 *Recuerdos de la Guacueria en el Quindio.* 2 vols. Bogota. Editorial de Cromos, Luis Tamayo & Co.

Arango Cano, Jesus

1976 *Mitos, leyendas y dioses chibchas.* Bogota.

1977 *Revaluacion de las antiguas culturas aborigenes de Colombia.* Bogota: Plaza y Janés. 4a.

Arbelaez Camacho, C., and S. Sebastian Lopez

1967 *Historia Extensa de Colombia.* vol. 20. Bogota.

Arboleda Llorente, José Maria

1942 "Memorias sobre los indigenas tributarios de la prov. de los Pastos, Año 1589." *Boletin de Historia y Antiguedades*, vol. XXIX, nos. 330–331. Bogota.

Arcila Robledo, Gregorio

1953 *Apuntes historicos de la provincio franciscana en Colombia.* Bogota: Imprenta Nacional.

Ardila, Gerardo

1980 Investigaciones arqueologicas en Chia. Manuscript. Bogota. Fundacion de Investigaciones Arqueologicas Nacionales, Banco de la Republica.

Ayala, Leonardo

1964 "Las tumbas de Tierradentro." *Revista Arco*, no. 31. Bogota.

1975 "Tierradentro, La serrania de los muertos." *Historia del arte colombiano.* Bogota: Salvat Editores Colombiana, S.A.

Ayerbe, Julio Manuel

1944 "Tradiciones indigenas de Tierradentro." *Revista de la Universidad del Cauca*, no. 5, pp. 227–228. Popayan.

Balcazar de Jacome, Stella

1973 "Resumen preliminar de informacion general sobre la zona arqueologica de Nariño." Bogota: Archivo de Museografia, Museo del Oro.

Barney Cabrera, Eugenio

1964 *El Arte Agustiniana. Boceto para una interpretacion estética.* Bogota: Escuela de Bellas Artes, Universidad Nacional de Colombia.

1975 "La fauna religiosa en el Alto Magdalena." *Colcultura, Biblioteca Basica Colombiana*, vol. 7. Bogota.

1975 "San Agustin, un pueblo de escultores." "San Agustin, centro religioso y artistico." "El Universo del Mito," *Historia del Arte Colombiano.* Bogota: Editorial Salvat.

Barriga Villalba, A. M.

1925 "Un nuevo alkaloide." *Boletin de la Sociedad Colombiana de Ciencias Naturales*, vol. 14, no. 79, pp. 31–36. Bogota.

1927 "El yagé: Bebida especial de los indios ribereños del Putumayo y el Amazonas." *Boletin del Laboratorio Samper-Martinez*, Special Issue no. 9. Bogota.

Behar, David

1976 Excavaciones Arqueologicas en las Fincas Padula y Emperatriz (Bolivar). Unpublished thesis. Bogota: Universidad de los Andes, Departamento de Antropología.

Bennett, Wendell Clark

1944 "Archaeological Regions of Colombia: A Ceramic Survey." *Yale Publications in Anthropology*, no. 30, New Haven: Yale University.

Bruhns, Karen Olsen

1967 Ancient Pottery of the Middle Cauca Valley, Colombia, Ph.D. dissertation in Anthropology. Berkeley: University of California.

1969 "Stylistic Affinities Between the Quimbaya Gold Style and a Little-Known Ceramic Style of the Middle Cauca Valley, Colombia." *Nawpa Pacha*, vols. 7–8, Institute of Andean Studies.

1976 "Ancient Pottery of the Middle Cauca Valley, Colombia." *Cespedesia.* Cali.

Cadavid, Gilberto, and Luisa F. Herrera de Turbay

1977 Manifestaciones culturales en el area tairona. Unpublished. Bogota: Instituto Colombiano de Antropología.

1977 *Arqueología de la Sierra Nevada de Santa Marta. Manifestaciones culturales en el area tairona.* Bogota.

Cadena, A., and Bouchard, J. F.

1980 "Las Figurillas Zoomorfas de Ceramica del Litoral Pacifico Ecuatorial (region de La Tolita, Ecuador y de Tumaco, Colombia)." *Bulletin de l'Institut Francais des Etudes Andines*, vol. 9, nos. 3–4, pp. 49–68.

Caldas, A. J.

1946 "Palabras del idioma Koaiker." *Revista de Historia*, vol. 7, pp. 136–37. Pasto.

Caldas, Ana Maria, Alvaro Chavez, and Marina Villamizar

1972 "Las Tumbas del Valle del Dorado." *Antropología*, vol. 5. Bogota: Universidad de los Andes.

Caldas, Francisco José

1966 *Obras completas.* Bogota: Universidad Nacional de Colombia, Imprenta Nacional.

Callela, Placido de

1935 "Los Indios Sionas del Putumayo." *Boletin de Estudios Historicos*, nos. 73–74, pp. 49–52. Pasto.

1936–37 "Apuntes etnograficos sobre el curaca y el yagé en los indios sionas del Putumayo. *Revista de Misiones*, vols. 12–13, nos. 131–43, 180–86, 161–69. Bogota.

1940–44 "Apuntes sobre los Indios Siona del Putumayo." *Anthropos*, vol. 35/36, pp. 737–50.

1944 "Datos mitologicos de los Huitotos de La Chorrera." *Amazonia Colombiana Americanista*, vol. 2, no. 48-8, pp. 33–37. Pasto.

1944 "Breves notas mitologicas de los Huitotos de Santa Clara (Amazonas-Colombia)." Ibid., pp. 38–40.

Canyes, Manuel

1939 "El yajé y sus relaciones con la americanistica." *Actas del VI Congreso Interamericano de Bibliografias y Bibliotecas*, vol. 2, pp. 301–17. Washington, D.C.

Cardale de Schrimpff, Marianne

1976 "Salt production in the Eastern Cordillera of Colombia before and after the Spanish Conquest, a preliminary survey." *Actas del XLI Congreso Internacional de Americanistas. Mexico 1974*, vol. 2, pp. 419–28.

1976 "Investigaciones arqueologicas en la zona de Pubenza. Tocaima, Cundinamarca." *Revista Colombiana de Antropología*, vol. 20, Bogota.

1978 "Informe preliminar sobre una mochila hallada en la region de Pisba." *Boletin del Museo del Oro*, vol. 1 (Jan.–Apr.), pp. 18–21. Bogota: Banco de la Republica.

1979 "Textiles arqueologicos de Nariño." *Revista Colombiana de Antropología*, vol. 21, pp. 246–82. Bogota.

1981 *Las salinas de Zipaquira, su explotacic indigena.* Bogota: Fundacion de Investigaciones Arqueologicas Nacionales, Banco d la Republica.

1981 "Ocupaciones humanas en el Altiplano Cundiboyacense." *Boletin Museo del Oro*, vol. 4 (Sept.–Dec.). Bogota: Banco de la Republica.

1982 *La Colina de la Sal. Zipaquira.* (Patrones de Asentamiento durante la épo precolombina y la colonia.) Unpublished report. Bogota: Fundacion de Investigaciones Arqueologicas Nacionales, Banco c la Republica.

1982 "Estudio de la cultura llama-Calima Temprano." Unpublished article. Bogota: Fundacion de Investigaciones Arqueologicas Nacionales, Banco de la Republica. Unpublished article. Bogota: Fundacion de Investigaciones Arqueologicas Nacionales, Banco de la Republica.

Castellanos, Juan
1886 *Historia del Nuevo Reino de Granada.* Published by don Antonio Paz y Melia. Colection de escritores castellanos. 2 vols. Madrid: Historiadores.
1955 *Elegias de varones ilustres de Indias.* Edition of the Presidency of the Republic. Bogota.

Castillo, Neyla
1981 *Excavaciones arqueologicas en Tunja.* Unpublished. Bogota: Fundacion de Investigaciones Arqueologicas Nacionales, Banco de la Republica.

Cespedesia
1976 *Boletin cientifico del Departamento del Valle del Cauca, Colombia*, vol. 5, nos. 17–18 (Jan.–Feb.). Cali.

Chaves, Alvarao
1972 "A notaciones sobre la ceramica Quillacinga." *Razon y Fabula*, no. 28. Bogota.

Chaves, Alvaro and Mauricio Puerta
1973–79 Excavaciones Arqueologicas en Tierradentro. Unpublished reports. Bogota: Fundacion de Investigaciones Arqueologicas Nacionales. Banco de la Republica.

Chaves Mendoza, Alvaro
1972 *Exploraciones y excavaciones arqueologicas en Tierradentro.* Reports presented to the Banco de la Republica. Bogota.
1972 "Reseņa etnografica de los Cobarias." *Casa Colonial*, no. 3. Pamplona.

Chaves Mendoza, Alvaro, and Mauricio Puerta Restrepo
1976 *Tierradentro.* Bogota: Ediciones Zazacuabi.
1976 Monumentos arqueologicos de Tierradentro. Unpublished. Bogota: Banco Popular.
1980 *Entierros Primaros de Tierradentro* (ed., Carlos Valencia). Bogota: Fundacion de Investigaciones Arqueologicas Nacionales, Banco de la Republica.

Chaves, Milciades
1945 "Mitos, tradiciones y cuentos de los indios Chami." *Boletin de Arqueología*, vol. 1, tomo 2, p. 150. Bogota.

Chen, A. L., and K. K. Chen
1939 "Harmine: The Alkaloid of Caapi." *Quarterly Journal of Pharmacy and Pharmacology*, vol. 12, pp. 30–38.

Cieza de Leon, Pedro de
1864 "The Travels of Pedro de Cieza de Leon, A.D. 1532–50." Contained in *The First Part of the Chronicle of Peru* (trans. and ed., Clements R. Markham), Hakluyt Society, series I, vol. 33. London.
1883 *The Second part of the Chronicle of Peru* (trans. and ed., Clements R. Markham), Hakluyt Society, Series I, vol. 68. London.
1947 *La Cronica del Peru.* Vol. 2. Madrid: Library of Spanish Authors.

Coe, Michael D.
1962 *Mexico: Ancient Peoples and Places.* London: Thames & Hudson.
1962 *Mexico: Viejos pueblos y logares.* Barcelona: Editorial Argos.
1970 *Olmec Jaguars and Olmec Kings.* Paper presented at the Dumbarton Oaks Conference on the Cult of the Feline. Washington, D.C.

Condamine, Charles Marie de la
1745 *Relation abrégée d'un voyage fait dans l'interieur de l'Amérique Méridionale.* Paris (first English edition, London, 1747).

Cooper, John M.
1949 "Stimulants and Narcotics." *Handbook of South American Indians*, vol. 5, pp. 525–58. Washington, D.C.

Coudreau, Henri A.
1887 *Voyage a travers les Guyanes et l'Amazonie, La France équinoxiale.* 2 vols. Paris.

Cubillos, Julio César
1945 "Arqueología de Rioblanco (Chapparal, Tolima)." *Boletin de Arqueología* I (6). pp. 519–30. Bogota.
1946 "Apuntes para el Estudio de la Cultura Pijao." *Boletin de Arqueología* II (1), pp. 47–81. Bogota.
1954 "Arqueología de las riberas del Rio Magdalena, Espinal-Tolima." *RCA* II (2), pp. 128–44. Tolima.
1954 "Arqueología de Rioblanco (Chaparral, Tolima)." Boletin de Arqueología, vol. 1, pp. 519–591, Bogota.
1980 *Arqueología de San Agustin — El Prador, El Estrecho y Mesita C.* Bogota: National Archaeological Research Foundation, Banco de la Republica.

Cuervo Marquez, Carlos
1920 *Estudios arqueologicos y etnograficos. Biblioteca de la Presidencia de Colombia*, vol. 27. Bogota.
1928 "Los Quillacs o Quillacingas." *2nd International Congress of Americanists*, pp. 329–34.
1930 "Razas desaparecidas: Los Tairona y los Quillacinga." *Annaes do XX Congresso International de Americanistas*, vol. 2. Rio do Janeiro.
1955 *Estudios arqueologicos y etnograficos. Colombian Anthropoligical Library.* Bogota.
1956 *Estudios arqueologicos y etnograficos. Biblioteca de la Presidencia de Colombia.* Bogota: Editorial Kelly.

David y Villota, F.
1938 "Costumbres indigenas." *Idearium*, vol. 1, no. 10. Pasto.

Dawson, Warren R.
1928 "Two Mummies from Colombia." *Man* (May), pp. 73–74.

Dobkin de Rios, Marlene
1970 "Banisteriopsis Used in Witchcraft and Healing Activities in Iquitos, Peru." *Economic Botany*, vol. 24, no. 35, pp. 296–300. New York.
1970 "A Note on the Use of Ayahuasca among Urban Mestizo Populations in the Peruvian Amazon." *American Anthropologist*, vol. 72, no. 6, pp. 1419–21.
1971 "Curanderismo con la soga alucinogena (ayahuasca) en la selva peruana." *América Indigena*, vol. 31, no. 3, pp. 575–91. Mexico.
1976 *The Wilderness of Mind: Sacred Plants in Cross-cultural Perspective. Sage Research Papers in the Social Sciences* (Cross-cultural Series #90-039). (Reprinted from 1973, "The Non-Western Use of Hallucinogenic Agents." *Drug use in America. Problem in Perspective. 2nd Report of the National Commission on Marihuana and Drug Abuse.* Washington, D.C.: U.S. Government Printing Office).
1985 *Hallucinogens: Cross-cultural Perspectives.* Albuquerque: University of New Mexico.

Drolet, Robert
1974 "Coqueros and shamanism: An analysis of the Capuli Phase ceramic modeled figurines from the Ecuadorian northern highlands, South America." *Journal of the Steward Anthropological Society*, vol. 5, no. 2 (spring).

Duque Gomez, Luis
1955 *Colombia, Monumentos Historicos y Arqueologicos.* Mexico: Instituto Panamericano de Geografia y Historia.
1958 *Notas Historicas sobre la metalurgia prehistorica en el litoral Caribe de Colombia.* Homenaje al profesor Paul Rivet. Bogota: Editorial ABC.
1958 *Notas Historicas sobre la Orfebreria Indigena en Colombia.* Homenaje al Profesor Paul Rivet, Academia Colombiana de Historia, Bogota, pp. 271–335. Bogota: Editorial ABC.
1963 *San Agustin: Reseña arqueologica Instituto Colombiano de Antropología.* Bogota: Imprenta Nacional.
1964 "Exploraciones Arqueologicas en San Agustin." *Instituto Colombiano de Antropologia, RCA,* supplement no. 1. Bogota: Imprenta Nacional.
1964–66 *Exploraciones arqueologicas en San Agustin.* Bogota: Imprenta Nacional.
1965 *Prehistoria, etnohistoria y arqueología Historia extensa de Colombia.* Bogota: Ediciones Lerner.
1965 "1a. Prehistoria; 2a. Las culturas indigenas colombianas." *Historia extensa de Colombia*, vol. 1. Bogota: Ediciones Lerner.
1966 *Exploraciones Arqueologicas en San Agustin.* Bogota: Instituto Colombiano de Antropología.
1967 *Exploraciones Arqueologicas en San Agustin.* Bogota: Instituto Colombiano de Antropología, Imprenta Nacional.
1967 "Tribus indigenas y sitios arqueologicos." *Historia Extensa de Colombia*, vol. 1, tomo 2, Bogota.
1967 "San Agustin." *Historia Extensa de Colombia*, vol. 1, no. 2. *Tribus indigenas y sitios arqueologicos.* Bogota: Ediciones Lerner.
1968 "Los hipogeos de San Andrés de Pisimbala." *El Tiempo, Lecturas Dominicales* (Jan. 28). Bogota.
1970 *Los Quimbayas: Reseña etnohistorica y arqueologica.* Bogota: Imprenta Nacional.
1977 "Tribus indigenas y sitios arqueologicos." *Historia Extensa de Colombia*, vol. 1, no. 2. Bogota: Ediciones Lerner.

Duque Gomez, Luis, and Julio César Cubillos
1979 *Arqueología de San Agustin. Alto de los Idolos, monticulos y tumbas.* Bogota: Fundacion de Investigaciones Arqueologicas Nacionales, Banco de la Republica, Carlo Valencia Editores.
1979 *Arqueología de San Agustin — La Estacion.* Bogota: Fundacion de Investigaciones Arqueologicas Nacionales, Banco de la Republica.

Dussan de Reichel, A.
1954 "Crespo, un nuevo complejo arqueologico del norte de Colombia." *Revista Colombiana de Antropologia*, vol. 2. Bogota.
1965–66 "Contribuciones al Estudio de la Cultura Calima en Colombia." *Revista del Museo Nacional, Lima*, vol. 34, pp. 61–67.

Eliade, Mircea
1971 "Spirit, Light, and Seed." *History of Religions*, vol. 2, no. 1, pp. 1–30. Chicago.

Ernst, A.
1889 "On the Etymology of the Word Tobacco." *American Anthropologist*, vol. 2, pp. 133–42. Washington, D.C.

Errazuriz, Jaime
1980 *Tumaco-La Tolita*. Bogota: Carlos Valencia, Editores.

Escobar, Fray Jeronimo de
1889 "Memorial al Real Consejo de Indias de lo que toca a la prov. de Popayan." *Anales de Instruccion Publica*, vol. 14, no. 665. Bogota.

Falchetti, Ana Maria, and
Clemencia Plazas de Nieto
1973 "El Territorio de los Muiscas a la llegada de los Españoles. *Cuadernos de Antropologia*, vol. 1. Bogota: Universidad de los Andes.
1975 *Arqueología de Sutamarchan, Boyaca*. Bogota: Biblioteca Banco Popular.
1976 The Goldwork of the Sinu Region, Northern Colombia. Unpublished thesis. London: University of London, Institute of Archaeology.
1979 "Colgantes Darién. Relaciones entre areas orfebres del occidente Colombiano y Centroamérica." *Boletin Museo del Oro*, vol. 2 (Jan.–Apr.). Bogota: Banco de la Republica.

Federman, Nicolas
1958 *Historia Indiana* (ed. J. Friede). Madrid: Artes Graficas.

Fernandez de Oviedo, and Gonzalo Valdes
1950 *Sumario de la natural historia de las Indias*. Mexico: F.C.E.
1951–55 *Historia general y natural de las islas y tierra firme del Mar Océano*. Edicion de la Real Academia de Historia, dirigida por José Amador de los Rios. Madrid: Imprenta de la Real Academia de Historia.

Fernandez de Piedrahita, Dr. Don Lucas
1831 *Historia general de las conquistas del Nuevo Reino de Granada*. Edicion hecha sobre la de Amberes de 1688. Bogota: Imprenta de Medardo Rivas.

Francisco, Alice E.
1969 *An archaeological sequence from Carchi, Ecuador*. Ph.D. dissertation, Department of Anthropology, University of California, Berkeley.
1961 *Vidas y luchas de Don Juan del Valle, primer obispo de Popayan y protector de indios*. Popayan.
1974 *Los chibchas bajo la dominacion española*. Bogota / Medellín: La Carreta.

Friede, Juan
1948 *Algunos apuntes sobre los Karijona-Huaque del Caqueta*. Minutes of the 28th International Congress of Americanists, Paris, 1947, pp. 255–63. Paris.
1951 "Breves Informaciones sobre la Metalurgia de los Indios de Santa Maria segun Documentos Encontrados en el Archivo de Indias, Sevilla." *Journal de la Société des Américanistes, N.S.*, vol. 40, pp. 197–202.
1954 "Errores de la relacion que escribio Fray Jeronimo de Escobar sobre la Gobernacion de Popayan." *Boletin de Historia y Antiguedades*, vol. 41, no. 481–2, (Nov.–Dec.). Bogota.
1955 *Documentos inéditos para la historia de Colombia*. Bogota: Academia Colombiana de Historia.
1956 *Documentos inéditos para la historia de Colombia*, vol. 4. Madrid: Academia Colombiana de Historia, Artes Graficas.
1957 "Documentos No. 1384. Real cedula dirigida al gobernador del Nuevo Reino sobre indios de Quito y Quillacinga que trajo Baltazar Gonzales (17 de marzo de 1540)." *Documentos ineditos para la historia de Colombia*, vol. 5 (1538/1540), p. 320. Sevilla: Archivo General de Indias.

Fulop, Marcos
1954 "Aspectos de la Cultura Tukana: Cosmogonia." *Revista Colombiana de Antropología*, vol. 3, pp. 99–137. Bogota.
1955 "Notas sobre los términos y el sistema de parentesco de los Tukano." Ibid., vol. 4, pp. 123–64.
1956 "Aspectos de la Cultura Tukana: Mitología." Ibid., vol. 5, pp. 337–73.

Furst, Peter T.
1968 "The Olmec Were-Jaguar Motif in the Light of Ethnographic Reality." *Dumbarton Oaks Conference on the Olmec* (ed., Elizabeth P. Benson), pp. 143–78. Washington, D.C.
1972 *Flesh of the Gods: The Ritual Use of Hallucinogens*. New York and Washington, D.C.: Praeger.

Gallo M., Carlos I.
1972 *Diccionario Tucano-Castellano*. Medellín.

Gamboa Hinestrosa, P.
1962 *Apuntes sobre el arte de Tumaco*. Bogota.
1971 "La escultura agustiniana." *Revista de Divulgacion cultural*, vol. 8. Bogota: Universidad Nacional de Colombia.
1972 "El trabajo artistico en la sociedad agustiniana." *Revista Aleph*, vol. 4. Manizales: Universidad Nacional.
1976 *Colombia: Arte y Cultura. San Agustin*. Limbro Film, 36 transparencies. Bogota: Ediciones Zazacuabi.

Garcia, Lieselotte y Sylvia de Gutiérrez
1982 Vacio Prehistorico en la Sabana de Bogota. Unpublished. Bogota: Fundacion de Investigaciones Arqueologicas Nacionales, Banco de la Republica.

Garganta Fabrega, Miguel de
1942 "Noticias sobre la coca en el occidente Colombiano." *Revista de Historia*, no. 2, pp. 215–32. Pasto.

Ghisletti, Louis V.
1954 "Los muiscas, una gran civilizacion precolombina." Bogota: *Revista Bolivar*.

Goldman, Irving
1940 "Cosmological Beliefs of the Cubeo Indians." *Journal of American Folklore*, vol. 53, pp. 242–47. New York.
1948 "Tribes of the Vaupés-Caquetá Region." *Handbook of South American Indians*, vol. 3, pp. 763–98. Washington, D.C.
1963 "The Cubeo: Indians of the Northwest Amazon." *Illinois Studies in Anthropology*, no. 2. Urbana.

Gomez, G., and Correal U. Gonzalo
1974 "Evidencias de cirugia craneana prehistorica en Colombia." *Revisto Colombiana de Antropología*, vol. 16, pp. 491–502. Bogota.

Grass, Antonio
1982 *Los Rostros del Pasado*. Edicion de Antonio Grass. Bogota: Lithographia Arco.

Grijalva, Carlos E.
1938 *La expedicion de Max Uhle a Cuasmal, o sea la protohistoria de Imbabura y Carchi*. Quito: Editorial Chimborazo.

Groot, Ana Maria
1974 *Excavaciones arqueologicas en Tierradentro, estudio sobre ceramica y su posible uso en la elaboracion de la sal*. Graduate thesis. Bogota: Universidad de los Andes.

Groot, Ana Maria, Luz Piedad Correa, and
Eva Maria Hooykaas
1976 Estudio etnohistorico y arqueologico de la zona andina nariñense con el fin de establecer los limites de ubicacion de los grupos indigenas "Pastos y Quillacingas" y los alcances geograficos de las incursiones del Imperio Incaico. Manuscript. Bogota.

Groot de Mahecha, Ana M., and
José Luis Mahecha
1978 Informe de actividades en el sitio "Buritaca-200" Año de 1977. Unpublished. Bogota: Instituto Colombiano de Antropología.

Guerra, Luis Alejando
1938 "La arqueología del sur de Colombia." *Idearium*, vol. 2, no. 14 (Oct.), pp. 78–87. Pasto.
1942 "Los territorios de los Pastos y de los Quillacingas." *Revista de Historia*, no. 2, pp. 210–14. Pasto.

Gutierrez V., Aristides
1923 "Un santuario indigena en el Eambo Pintado." *Revista Don Quijote*, vol. 1. Pasto.
1928 "Tribus y naciones indigenas del tiempo de la conquista." *Boletin de Estudios Historicos*, vol. 1. Pasto.

Hagen, Victor W. von
1974 *The Golden Man: The Quest for El Dorado*. Farnborough: Saxon House.

Hamilton, Colonel J. P.
1827 *Travels through the Interior Provinces of Colombia*. London: John Murray.

Harner, Michael J.
1973 *Hallucinogens and Shamanism*. London: Oxford University Press.

Haury, Emil y Cubillos, and Julio César
1952 *Investigaciones arqueologicas en la Sabana de Bogota*. Tucson: Ediciones de la Universidad de Arizona.

Hernandez de Alba, Gregorio
1938 "Investigaciones arqueologicas en Tierradentro." *Revista Indias*, vol. II, no. 9 (Apr.), Bogota.
1938 "Descubrimientos arqueologicos en Inza." *Revista de Indias*, vol. 2, no. 2. Bogota.
1938 "Investigaciones arqueologicas en Tierradentro, II." *Revista de Indias*, vol. II, no. 10 (Aug.). Bogota.
1940 "Nouvelles decouvertes arqueologiques a San Agustin et Tierradentro (Colombie)." *Journal de la Société des Americanistes*, vol. 32 p. 57–67. Paris.
1944 "Etnología de los Andes del sur de Colombia." *Revista de la Universidad del Cauca*, no. 5 (Oct.–Dec.), pp. 141–266. Popayan.
1946 "The Archeology of San Agustin and Tierradentro." *Handbook of South American Indians*, vol. 2. Washington, D.C.: Smithsonian Institution.

1946 "The Highland Tribes of Southern Colombia." *Handbook of South American Indians*, vol. 2, pp. 915–60. Washington, D.C.
1978 *La cultura arqueologica de San Agustin*. Bogota: Carlos Valencia Editores.

Herrera, Antonio de
1730 *Descripcion de las Indias Occidentales*. Madrid: Oficina Real de Nicolas Rodriguez Franco.
1730 *Historia general de los hechos de los castellanos en las islas y tierra firme del Mar Océano; que llaman Indias Occidentales*. 2 vols. Madrid: Editorial de Nicolas Rodriguez Franco.

Hultgren, Axel
1931 "The hardness of Colombian tools made from copper-gold-silver alloys." *Comparative Ethnographical Studies*, vol. 9, pp. 108–12. Gothenburg.

Humboldt, Alexandre von
1822 *Voyage aux régions equinoxiales du Nouveau Continent*. Paris.

Igualada, F. de, and Marcelino de Castellvi
1940 "Classificion y estadistica de las lenguas habladas en el Putumayo, Caqueta y Amazonas." *Amazonia Colombiana Americanista*, vol. 1, nos. 2–3, pp. 92–101. Sibundoy.

Instituto Agustin Codazzi
1967 *Atlas de Colombia*. Bogota: Litografia Arco.

Jijon y Caamaño, Jacinto
1938 "Las naciones indigenas que poblaban el occidente de Colombia al tiempo de la conquista, segun los cronistas castellanos." *Sebastian de Belalcazar*, vol. 2. Quito.
1974 "Las culturas andinas de Colombia." *Biblioteca del Banco Popular*, vol. 60. Bogota.

Koch-Grunberg, Theodor
1906 "Die Indianerstamme am aberen Rio Negro und Yapura und ihre sprachliche Zugehorigkeit." *Zeitschrift für Ethnologie*, vol. 1–2, pp. 167–205.
1908 "Einige Bemerkungen zu der Forschungsreise des Dr. H. Rice in den Gebieten zwischen Guaviare und Caqueta-Yapura." *Globus*, vol. 93, no. 19. Braunschweig.
1922 "Die Volkergruppierung zwischen Rio Branco, Orinoco, Rio Negro und Yapura. *Festschrift Eduard Seler* (ed., Walter Lehmann), pp. 205–66. Stuttgart.

Krickeberg, Walter
1974 *Etnología americana*. 1st printing of the 1st edition. México: F.C.E.
1975 *Mitos y leyendas de los aztecas, incas, mayas y muiscas*. México: F.C.E.

Kuhne, Heinz
1955 "Der Jaguar im Zwillingsmythus der Chiriguano und dessen Beziehung zu anderen Stammen der Neuen Welt." *Archiv für Volkerkunde*, vol. 10, pp. 16–135.

Kunike, H.
1915 *Jaguar und Mond in der Mythologie des andinen Hochlandes*. Leipzig.

La Barre, Weston
1964 "The Narcotic Complex of the New World." *Diogenes*, pp. 125–38.
1970 "Old and New World Narcotics: A Statistical Question and an Ethnological Reply." *Economic Botany*, vol. 20, no. 1, pp. 73–80. New York.
1972 "Hallucinogens and the Shamanic Origins of Religions." *The Flesh of the Gods: The Ritual Use of Hallucinogens* (ed., Furst, Peter T.), pp. 261–78. New York and Washington, D.C.: Praeger.

Labbé, Armand J.
1980 "The Esoteric Side of Exotic Symbols in Art." *Bowers Museum Foundation Bulletin*, Jan. / Feb. Santa Ana: Bowers Museum Foundation Press.
1980 "The Hopi: Reflections on Clay (Anasazi Geometric Symbol Tradition)." *Bowers Museum Foundation Bulletin*, Mar. / Apr. Santa Ana: Bowers Museum Foundation Press.
1980 "Moche Art and Culture." *Bowers Museum Foundation Bulletin*, May / June. Santa Ana: Bowers Museum Foundation Press.
1980 "Windblown Sand: The Trumpets, Horns and Flutes of Nariño, Colombia." *Bowers Museum Foundation Bulletin*, Sept. / Oct. Santa Ana: Bowers Museum Foundation Press.
1980 "Art or Artifact?" *Bowers Museum Foundation Bulletin, Nov. / Dec.* Santa Ana: Bowers Museum Foundation Press.
1981 "Arte o Artefacto: Textiles Peruanos." *La Opinion*. Los Angeles.
1982 *Religion, Art and Iconography: Man and Cosmos in Prehispanic Mesoamerica*. Santa Ana: Bowers Museum Foundation Press.
1983 *Skywatchers of Ancient California* (co-authored with D. Travis Hudson, Ph.D., and Christopher Moser, Ph.D.). Santa Ana: Bowers Museum Foundation Press.

Langegg, F.A. von
1888 *El Dorado: Geschichte der Entdeckungsreisen nach dem Goldlande El Dorado*. Leipzig.

Lathrap, Donald
1980 *El Ecuador Antiguo. Cultura, ceramica y creatividad 3000–300 A.C.* Guayaquil: Chicago Field Museum of Natural History.

Legast, Anne
1980 *La Fauna en la Orfebreria Sinu*. Bogota: Fundacion de Investigaciones Arqueologicas Nacionales, Banco de la Republica.

Lehman, Henri
1953 "Archeologie du sud-ouest Colombien." *Journal de la Société des Américanistes*, vol. 42, pp. 199–270. Paris.
1959 "Reseña a Tierradentro, archeologie et etnographie d'une contrée de la Colombie." *L'Anthropologie*, vol. 63, nos. 3 and 4. Paris.

Levi-Strauss, Claude
1963 "The use of wild plants in tropical South America." *Handbook of South American Indians*, vol. 6, p. 469 (Chonta). New York: Cooper Square Publishers. (original version: 1950)

Londoño, Julio
1955 "La geografía y el hombre de Tierradentro." *Revista Colombiana de Antropología*, vol. 4, pp. 111–20. Bogota: Editorial Antares.

Long, Stanley
1967 "Formas y distribucion de tumbas de pozo con camara lateral. Razon y Fabula." *Revista de la Universidad de los Andes*, no. 1 (May). Bogota.

Long, Stanley, and Juan Yanguez
1970–71 "Excavaciones en Tierradentro." *Revista Colombiana de Antropología*, vol. XV, pp. 11–127. Bogota.

Lopez, Tiberio
1946 *Compilacion de estudios arqueologicos etnograficos, etnologicos, geograficos y estadisticos de San Agustin*. Bogota.

Lopez de Gomara, Francisco
1965 *Historia General de las Indias*. Barcelona: Editorial Iberia.

Lopez de Velazco, Juan
1894 "Geografía y descripcion universal de las Indias, recopiladas por el cosmografo-cronista . . . desde el año 1571 al 1574." *Boletin de la Sociedad Geografica de Madrid*. Madrid.

Lowie, Robert H.
1946 "The Tapuya." *Handbook of South American Indians*, vol. 1, pp. 553–56. Washington, D.C.
1948 "The Tropical Forests: An Introduction." Ibid., vol. 3, pp. 1–56.

Lunardi, Federico
1933–34 'Tradiciones Paez." *Boletin Historico del Valle*, vol. 1, pp. 241–84, 553–56; vol. 2, pp. 49–191. Cali.
1935 *La vida en tumbas-arqueología del macizo colombiano*. Rio de Janeiro.
1936 "Costumbres mortuorias del macizo colombiano." *Revista del Museo Nacional*, vol. 3, pp. 32–64. Lima.

Mallol de Recasens, Maria Rosa
1963 "Cuatro representaciones de las imagenes alucinatorias originadas por la toma de yajé." *Revista Colombiana de Folklore*, vol. 8, pp. 61–81. Bogota.

Mallol de Recasens, Maria Rosa, and José de Recasens T.
1964–65 "Contribucion al conocimiento del Cacique-Curaca entre los Siona." *Revista Colombiana de Antropología*, vol. 13, pp. 93–145. Bogota.

Markham, Clements R. (ed.)
1864 "The Travels of Pedro Cieza de Leon." *The Hakluyt Society*, First Series, no. 33. New York: Burt Franklin.

Marquez, Fidel
1949 "Cultura indigena americana y diccionario etnografico." *Revista de Historia*, vol. 4, nos. 19, 22–25. Pasto.

Martinez, Eduardo N.
1956 "Los Pastos." *Llacta*, vol. 2, pp. 139–67. Quito.
1977 *Etnohistoria de los Pastos*. Quito: Editorial Universitaria.

Mason, J. Alden
1931 "Archaeology of Santa Marta, Colombia. The Tairona Culture. Pt. 1: Report on Field Work." *Field Museum of Natural History, Publ. 304, Anthropological Series*, vol. 20, no. 1. Chicago.
1936 "Archaeology of Santa Marta, Colombia. The Tairona Culture. Pt. 2, Sec. 1: Objects of Stone, Bone, and Metal. *Field Museum of Natural History, Publ. 358, Anthropological Series*, vol. 20, no. 2. Chicago.
1939 "Archaeology of Santa Marta, Colombia. The Tairona Culture. Pt. 2, Sec. 2: Objects of Pottery." *Field Museum of Natural History, Publ. 446, Anthropological Series*, vol. 20, no. 3. Chicago.

Mejia y Mejia, Justino
1934 *Ensayo sobre prehistoria nariñense.* Pasto: Imprenta de la Diocesis.
1949 "A puntaciones sobre arqueología del sur de Colombia." *Revista de Historia*, vol. 4, Pasto.

Mendoza, Alvaro Chaves
1981 *Los Animales Magicos en las urnas de Tierradentro.* Bogota.

Montana de Silva Celis, Lilia
1970 *Mitos, leyendas, tradiciones y folcior del Lago de Tota.* 1st edition. Tunja: Universidad Pedagogica y Tecnologica de Colombia.

Murdy, Carson
1975 *La economia y densidad de poblacion en los asentamientos de la cultura tairona en la arida zona litoral de la Sierra Nevada de Santa Marta.* Santa Marta: Primer Congreso Nacional de Historiadores y Antropologos.

Nachtigall, Horst
1955 *Tierradentro, Archaeologie und Ethnographie einer kolumbianischen Landschaft.* Zurich: Origo Verlag.
1955 "The cave tombs of Tierradentro." *Ethnos*, vol. 20, nos. 2 and 3. Estocolmo.
1955 Tierradentro: Archaeologie und Ethnographie einer kolumbianischen Landschaft." *Mainzer Studien zur Kultur- und Volkerkunde*, vol. 2. Zurich.
1955 "Schamanismus bei den Paez Indianern." *Zeitschrift für Ethnologie*, vol. 78, no. 2, pp. 210–23. Braunschweig.

Noble, G. Kingsley
1965 "Proto-Arawakan and its descendants." *International Journal of American Linguistics*, vol. 31, no. 3, Part II.

Ortiz, Sergio Elias
1928 "Participacion de Pasto en la dominacion de los indios Pijaos." *Boletin de Estudios Historicos*, vol. 1. Pasto.
1934 "Los petroglifos de Negrohuiaco." *Boletin de Estudios Historicos*, vol. 5, nos. 56–60. Pasto.
1936 "Notes sobre los indios Coaiqueres." *América Española*, vol. 5, pp. 88–96. Madrid.
1937 "Notas sobre los indios Koaikeres." *Idearium*, vol. 1, no. 1, pp. 24–33. Pasto.
1937 "Sobre la antigua provincia de los Pastos." *Idearium*, vol. 1, pp. 260–63. Pasto.
1937 "Notas: Excavaciones arqueologicas en el Campo de la Aurora." *Idearium*, vol. 1, no. 1. Pasto.
1937 "Hallazgos arqueologicos en el sur de Colombia (Excavaciones en la Normal de Pasto)." *Boletin de Estudios Historicos*, vol. 7. Pasto.
1938 "Nuevos hallazgos arqueologicos en el depto. de Nariño." *Idearium*, vol. 1, no. 10. Pasto.
1943 "Un nuevo cronista de Indias. La ciudad de San Juan de Pasto en los primeros tiempos coloniales." *Ilustracion Nariñense*, Series 7, no. 85. Pasto.
1946 "The native tribes and languages of southwestern Colombia." *Handbook of Southamerican Indians* (ed., Julien Steward), vol. 2, pp. 911–914. Washington, D.C.
1946 "The modern Quillacinga, Pasto and Coaiquer." *Handbook of Southamerican Indians* (ed., Julien Steward), vol. 2, pp. 961–68. Washington, D.C.
1960 "Sobre el dominio de los Incas en nuestros territorios del sur." *Boletin de Historia y Antiguedades*, vol. 48. Bogota.

Osborn, Harold
1968 "Southamerican mythology." Feltham, Middlesex: Hamlyn.

Oviedo y Valdes, Gonzalo Fernandez de
1851–55 *Historio general y natural de las Indias, islas y tierra firme de la mar océano.* 4 vols. (ed., José Amador de los Rios). Madrid.

Parsons, James
1970 "Los Campos de Cultivo Prehispanicos del Bajo San Jorge." *Revista de la Academia Colombiana de Ciencias*, vol. 12, no. 48. Bogota: Editorial Voluntad.

Parsons, James, and William Bowen
1966 "Ancient Ridged Fields in the San Jorge River Floodplain, Colombia." *The Geographical Review*, vol. 56, no. 3, pp. 317–43.

Patterson, Thomas
1965 "Ceramic sequences at Tierradentro and San Agustin, Colombia." *American Antiquity*, vol. 31, no. 1, pp. 66–73. Salt Lake City.

Pazos, Arturo
1972 "Algunos instrumentos musicales autoctonos." *Cultura Nariñense*, vol. 5, no. 44. Pasto.

Pedrahita, Lucas Fernandez
1881 *Historia general de las Conquistas del Nuevo Reino de Granada.* Bogota (first edition, Amberes, 1688).

Perdomo, Lucia de, Luisa F. de Turbay, and Lauricio Londoño
1974 "Estudio preliminar sobre la zona arqueologica de Pupiales." *Revista Colombiana de Antropología*, vol. 17, 2nd biannual. Bogota.

Perdomo, Lucia R. de, Luisa Fernanda de Turbay, and Londoño P. Lauricio
1974 "Estudio Preliminar sobre la Zona Arqueologica de Pupiales (Nariño). *RCA*, vol. 17, pp. 145–83.

Perdomo, Lucia R. de
1975 "Excavaciones arqueologicas en zona Panche, Guadruas-Cundinamar." *RCA*, vol. 19, pp. 247–89.
1977 *Aspectos de la cultura muisca.* Bogota: Instituto Colombiano de Cultura.
1977 *Muiscas.* Bogota: I.B.M. de Colombia.

Perez de Barradas, José
1936 "Interpretacion de un mito chibcha." *Revista de Indias*, no. 4, pp. 12–16. Bogota.
1937 *Arqueología y Antropología Precolombinas de Tierra Dentro.* Ministerio de Educacion Nacional, Publicaciones de la Seccion de Arqueología, no. 1. Bogota: Imprenta Nacional.
1937 "Mascara de oro de Inza." *Revista de las Indias*, no. 1, pp. 3–7.
1943 *Colombia de norte a sur.* Madrid: Ministerio de Asuntos Esteriores.
1943 *Arqueología Agustiniana.* Bogota: Ministry of Education.
1950 "Drogas ilusionogénicas de los indios americanos." *Antropología y Etnología*, vol. 3, pp. 9–107.
1950–51 *Los Muiscas antes de la Conquista.* Madrid: Instituto Bernardino de Sahagun, Consejo. Superior de Investigaciones Cientificas.
1954 *Orfebreria Prehispanica de Colombia: Estilo Calima.* Madrid: Banco de la Republica, Museo del Oro, Bogota, Talleres Graficos 'Jura.'
1957 *Plantas magicas americanas.* Madrid: Consejo Superior de Investigaciones Cientificas, Instituto Bernardino de Sahagun.
1958 *Orfebreria Prehispanica de Colombia: Estilos Tolima y Muisca.* Madrid: Banco de la Republica, Museo del Oro, Bogota, Talleres Graficos "Jura."
1966 *Orfebreria Prehispanica de Colombia: Estilos Quimbaya y Otros.* Madrid: Banco de la Republica, Museo del Oro, Bogota, Talleres Graficos "Jura."

Perrot, E., and R. Hamet
1927 "Le yagé, plante sensorielle des indiens de la région amazonienne de l'Equateur et de la Colombie." *Comple Rendu de l'Academie des Sciences*, vol. 184, p. 1266. Paris.

Pineda Giraldo, Roberto
1945 "Material arqueologico de la zona Calima." *Boletin de Arqueología*, vol. 1, no. 6, pp. 491–518. Bogota.

Plazas, Clemencia
1977–78 "Orfebreria Prehispanica del altiplano nariñense, Colombia." *Revista Colombiana de Antropología.* vol. 21, pp. 197–244. Bogota: Instituto Colombiano de Antropología. Italgraf.

Plazas, Clemencia, Ana Maria Falchetti, and Juanita Saenz
1979 Investigaciones Arqueologicas en Montelibano (Cordoba). Partial report; unpublished. Bogota.

Plazas de Nieto, Clemencia, and Ana Maria Falchetti de Saenz
1978 *El Dorado: Colombian Gold.* Australian Art Exhibitions Corporation.

Plazas de Nieto, Clemencia
1979 "Orfebreria prehispanica del altiplano nariñense, Colombia." *Revista Colombiana de Antropología*, vol. 21, pp. 197–244.

Preuss, Konrad Theodor
1921 *Religion und Mythologie der Uitoto.* Gottingen / Leipzig.
1926 *Forschungsreise zu den Kagaba. Beobachtungen, Textaufnahmen und sprachliche Studien bei einem Indianerstamm in Kolumbien, Sudamerika.* St. Grabriel-Modling: Anthropos Verlag.
1929 *Monumentale vorgeschichtliche Kunst, Ausgrabungen im Quellgebiet des Magdalena in Kolumbien, und ihre Ausstrahlungen in Amerika.* Gottingen: Vandenhoeck & Ruprecht.
1931 *Arte Monumental Prehistorico Excavaciones, hechas en el Alto Magdalena y San Agustin.* Translated from the German by Dr. Cesar Uribe Piedrahita and H. Walde Waldegg. Bogota.

Puerta Restrepo, Mauricio
1973 *Excavaciones arqueologicas en la region de Tierradentro.* Graduate thesis (Feb. 1973). Bogota: Universidad de los Andes.

Ramirez, German
1973–74 "Analisis filosofico de la mitología chibcha." *Revista Franciscanum*, vol. 15, no. 45 (Sept.–Dec. 1973), pp. 257–350. Bogota.

Ramos Pierez, Demetrio
1973 "El mito del Dorado: su génesis y proceso." Biblioteca de la Academia Nacional de la Historia, vol. 116. Caracas: Fuentes para la Historia Colonial de Venezuela.

Recasens, Maria Rosa de
1963 "Cuatro Representaciones de las Imagenes Alucinatorias originadas por la toma de yagé." *Revista Colombiana de Folclor*, vol. 3, no. 8, pp. 59–78. Bogota.

Reichel-Dolmatoff, Gerardo
1944 "La cultura material de los Indios Guahibo." *Revista del Instituto Etnologico Nacional*, vol. 1, no. 1, pp. 437–506. Bogota.
1945 "Mitos y cuentos de los Indios Chimila." *Boletin de Arqueología*, vol. 1, no. 1, pp. 4–30. Bogota.
1950–51 *Los Kogi: Una tribu indigena de la Sierra Nevada de Santa Marta, Colombia*. 2 vols. Bogota.
1951 *Datos historico-culturales sobre las tribus de la antigua gobernacion de Santa Marta*. Bogota: Imprenta del Banco de la Republica.
1953 "Contactos y cambios culturales en la Sierra Nevada de Santa Marta." *RCA*, vol. 1, no. 1, pp. 15–122.
1965 *Colombia*. Ancient Peoples and Places Series. London: Thames & Hudson.
1965 *Excavaciones arqueologicas en Puerto Hormiga*. Bogota.
1967 "Recientes investigaciones arqueologicas en San Agustin." *Revista Razon y Fabula*, vol. 2. Bogota: Universidad de los Andes.
1967 "A Brief Field Report on Urgent Ethnological Research in the Vaupés Area, Colombia, South America." *Bulletin of the International Committee on Urgent Anthropological and Ethnological Research*, no. 9, pp. 53–61. Vienna.
1969 "El contexto cultural de un alucinogeno aborigen." *Revista de la Academia Colombiana de Ciencias Exactas, Fisicas y Naturales*, vol. 13, no. 51, pp. 327–45. Bogota.
1971 *Amazonian Cosmos: The Sexual and Religious Symbolism of the Tukano Indians*. Chicago: University of Chicago.
1972 *San Agustin: A Culture of Colombia*. New York and Washington, D.C.: Praeger.
1972 "The Cultural Context of an Aboriginal Hallucinogen: Banisteriopsis Caapi." *Flesh of the Gods: The Ritual Use of Hallucinogens* (ed., Peter T. Furst), pp. 84–113. New York and Washington, D.C.: Praeger.
1975 *El Chaman y el jaguar*. Mexico: Siglo XXI Editores.
1975 *Contribuciones al conocimiento de la estratigrafia ceramica de San Agustin*. Colombia. Bogota: Biblioteca del Banco Popular.
1978 "Colombia Indigena. Periodo Prehispanico." *Manual de Historia de Colombia*, vol. 1. Bogota: Biblioteca Colombiana de Cultura.
1978 "Colombia Indigena. Periodo Prehispanico." *Manual de Historia de Colombia*, vol. 1. Bogota: Colcultura.
1985 *Los Kogi*, vols. 1, 2. Bogota: Nueva Biblioteca Colombiana de Cultura.
1985 *Monsu: un sitio arqueologico*. Bogota: Biblioteca Banco Popular Textos Universitarios.

Reichel-Dolmatoff, Gerardo, and Alicia Dussan de Reichel
1943 "Las Urnas Funerarias de la Cuenca del Rio Magdalena." *Revista del Instituto Etnologico Nacional*, pp. 209–81. Bogota.
1954 "Contribuciones a la Arqueología del Bajo Magdalena (Plato-Zambrano, Tenerife)." *Divulgaciones etnologicas*, vol. 3, no. 5, pp. 145–63. Barranquilla.
1954 "Investigaciones arqueologicas en la Sierra Nevada de Santa Marta," Parts 1 and 2. *Revista Colombiana de Antropología*, vol. 2, no. 2. Bogota.
1954 "Investigaciones arqueologicas en la Sierra Nevada de Santa Marta," Part 3. *Revista Colombiana de Antropología*, vol. 3. Bogota.
1955 "Investigaciones Arqueologicas en la Sierra Nevada de Santa Marta," Part 4. *Revista Colombiana de Antropología*, vol. 4. Bogota.
1956 "Reseña, Julio Cesar Cubillos, Tumaco: Notas arqueologicas." *Revista Colombiana de Antropología*, vol. 5, pp. 384–85. Bogota.
1957 "Reconocimiento Arqueologico de la Hoya del rio Sinu." *Revista Colombiana de Antropología*, vol. 6. Bogota
1958 "Notas sobre la metalurgia prehistorica en el litoral Caribe de Colombia." Tribute to Prof. Paul Rivet. Bogota: Editorial ABC.
1959 "Reseña a: Horst Nachtigall. Tierradentro." *American Antiquity*, vol. 22, no. 21, p. 120. Salt Lake City.
1960 "Notas etnograficas sobre los Indios del Choco." *Revista Colombiana de Antropología*, vol. 11, pp. 75–158. Bogota.
1961 "The agricultural basis of the Sub-Andean Chiefdoms of Colombia." *Antropologica*, Supplement no. 2, pp. 83–100. Caracas.
1963 "Apuntes etnograficos sobre los indios del alto rio Sinu." *Revista de la Academia Colombiana de Ciencias Exactas, Fisicas y Naturales*, vol. 12, no. 45, pp. 29–40. Bogota

Reinburg, P.
1921 "Contribution a l'étude des boissons toxiques des indiens du Nordouest de l'Amazone: l'ayahuasca, le yajé, le huanto." *Journal de la Société des Américanistes, N.S.*, vol. 13, p. 25–54, 197–216. Paris.

Restrepo, Vicente
1895 *Los muiscas antes de la conquista española, y Atlas arqueologico, 1895*. With map, 46 laminations, and index. Biblioteca del Banco Popular, vol. 26, Bogota, 1972.

Restrepo Tirado, Ernesto
1892 *Estudios sobre los aborigenes de Colombia*. Bogota: Imprenta de la Luz.
1919 *Descubrimiento y conquista de Colombia*. 2 vols. Bogota: Imprenta Nacional.
1953 *Historia de la provincia de Santa Marta*. Bogota.

Rivet, Paul
1924 *L'Orfevrerie Colombienne (Technique, Aire de Dispersion, Origine)*. Proceedings of the 21st International Congress of Americanists, Part 1, pp. 15–28. The Hague.

Rocherau, Henri, R. Monsalve, and Nestor Parra
1914 "Los Indios Tunebos." *Boletin de la Sociedad de Ciencias Naturales*, vol. 2, no. 6, pp. 163–69, 195–97, 229–30. Bogota.
1919 "Les Indiens Tunebos et Pedrazas." *Journal de la Société des Américanistes, N.S.*, vol. 11, no. 2, pp. 513–24. Paris.

Rodriguez Freile, Juan
1935 *El Carnero. Conquista y descubrimiento del Nuevo Reino de Granada de las Indias Occidentales del Mar Océano y Fundacion de la Ciudad de Santafe de Bogota....* Preface and Notes by J. M. Henao. Bogota.

Rodriguez Lamus, Luis Raul
1958 "La arquitectura de los Tukano." *Revista Colombiana de Antropología*, vol. 7, p. 251–70. Bogota.
1962 "Aspectos arquitectonicos de las tumbas de Tierradentro." *Revista Colombiana de Antropología*, vol. 10. Bogota.

Rodriguez Lamus, Luis Raul, and Antonio Vidal Rozo
1974 *La Ceramica en Colombia*. Banco Popular, Museo Arqueologico de la Casa del Marques de San Jorge. Bogota: Litografia Arco.

Romoli de Avery, Kathleen
1965 "Apuntes sobre los pueblos autoctonos del litoral Colombiano del Pacifico en la epoca de la conquista espanola." *Revista Colombiana de Antropología*, vol. 12, pp. 259–92. Bogota.

Root, William C.
1964 "Pre-Columbian Metalwork of Colombia and its Neighbors." *Essays in Pre-Columbian Art and Archaeology* (ed., S. K. Lothrop), pp. 242–57. Cambridge: Harvard University Press.

Rozo, Dario
1938 *Mitología escritura de los Chibchas*. Bogota.

Rozo, José
1977 *La Cultura material de los muiscas*, p. 99. Bogota: Ediciones Ideas.
1978 *Los Muiscas, organizacion social y regimen politico*. Bogota: Editorial Suramerica.

Saake, Willhelm
1922 *Daturas of the Old World and New: An Account of Their Narcotic Properties and Their Use in Oracular and Initiatory Ceremonies*. Smithsonian Institution Annual Report for 1920, pp. 537–67, Washington, D.C.

Sahagun, Bernardino de
1959 *Florentine Codex: General History of the Things of New Spain* (eds. C. E. Dibble and A. J. O. Anderson). Book 9, Monographs of the School of American Research and the Museum of New Mexico, no. 44, Part 10, Santa Fe.

Salvat
1977 *Arte Colombiano*. Vols. 1–3. Bogota: Editores Salvat.

Santa Gertrudis, Fr. Juan de
1956 *Maravillas de la Naturaleza*. Colombian Presidential Library. Bogota.
1970 *Maravillas de la Naturaleza*. Bogota: Biblioteca del Banco Popular, vol. 10, Editorial Kelly.

Sauer, Carl O.
1963 "Cultivated Plants of South and Central America." *Handbook of South American Indians*, vol. 6, p. 487–543. New York: Cooper Square Publishers (original version: 1950).

Schottelius, J. W.
1942 "Ceramica de la region de Pedregal, Cauca." *Publicacion de la Escuela Normal Superior*, vol. IV (Mar.–Apr.), pp. 332–41. Bogota: Imprenta Nacional.

Schultes, Richard Evans
1954 "A New Narcotic Snuff from the Northwest Amazon." *Botanical Museum Leaflets*, Harvard University, vol. 16, no. 9, pp. 241–60.
1961 "Native Narcotics of the New World." *Texas Journal of Pharmacology*, vol. 2, p. 141.
1967 "The Botanical Origins of South American Snuffs." Ibid., pp. 291–306.
1969 "The Unfolding Panorama of the New World Hallucinogens." *Current Topics in Plant Science* (ed., J. E. Gunckel), pp. 336–54. New York.
1972 "An Overview of Hallucinogens in the Western Hemisphere." *Flesh of the Gods: The Ritual Use of Hallucinogens* (ed., Peter T. Furst), pp. 3–54, New York and Washington, D.C.

Seijas, Haydee
1969 *The Medical system of the Sibundoy indians of Colombia*. Ph.D. thesis, Tulane University. (30/06B/2516, order no. 69-20, 502). Ann Arbor: University Microfilms.

Silva Celis, Eliecer
1943 "La arqueología de Tierradentro." *Revista del Instituto Etnologico Nacional*, vol. 1, no. 1, pp. 117–30. Bogota.
1943 La arqueología de Tierradentro. *Revista del Instituto Etnologico Nacional*, vol. 1, no. 2, pp. 521–89. Bogota.
1944 "La Arqueología de Tierradentro (continuation)." *Revista del Instituto Etnologico Nacional*, vol. 1, no. 2, pp. 521–89. Bogota.
1946 "Relacion preliminar de las investigaciones arqueologicas realizadas en 'La Belleza', Santander." *Boletin de Arqueología*, vol. 2, no. 1, pp. 33–41. Bogota.
1961 "Pinturas rupestres precolombinas de Sachica." *Revista Colombiana de Antropología*, vol. 10. Bogota.
1961 "Antiguedad y relaciones de la civiliza cion chibcha. *Revista Colombiana de Antropología*, vol. 13, pp. 239–65.
1961 "Una inspeccion arqueologica por el Alto Rio Minero." *Revista Colombiana de Antropología*, vol. 13, pp. 9–26. Bogota.
1968 *Arqueología y prehistoria de Colombia*. Tunja: Universidad Pedagogica y Tecnologica de Colombia.

Simon, Pedro
1882–92 *Noticias historiales de las conquistas de Tierra Firme en las Indias Occidentales*. 5 vols. Bogota.

Spruce, Richard
1874 "On Some Remarkable Narcotics of the Amazon Valley and Orinoco." *Geographical Magazine, N.S.*, vol. 1, pp. 184–93.
1908 *Notes of a Botanist on the Amazon and the Andes* (ed., Alfred Russel Wallace). Vols. 1, 2. London: MacMillan.

Steward, Julian H., and Louis C. Faron
1959 *Native Peoples of South America*. New York.

Stoddart, D. R.
1962 "Myth and Ceremonial among the Tunebo Indians of Eastern Colombia." *Journal of American Folklore*, vol. 75, pp. 147–52.

Suarez, V. (ed.)
1913 *Cedulario de las Provincias de Santa Marta y Cartagena de Indias (Siglo XVI): Tomo primero, Añois 1529–1535* (vol. 14, Coleccion de Libros y Documentos Referentes a la Historia de America). Madrid: Librería General de Victoriano Suarez.

Sutherland, Donald R.
1971 Preliminary Investigations into the Prehistory of Santander, Colombia. Ph.D. thesis, Tulane University.

Triana, Miguel
1924 *Petroglifos de la Mesa Central de Colombia*. Album with 56 laminations. Bogota: Woeckner.
1959 *La civilizacion chibcha*. Bogota: Editorial A.B.C.
1970 *El jeroglifico chibcha*. Bogota: Biblioteca Banco Popular.
1972 *La civilizacion Chibcha*. Bogota: Ediciones Banco Popular.

Trimborn, Hermann
1943 "Tres Estudios para la Etnografía y Arqueología de Colombia: Los Reinos de Guaca y Nore." *Revista de Indias*, vol. 4, no. 11, pp. 43–91; no. 12, pp. 331–47; no. 13, pp. 441–56; no. 14, pp. 629–81. Bogota.
1944 "Tres Estudios para la Etnografía y Arqueología de Colombia: Las Minas de Buritica." *Revista de Indias*, vol. 5, no. 15, pp. 27–39; no. 16, pp. 199–226. Bogota.

Uribe, Alarcon, Maria Victoria
1976 "Relaciones Prehispanicas entre la Costa del Pacifico y el Altiplano. Nariñense, Colombia." *RCA*, vol. 20, pp. 11–20.
1977 Asentamientos Prehispanicos en al Altiplano de Ipiales, Colombia. Unpublished Master's thesis. Escuela Nacional de Antropología e Historia, Universidad Nacional Autonoma de Mexico.
1979 "Asentamientos prehispanicos en el altiplano de Ipiales, Colombia." *Revista Colombiana de Antropología*, vol. 21, pp. 57–195. Bogota.

Uscategui, M. Nestor
1959 "The Present Distribution of Narcotics and Stimulants Amongst the Indian Tribes of Colombia." *Botanical Museum Leaflets*, Harvard University, vol. 18, no. 6, pp. 273–304.

Vargas, Fray Martin de
1948 "Notas sobre los indios Cuaiqueres del sur de Colombia." *Trabajos del Instituto Bernardino de Sahagun de Antropología y Historia*, vol. 6, pp. 117–25. Madrid.

Vargas Machuca, Bernardo de
1892 *Milicia y descripcion de las Indias*. 2 vols. Coleccion de libros raros o curiosos que tratan de America, vols. 8, 9. Madrid (first edition: Madrid, 1599).

Wassen, S. Henry
1936 "An archaeological study in the western Colombian cordillera." *Etnologiska Studier*, vol. 2, pp. 30–67.
1964 "Some General Viewpoints in the Study of Native Drugs, Especially from the West Indies and South America." *Ethnos*, no. 1–2, p. 97–120. Stockholm.
1965 "The Use of Some Specific Kinds of South American Indian Snuff and Related Paraphernalia." *Etnologiska Studier*, no. 8, Goteborg.

Wilbert, Johannes
1960 "Nachrichten uber die Curipaco." *Ethnologica, N.S.*, vol. 2, pp. 508–21. Cologne: Sonderdruck aus Festband M. Heydrich.
1961 *Indios de la Region Orinoco-Ventuari*. Caracas: Instituto Caribe de Antropología y Sociología.

Willey, Gordon R.
1967 *An Introduction to American Archaeology South America*. Englewood Cliffs: Prentice Hall.

INDEX